NATIONALISM WITHOUT WALLS

RICHARD GWYN

NATIONALISM
WITHOUT
WALLS

THE UNBEARABLE LIGHTNESS OF

BEING CANADIAN

M&S

Canadian Cataloguing in Publication Data

Gwyn, Richard, 1934-
    Nationalism without walls : the unbearable lightness of being Canadian

Includes index.
ISBN 0-7710-3717-1

1. Nationalism – Canada.   2. Multiculturalism – Canada.
3. Regionalism – Canada.   4. Canada – Politics and government –
1993-   .*   I. Title.

FC98.G89   1995   971.064'8   C95-932164-0
F1034.2.G89   1995

The publisher acknowledges the support of the Canada Council and the Ontario Arts Council for its publishing program.

Design by Stephen Kenny
Typesetting by M&S, Toronto
Printed and bound in Canada on acid-free paper

McClelland & Stewart
The Canadian Publishers
481 University Avenue
Toronto, Ontario
M5G 2E9

1 2 3 4 5   99 98 97 96 95

CONTENTS

To my lifelong love

AUTHOR'S NOTE

Sandra and I have always performed as editor and critic and cheerleader for each other on all our major projects such as books and magazine articles. Because of circumstances, we were able to work more closely together on this project than on any earlier one. Every word in the book but these has passed under Sandra's pen or through her mental word-processor. The dedication expresses, but still hopelessly inadequately, the magnitude of my debt to her.

A number of friends helped on points of detail. Two went far beyond the call of duty. David Hilton and Maureen O'Neil read a number of chapters in draft, identifying errors and misjudgements and infelicities. The many that remain are entirely my own responsibility.

Toronto Star publisher John Honderich and Editorial Page Editor Haroon Siddiqui generously made it possible for me take a "semi-sabbatical" that enabled me to attach myself to the book at the same time as not completely detaching myself from the *Star*.

Because this is not a work of scholarship, I haven't cluttered up the bottoms of pages with footnotes. However, the reasonably comprehensive list of sources will serve as a guide for those who want to study specific issues and topics in greater detail.

Toronto, August 1995

INTRODUCTION

This book began life as a speech, "Canada as the First Postmodern Nation," delivered on November 23, 1994, at Brock University in St. Catharines, Ontario, as part of the D. G. Wilmot Distinguished Lecture series. Fulfilling that invitation required me to stitch together into a coherent form a series of observations I'd been making in my regular columns about the changes – economic, social, political, cultural – taking place in Canadian society. The *Toronto Star* reprinted much of the text, so it reached a sizeable readership. Many responses were along the lines of "Interesting. But prove it." This book is an attempt to do so.

The idea of questing for framework ideas about my country had occurred more than two years earlier, though, in mid-1992. This was right after Sandra and I had come home to live in Toronto from London, England, where I'd been posted for nearly seven years as the *Star*'s international affairs columnist. No sooner were we back than we went through a culture shock as severe as the one we'd experienced as new arrivals in Britain when we'd had to learn to not get mad, although often to look for ways to later get even, when time and again the words "Canadian" and "boring" were used as synonyms. We realized quickly that a good deal of the Canada we'd left behind in 1985 had evaporated. In its place a quite different kind of society was emerging, far more diverse, and funkier and livelier, but also far more stressed out, self-doubting, and, above all, far more fractured.

An early assignment to survey the hinterland – Cape Breton, Northern Ontario, southern Saskatchewan – taught me that in much of the country little had changed, although these regions were acutely anxious now about being hollowed out by population decline and economic contraction. In southern Saskatchewan, people were wondering whether John Palliser might not have been right and that the wild grasses of the parched flatlands should never have been broken to grow grain. In Northern Ontario, there was near-despair at the way urban Canada had lost almost all connection with the hard-rock trades of forestry and mining upon which the very country had once been built; indeed, it had developed a virtual contempt for them. My melancholy impression – magnified in a way that touched me personally (Sandra much more so) when Newfoundland's fishery was struck down as if by some biblical plague – was that this old foundation Canada was becoming almost meaningless to the emerging, polyglot, urban Canada.

Ottawa itself – where we had lived for nearly a quarter-century – had changed little. It was still cosy yet spacious, had even become elegant in spots with the glittering galleria of the National Gallery and the sinuous curves of the Museum of Civilization now superimposed upon its cityscape. It was still the best city in the country – one of the best in the world – to get out of quickly, to the thickly wooded Gatineau Hills or to the rolling Ontario countryside of the Ottawa Valley. Disturbingly, Official Ottawa had changed scarcely at all. No differently from the early 1980s, no conversation could proceed for more than a few minutes before the phrase "national unity" popped out to frame all future discussion. Everywhere else, people were talking about jobs, employment insecurity, contracting incomes, falling real estate values, crime; or else they were talking about the Internet. The gulf between governing and governed was becoming so wide it was easy to guess that the forthcoming Charlottetown referendum would fail unless Mulroney could guilt-trip everyone into saving Canada yet again; even easier to guess that Mulroney no longer commanded the credibility to do this, or almost anything.

This impending revolt against the élite would constitute a break with our entire tradition of deference to authority. It would be confirmed later by the electoral success of the Reform Party, by the popularity of the spending-cutting policies of Alberta's Ralph Klein and by Conservative Mike Harris's remarkable victory in Ontario. In a parallel break from the past, a new resistance, stubborn and sullen, had developed to paying taxes: first the GST and later to tax increases of any kind.

More significant was the way Canadians now looked at themselves, and at each other. Above all, the new attitude was unsentimental. No more guilt about Quebec, a new scepticism about entrenched "caring and sharing" programs (welfare, unemployment insurance, foreign aid), and outright cynicism about most institutions, almost all politicians, and much of the media. People talked, unsentimentally, about what they needed to do to survive in the encroaching jungle of the global economy, of headlong technological change, of the shredding of social safety nets.

The most obvious economic change between past and present was the persistence of high unemployment; Kim Campbell would get into terrible trouble in the 1993 election for saying it might not come done much before the century's turn; she was of course dead right. This, though, masked a deeper economic change. The nature of jobs was changing radically, dividing ever more sharply between high-paid, high-tech ones and impermanent, semi-skilled ones. In turn, this phenomenon masked a profound social change: Our great postwar achievement of a rough and ready egalitarianism, particularly in contrast to the United States, was being gnawed away. Destabilizing it further would be the cuts in government spending forced by the imperatives of reducing the debt and deficits, a necessity Canadians began to accept as inevitable from about the spring of 1993 on. We were on our way to becoming, as we hadn't been in half a century, a polarized country shaped like an hourglass containing two separate economic nations.

Trying to get a handle on these politico-economic changes involved conventional punditry, even if more demanding than usual because so much was so novel. It was at the level of the personal that I began to sense that Canada was becoming a fundamentally different kind of country from the one I'd once known pretty well.

Having unfurled the word "personal," let me wave it around a bit. As a self-appointed observer attempting to probe the contemporary Canadian psyche, my qualifications are decidedly skimpy. I'm a white, sexagenarian (just), anglophone male who emigrated here in the mid-1950s and then slipped sideways into journalism after spending what otherwise would have been my university years selling magazines door-to-door around the Atlantic provinces. My life, much of it spent in Ottawa, has been mostly as cosy as that city. I've never been poor. I've never been discriminated against, except once way back in 1960 when I was refused a job at CBC Radio in Ottawa because of "your British accent." (Where was the Human Rights Commission when I needed it?)

My only offsetting assets are a certain familiarity with other countries, and therefore a certain ability to make comparisons. Also, as is common among journalists, a jackdaw facility for gathering up oddments of facts and ideas. Lastly, that I have eyes and ears.

What I began seeing and hearing soon after our return were

the faces and voices of the emerging, polyglot, urban Canada. At times, they were very angry indeed. Just before our homecoming flight landed, the one and only "echo riot" in North America of those in south-central Los Angeles occurred in Toronto as black youths (and some white) went on a rampage up and down Yonge Street. In anguish, Stephen Lewis, former ambassador to the United Nations, would produce a report to the Ontario government describing Canada as a "systemically racist" society.

What unsettled me about the Yonge Street riot wasn't the nihilistic rage of the black youths or the counter-annoyance of the respectable citizenry. It was that the far worse riots that had broken out in Britain, as in Brixton and Toxteth in the early 1980s, were history now, while, apparently, they were just starting here.

In fact, no other race riots would take place here (indeed, some later reoccurred in Britain, in Bradford). But as cures for Canada's supposed "systemic racism" would come the world's most comprehensive employment equity regime, proposals for a "cultural defence" to exempt ethnic and religious believers from the general laws and for separate, state-supported schools for all religions, and a conference for writers of colour from which white writers were excluded.

As the race issue went, so multiculturalism seemed to be going. Terms like Italian-Canadian and Sikh-Canadian and the rest weren't new in themselves. But these now seemed to carry an emphatic, exclusionary quality, as if those who belonged to ethnic groups had acquired the right to define the terms of their citizenship.

Native people were similarly redefining themselves. They wanted to separate themselves from other Canadians now, in self-governing territories. In the past, we of course had separated them from us – in reserves. Even if the motive was different, there was nevertheless a disturbing parallel between what was happening here and what had happened in South Africa, in its now disappearing Bantustans, or tribal territories.

Lastly, the sexes seemed to be distancing themselves in a ferocious, intimate war – victories and defeats chronicled in "WAR AGAINST WOMEN" headlines about endemic male violence – for which little in Britain and almost nothing at all in the rest of Europe had prepared me. Personally, I had to learn to say gender rather than sex, even though, curiously, no one spoke about "same-gender benefits."

The new cultural creeds seemed to be those of moral absolutism and of cultural apartheid.

Such were my early, gloomy thoughts while walking around Toronto's central streets – walking for a good deal longer than I'd expected because of a strike at the *Star*. During that span of downtime, my eyes and ears began picking up quite different signals.

Wandering around those inner-city streets, I gradually became aware of a remarkable phenomenon. I began to notice that a strikingly high number of the couples walking together were made up of one white person and another who was black or brown or Asian. Less common, but by no means rare, were couples of whom one member was black and the other brown or Asian. In all their colours, there were far more of these pairs and groups than I'd ever noticed in London (almost as polyglot a city as Toronto) or Paris, Berlin, Rome or, as I would later observe, in New York, Los Angeles, or Washington.

It was the unselfconsciousness of these couples – I noticed them later also in Vancouver – that struck me most. They weren't making a statement; they were simply *unaware* of each other's colour.

A fundamental disconnection existed, it seemed to me, between Canada's supposed character as "systemically racist" and the reality that more people of the rainbow were more at ease in each other's company here than in any other society I've ever been in.

Of course most of these people were young, to whom the novel is always a delight, or isn't noticed at all. And Toronto and Vancouver aren't the whole country. But if these Canadians can do it, surely others can, including, far from least, those ethnic communities that have been retreating into self-constructed ghettos.

We were poised, it seemed to me, on the brink of creating a society like none other in the world. Hence my – later – notion of Canada as the first postmodern nation. What postmodern actually means, though, no one has yet been able to define. The risk is that we may progressively lose our sense of solidarity and cohesion until we cease to be a national community in any worthwhile meaning of that term. Inevitably, Canadians possess a far lighter sense of national identity than citizens of ethnic nations, Ireland, Poland, Thailand, whatever. At some point, the lightness of identity may become unbearable, as in the title of Milan Kundera's novel, and we'll let it slip away, scarcely noticing that it's gone.

Quebec, to commit the ultimate Canadian heresy, didn't concern me, then or later, nearly as much as this progressive loss of national stuffing. My operating presumption was that either Quebec would go or, much more probably, that it would not. Whichever, Quebeckers themselves would make up their own minds. Afterwards, other Canadians would either have to pick up the pieces and stitch together a country out of what remained or, in the more likely event of a vote by Quebeckers for federalism, would have to find a way to reach out so that all Quebeckers would feel, and would be in fact, fully included in the larger community.

Viewing Quebec as a self-contained problem, even if this was misguided, did liberate me to focus on the alternative threat of a slow unravelling of the national fabric.

The possibility that Canada might gradually fade away, not with the enigmatic smile of a Cheshire cat but with a kind of regretful sigh, is almost never discussed in public. It does come up, though, often quite candidly, in private conversations. The people's mood *is* unsentimental. If, as is the case, the primal social unit of the family is no longer what it was, why should national units be immutable? If lifelong employment no longer exists, why should nation-states exist in perpetuity?

Some outsiders may know us better than ourselves, or at least be less inhibited by a need to maintain a public posture of denial. A 1991 special report on Canada in *The Economist* concluded, "Sooner or later, Canadians are going to become Americans. Too bad." Lansing Lamont, a sympathetic American observer, began his 1994 book, *Breakup*, with the arresting line "Nations, like stars, burn out." He made the melancholy guess that "Maybe Canada is not meant to survive. Maybe it isn't destined to live out its span as a nation."

Maybe not. That an ever-increasing number of Canadians are determining the terms of their citizenship is one thing. Quite another is our progressive loss of control over the character of our collective citizenship. Like all nation-states, the authority and effectiveness of ours has been eroded by the global economy. Our state's down-going matters more to us than to any other people, though, because, lacking a distinctive ethnic identity, we've used the state to give us collective shape. As the state weakens, the "caring and sharing" concept of Canadianism – the phrase is usually used derogatorily now; it ought to be used with pride – becomes less and less able to resist the polarizing effect of globalism and technology upon incomes and jobs; the impact of both of these is being magnified further by the contemporary dominance of neo-conservative, free-market ideology. As Canadians become more and more different from each other – not as a function of demography but as a function of their rising demands to be treated as "differentiated citizens" on the basis of their cultures and values – the less Canadians will be interested in, let alone care about, each other. It cannot be a coincidence that the higher the various cultural walls have gone up inside Canada, the stronger popular resistance to paying taxes has become.

That the external walls once protecting Canada have been largely levelled by continental free trade and by the global economy magnifies our national challenge. Hence the book's title. The phrase "nationalism without walls" was minted by Finance Minister Paul Martin during his 1990 run for the Liberal leadership. It didn't work for him then. But it fits this book's purpose exactly.

A glance backwards may help us plot a way ahead. The political debate that perhaps best defines contemporary Canada took place during the federal election of 1979. It pitted Joe Clark against Pierre Trudeau.

In opposition to Trudeau's vision of "One Canada," Clark, in a speech in High River, Alberta, raised the alternative vision of Canada as "a community of communities." Trudeau won the debate, as he did all his verbal encounters, scorning Clark's concept as reducing Canada to "a string of shopping centres."

The debate between Trudeau and Clark was a defining one because both were right. History has proven Clark the better prophet. The country today is much nearer to being his community of communities than to Trudeau's one nation. Yet history has also overtaken Clark. By "communities," he meant the historic ones of province and region. Crisscrossed over them now, though, are all the new identity communities, and the still more divisive ones caused by the widening income gaps.

Trudeau's "One Canada" concept hasn't ended up on history's trash heap. When asked to name the best country in the world to live in, more Canadians cite their own country than do citizens of any other country. If Canadians care less for each other than they used to, they care as much as ever about their community as a whole.

The thesis of this book is that it's time to turn our attention to that over-arching community. A paraphrase of one of John F. Kennedy's best-known lines may apply to us today: "Ask not what the community can do for your community, but what you can do for the community." The rest of the book amounts to an attempt to describe how we got to where we are, and to point out some stepping-stones that may help to move us, a way at least, out of the swamp.

A last point needs to be made about the nature of the book itself. It's a book about ideas.

Supposedly, this is about as un-Canadian as it's possible to get. As we constantly tell ourselves, we are pragmatists (and survivalists); the conventional wisdom is that we're a bit provincial and spend most of our time looking at 'great events' from the sidelines. All of which is true, most of the time.

In the manner of the discovery by Molière's M. Jourdain that he'd been speaking prose his entire life, Canadians have been discussing ideas a good deal more than they realize. Free trade. Then Meech Lake and Charlottetown. Later, the Reform Party's ideas about direct democracy, which prefigured many of those by the new Republicans of 1994. Now, inevitably, national unity yet again. That's a lot of abstract ideas for a prosaic crowd. The European Union's Maastricht Treaty of 1992 is roughly equivalent to the Meech constitutional package *plus* free trade. Yet that long constitutional step towards Euro-federalism was debated publicly in advance in only one country – Britain. Germans only discovered by way of a tabloid headline on the same day that Chancellor Helmut Kohl signed the treaty on their behalf that a single European currency would mean the end of their prized deutschemark. No wonder so many Europeans, and no longer just the Brits, have lost their enthusiasm for Euro-federalism.

Nevertheless, ideas are un-Canadian. I can't deny this. What this book is about is the idea of Canada.

PART I

The Economics of the Matter

1

L'État C'est Nous

"The nation-state has become an unnatural, even a dysfunctional unit for organizing human activity and managing economic endeavour."

> — Kenichi Ohmae, *The Borderless World*, 1990

When John Turner, former prime minister and Liberal leader, was awarded an honorary degree by his alma mater, the University of British Columbia, in November 1994, he spoke on the conventional topic of the global economy. Midway through the usual pieties about the challenges and opportunities created by the opening up of markets everywhere, a fresh thought occurred to him. Turner tossed it out: "Go global, because you're going have to. But, do me a favour. Stay Canadian." Seconds passed before there was any response. Suddenly, the students jumped to their feet, pulling up with them parents, professors, and other guests. The ovation went on and on as if no one wanted to be the first to sit down. On the podium and in the audience, quite a few eyes were damp.

A few months later, the same thing happened right across the country. With considerable daring and a fair bit of political calculation, Fisheries Minister Brian Tobin dispatched patrol vessels to seize a Spanish trawler, the *Estai*, that had been overfishing its quota of turbot on the tail of the Grand Banks. The European

Union denounced the deed as "piracy." Again there was a momentary pause. Commentators worried we had damaged our reputation as a role model of rational diplomacy. Then the public spoke up: Polls measured an unprecedented 90 per cent support for Tobin's actions. No doubt it helped that Tobin had astutely cast the issue as one of conservation versus international legalisms. No doubt people relished the fact that Canada, for once, wasn't behaving like an international Boy Scout. Nevertheless, Tobin's pugnacity and eloquence touched a national nerve. "It's not really about fish," New Brunswick Liberal MP Paul Zed remarked shrewdly to *Globe and Mail* reporter Edward Greenspon. "It's about sovereignty. It is awakening a Canadian giant of national identity."

For about a decade now, Canada's national consciousness has been ground down in-between two millstones. The upper one is the effect upon us of the global economy, and, particular to us, the effect of continental free trade. These have worn away most of the walls that once kept us at a distance from the rest of the world and its systems, practices, and values, which, no matter whether positive (the free-market rules) or negative (the polarizing of incomes), challenge our national distinctiveness. As for the lower millstone, it is made up of the effect upon us of both our own historic internal divisions of regions and language (heightened incomparably now that Quebeckers are about to decide, yet again, whether they want to continue to be Canadians at all) and, added to these, the new faultlines created by the "identity politics" of ethnicity, race, colour, and gender.

Cheering Turner for urging students to "stay Canadian" and cheering on Tobin as he battled for us against the Europeans were spontaneous acts of national pride. Yet the very eagerness with which each opportunity for symbolic flag-waving was seized upon revealed the extent of the public's doubt whether this curious nation-state can endure, and in what form for how long.

The conventional wisdom of our time is that nation-states are no longer what they were. Globalism – economic, financial, technological, and audio-visual – has made these entities "dysfunctional," in Kenichi Ohmae's phrase. As the analysis continues, they are at the same time too small now to be able do the big things, such as guaranteeing the economic and social well-being of their citizens, and too big to do the essential small things, like operating schools and hospitals. Some believe that nation-states will simply fade away, to be replaced by a new constellation of supranational agencies (the UN, the World Trade Organization), of regional federations of previously sovereign states (the EU, NAFTA), and beneath these a mix of geo-economic regions, of ethnic provinces, of city-states. As Latin once was, data may become the new universal language – or more exactly English will, since 80 per cent of all the data stored in the world's computers is in that language; all other languages may become private, or strictly local, like Celtic, Piedmontese, or Inuktitut.

Politics has made as much difference as economics and technology. The Cold War's end has liberated everyone to be what they want to be. Specifically, it has ended the existence of the Soviet Union, Yugoslavia and Czechoslovakia. In part because the superpowers no longer care what's happening there, several countries – Somalia, the Sudan, Afghanistan, Bosnia – have slipped into a new international category known as "failed states." Around the world there are more than two thousand "nation-peoples" but, so far, less than one-tenth that number of nation-states.

Not even size and power guarantee permanency. Many observers believe that the death of the last of the "Red Emperors," Deng Xiaoping, will be followed by China's fragmentation, at the very least, into economic equivalents of old-style warlordism or, if the central authorities try to bind the provinces too closely, perhaps into outright civil war. Unbelievable as it may sound, some commentators foresee the same process happening – entirely peaceably – to the United States. "Our nation is no longer manageable. The time has come for both individual states and the federal government to begin planning the rational downsizing of America," Duke University economist Thomas Naylor argues in *Challenge* magazine. "We need to begin thinking about a new Confederation of American states to replace the old Union." One professor's opinion doesn't amount to much, except that, even for the sake of being provocative, such an opinion would have been inexpressible a few years ago. Indeed, a June 1995 *Newsweek* poll found that one in three Americans doubt that their country will still be around in one piece in a century's time. More to the practical point, the devolution agenda of the new Republicans may create at least a quasi-confederacy as power is shifted from the centre to the states.

Before considering Canada's condition, it may be useful to set it in the context of the condition of all nation-states today. Much that is happening to them is also happening to us; because of the way we are, we are also walking alone a good deal of the time.

The 185 member-states of the UN come in all shapes and sizes, from Palau (pop. 15,000) to the solitary superpower, the United States. They go as well as come: Belarus appeared on the international map for the first time four years ago when the Soviet Union broke up and now it may soon disappear from the map by rejoining Russia; Bosnia's life span as a nation-state will probably be even shorter. They come in all kinds. The United States is an idea-state, founded on "life, liberty and the pursuit of happiness" and the rest of it. In a different way, Israel is also an idea-state. China is more a civilization than a state.

Among the crowd, Canada is unusual because we encompass within ourselves a nation perfectly capable of becoming a separate nation-state, if at considerable cost to itself. The same circumstance applies, though, to Belgium, Spain, Russia, and India; it also once applied to Czechoslovakia and Yugoslavia.

We're unusual also because our principal language isn't distinct to us. The same is true, though, for Ireland, Australia, and Austria;

the spoken languages of Pakistanis and Indians, Urdu and Hindi, are virtually the same; Serbo-Croat is common to Serbs and Croats, although neither cares to admit it. Russian is still more widely spoken in official circles in the Ukraine than Ukrainian. We're unusual, lastly, because we've never had to fight for our independence. (Despite some patriotic revisionism, the War of 1812 was fought for us by the British.) We've been denied, therefore, the sustaining myths of martyrdom and of a struggle against occupation and oppression that are such powerful bonding agents in most nation-states, including the people-nation of Québécois.

One characteristic that makes us just about unique is that we've always had available to us an "alternative national option." Joining the United States has always been both an attractive proposition and one made seemingly inevitable by the logic of geography and economics. Many knowledgeable observers have taken for granted that that union was only a matter of time. "Canada is fighting a rearguard action against the inevitable," wrote former U.S. undersecretary of state George Ball in his 1968 memoir, *The Discipline of Power*. Ball foresaw Canada–U.S. free trade two decades before it actually happened, and understood that to realize its full potential would require "a progressively expanding area of political cohesion." A century earlier, in 1877, Goldwyn Smith made an identical prediction: "Canadian nationality being a lost cause, the ultimate union of Canada with the United States appears now to be morally certain." One primal definition of Canadianism has to be that we are among the few peoples in the world who, given a chance to become Americans, have chosen not to.

The characteristic that really distinguishes Canada from all other UN members is that we aren't really a nation-state at all. We possess all the conventional accoutrements: A national government and parliament, armed forces, and a seat at the General Assembly marked by a placard and a maple leaf flag. Rather than a nation-state, though, we are really a *state-nation*. Our state has formed us and has shaped our character in a way that is true for no other people in the world. To paraphrase Louis XVI, "*L'état, c'est nous.*"

From our very beginning, we've been defined from the top down. The Loyalists came north so they could continue to be ruled by a monarch rather than, in their terms, "by the mob"; the *Canadiens* remained loyal (ignoring the appeal of Benedict Arnold after he'd marched his army to Quebec City) because they trusted the state to guarantee all that then mattered to them, their religion. As early as the 1820s, the construction of the Welland Canal as a public enterprise left the colony as deeply in debt as its successor-state today. The deference of Canadians to the Family Compact was matched by the deference of the *Canadiens* to their "domestic" state of the Church. In the west and north, law and order was maintained not by vigilantes but by the North West Mounted Police. Soon after the century's turn, in a manner quite alien to the American political culture (uncommon even in Europe then), Canadian governments created state-enterprises like Canadian National Railways (CNR) and Ontario Hydro to fill up the cracks – chasms – in our marketplace.

While counting on our state, and ourselves, to be "kinder and gentler" than those south of the border is now one of the principal sources of our national distinctiveness, the opposite may have been true for the greater part of our history. Until well into this century, our self-image was that we were more rugged, more manly, because we were more northern. As may surprise today's young Canadians, we used to take pride in being more militaristic, having entered both world wars far earlier than the Americans. Until the postwar years, we were much less welcoming to strangers, particularly to Jews and Asians. Our New Deal was far less ambitious than Franklin D. Roosevelt's.

The gentler qualities had to have always been latent. Every now and then they surfaced: The Social Gospel movement at the turn of the century; the son-of-the-manse tradition of public service personified by Lester Pearson; the mid-Depression social democracy of the CCF and the Antigonish co-operative movement of Monsignor Moses Michael Coady in contrast to the angry populism of Father Charles Coughlin, and of Huey Long.

From the mid-1940s on, our potential became our reality. Our state began to take on its contemporary character as a welfare, or "provider," state. At the same time, our character changed. We first delighted in being looked after; we then delighted in looking after each other. If Canadian consciousness dates from the victory at Vimy in 1917, and the Canadian nation-state's status as an international entity from the Statute of Westminster of 1926, we transformed ourselves into the distinctive state-nation we are now by our actions during the half-century since the end of the Second World War.

Before following our own path further, it's worth taking a sideways glance at those taken by all the others. Although nation-states are now central to our political consciousness and are the foundation of the entire international order, these entities are a comparatively recent political invention. Only a handful – England, Holland, Japan, maybe Poland and Russia (Muscovy), and Spain and Portugal – predate the 19th century by any consequential amount of time. France created itself, by its revolution, just before that century's turn.

The decline of religious belief was the crucible out of which nation-states emerged: Ethnicity provided an alternate opportunity for commitment to, and a sense of belonging to, a collectivity larger than family, clan, sept, tribe, guild, village, neighbourhood. For some, it was the only source of belonging. "The nation exists before all things, and is the origin of all things," pronounced revolutionary philosopher Abbé Sieyès.

The Enlightenment doctrine of the perfectibility of the naturally good, Rousseauean man by the application of reason and science, played a key part. Crucial also was the Industrial Revolution: Its railways and canals, later automobiles and highways, made it possible, and necessary, for an extended geographical area to be administered by a centralized state. Napoleon's military genius mattered a good deal: His armies seeded the transformational ideas of liberty, fraternity, and equality across Europe, and, as the only political structure within which these could be realized, that of nationalism.

Scholars have devoted protracted, often obsessive, study to trying to determine the qualities that actually define a nation. Ethnic homogeneity is the most obvious characteristic, although even in Japan, the world's most homogeneous society, there have always been ethnically distinct aboriginals. As a technique to achieve homogeneity, there is, sadly, nothing new about the kind of "ethnic cleansing" now happening in the Balkans, nor in Hitler's quest for *lebensraum*. Earlier examples include the mass transfer of Greeks and Turks after their war in 1922, Stalin's reshaping of Poland during and after the Second World War to add all Ukrainians to the Soviet Union and to evict all Germans, and the mass cross-movement of Muslims and Hindus before India's Partition in 1947. While a common historical experience is often cited as a necessity, the memories of Lowland and Highland Scots could scarcely be less alike; nor has a common national history united Belgium's Walloons and Flemings.

The finest analysis of the origins of nation-states is contained in Benedict Anderson's *Imagined Communities*. Even in the smallest nation-state, few citizens know each other personally, he writes, "yet in the minds of each lives the image of this communion." History – imagined history – is vital. Each nation's Tomb of the Unknown Soldier is "saturated with ghostly national imaginings." Antiquity, no matter how fraudulent objectively, justifies the present collectivity and therefore its future. Language is critical, above all in its printed form: "Print-language laid the basis for

national consciousness." (Language itself isn't always the communal precondition it's commonly assumed to be: Scarcely 5 per cent
of Italians spoke Italian at the time of its unification.) Anderson
makes a vital distinction between benign nationalism, or patriotism, and its racist variant: "Nationalism thinks in terms of historical destinies, while racism dreams of eternal contaminations."
And he comments shrewdly, "Racism justifies not so much
foreign wars as domestic repression and domination."

All nation-states exist therefore as exercises in the collective
imagination. They exist because their people want to have something they can call their own.

Over the years, nationalism's reputation has oscillated wildly.
In the 19th century, it was seen as liberating and progressive –
Byron in Greece as romantic forerunner to Che Guevara. It
blighted Europe in the First World War, and turned much of the
world into the charnel-house of the Holocaust during the Second
World War. Postwar, though, as in the decolonization of Africa
and Asia – the triumphant realization of President Woodrow
Wilson's creed of "self-determination" – nationalism was again
seen as liberating and progressive. It was seen again in this light
during the *annus mirabilus* of 1989 and the fall of the Wall. Today,
from the Balkans to Rwanda and Burundi, nationalism is once
again perceived as destructive and mindless.

During this long span, only two rival doctrines have challenged
the supremacy of nation-states. (A third rival, nazism and fascism,
amounted to an attempt to internationalize ethnic-nationalism).
The serious rival was communism. Until brought down by its
internal contradictions, communism's creed that all workers were
"brothers" held down by the chains of their bourgeois nation-
states exercised immense appeal.

The other rival doctrine has been postwar liberal internationalism. Revealingly, the UN's Declaration of Universal Rights makes
no reference to ethnic rights (nor to self-determination). The

ideal was to be a "Citizen of the World." It was exemplified by a young French-Canadian, Pierre Elliott Trudeau, who deliberately left his parochial nation-state to study at Harvard, London, Paris, then to travel the world over from the Middle East to India to China. Yet while the UN, and all other optimistic postwar international institutions, may have exercised authority, they could never command allegiance. As the Cold War's end demonstrated, all that had happened during the intervening decades was that ethnic nationalism had gone into hibernation.

One legacy of the ideal of liberal internationalism is the practice of dividing nation-states into those that are "civic," or which offer their benefits to all citizens no matter their origins, and the narrower, and cruder, "ethnic" nation-states. Canada in this sense is a civic state, as is the United States and the states of Western Europe, most of which have long ago transcended their strictly ethnic origins. At least formally, Japan possess many of the characteristics of a civic state, perhaps also Singapore. So, once, within Bosnia, did Sarajevo.

Mostly, though, this amounts to distinguishing between rich states and poor ones. The practice exaggerates the extent to which nationalism can be detached from ethnicity: Even while a citizen of the world, Pierre Elliott Trudeau was a French-Canadian through and through. Michael Ignatieff, a Canadian writer now living in London, makes a useful point about this distinction in his book *Blood and Belonging*. Ignatieff recoils from the savagery of the ethnic nationalism he encountered in Yugoslavia and Northern Ireland and among the skinheads in Germany. But, he admits, "Cosmopolitans like myself are not beyond the nation, and a cosmopolitan, post-nationalist spirit will always depend in the end on the capacity of nation-states to provide security and civility for their citizens."

We all need to belong, to have a place where we feel "*maîtres chez nous.*" The resonance of the words that fix the site of ethnic identity, *patria, patrie,* homeland, fatherland, *heimat,* confirm the

power of the idea. Even those who are affluent enough and cosmopolitan enough not to need to wear their identity on their
sleeves risk becoming global tumbleweeds if they detach themselves entirely from their ethnic roots. Ignatieff ends his 'confes-
sion' by remarking that while himself a civic nationalist, he
"believe[s] in the necessity of nations."

However they were formed, and whatever form they took, all
nation-states have demonstrated astonishing durability. "Nation-
ness is the most universally legitimate value in the political life of
our times," Benedict Anderson writes. Ethnic loyalty was the
initial bonding agent. Nation-states then fulfilled themselves by
protecting their citizens, either by winning wars or by losing them
appropriately heroically. Always, they could bind influential citizens to them by honours, patronage, profits. Postwar, most
nation-states have done a good deal more for their citizens: They
have looked after them, economically and socially.

    Although, by the Second World War's end, all democratic states
had succeeded in fulfilling their prime purpose of protecting their
citizens, almost all – the perverse exception being Nazi Germany
– had failed utterly to protect their people during the murderous
economic civil wars of the Depression. Postwar, all set out to
rectify their failure by turning themselves into welfare states and
by applying the anti-cyclical economic theories of John Maynard
Keynes. Whether the prolonged postwar boom was in fact caused
by counter-cyclical pump-priming or by the new mass consumerism and the piggybacking of new mass technologies (jet
airliners) on wartime inventions or was a by-product of the prolonged peace guaranteed, paradoxically, by the bomb mattered
little to the fact that transferring Keynesianism from out of the
pages of *The General Theory* into practical political life worked.
By 1971, even President Richard Nixon could proclaim, "We are all
Keynesians now."

    The magic worked doubly. Welfare made people both grateful

to their states and dependent upon them since all social security systems applied only within national boundaries. Welfare Keynesianism thus became a new dimension of citizenship. It's in this sense that, for Canadians, *l'état c'est nous.*

As always, the Canadian welfare or "provider" state was conceived out of a mix of self-interest and idealism. The Liberals were worried that if they didn't do the job the CCF might be given the chance to – as Labour had in Britain. Civil servants – this was the heyday of the famous "Ottawa Man" – had discovered new abilities and ambitions by having managed successfully the immensely expanded wartime administration. It helped a lot that as soon as the guns stopped firing, the economy boomed. Also that the prevailing intellectual theory of those times was collectivist and interventionist (and high-minded): The same top-down, rational planning that had defeated Nazi Germany could, surely, defeat all internal enemies – poverty, unemployment, sickness, illiteracy, underdevelopment.

Once the Canadian state had made up its mind to turn theory and idealism into a challenge and obligation, it moved with remarkable speed. First, family allowances and pensions. Thereafter, comprehensive welfare (the Canada Assistance Plan of 1966), medical care, hospital care, the Canada/Quebec Pension plans supplemented by Old Age Security and the Guaranteed Income Supplement, an unemployment insurance scheme utterly transformed from its original quite modest scope, subsidized higher education (to about four-fifths of students' costs), job retraining, regional development, equalization, and a host of specialized social services. Starting later than Germany, Sweden, and Britain, we developed within three decades one of the world's most comprehensive social security systems.

This achievement became a definition of Canadianness itself. Distinctive to this country, measured not just against the United States but also Britain, where so many of our social policy ideas originated, all these schemes were structured on the principle of universality. Everyone contributed; everyone benefited, on the basis of their need rather than of their contributions. This rejection of the alternative of two-tier social systems was decisively different from Britain (private schools, private medicine), as well as more dramatically from the United States (private schools and universities, private medicine, private personal security). Sharing out our wealth became a conscious redefinition by Canadians of what being a North American could mean; it also knitted us together as a subcontinental community as we had never been before, except in wartime, and even then a unity that encompassed only English-Canadians.

Our new provider-state also knitted Canadians together by using Keynesian pump-priming to flatten out the business cycles and to mop up periodic unemployment. American economist John Kenneth Galbraith describes Canada as "perhaps the first country to commit itself unequivocally to a Keynesian economic policy." The state acted as well to fill up the cracks in our marketplace by creating a network of new state enterprises, a vastly expanded Canadian Broadcasting Corporation (CBC) and Air Canada, Teleglobe, Atomic Energy of Canada, the Canada Development Corporation, and Petro-Canada. It challenged the "invisible hand" of the market economy by handing out equalization and regional development subsidies, and it nurtured nascent industries by grants and subsidies.

Through the adult lifetimes of almost all contemporary Canadians, this provider-state has reshaped Canada and the consciousness of its citizens. Its own lifetime – more exactly, its full bloom – was ended by Finance Minister Paul Martin's budget of February 27, 1995.

Once all Martin's cuts have gone into effect, by the fiscal year 1996-97, federal spending on programs – on people and things as opposed to paying interest charges on the debt – will decline to 13.1 per cent of the gross national product (GNP). This will be the lowest percentage in any year since 1950-51. That comparison exaggerates the extent of the reduction: Back then, Ottawa spent disproportionately on defence and veterans' benefits and so spent comparatively less on everything else. It is today's trend that matters. Ottawa's downsizing will continue through the rest of the 1990s. Simultaneously, all provincial governments, with only Quebec still on the sidelines until after the referendum and with Ontario, post-election, jostling to get to the head of the queue, are engaged similarly in what's been called a "governmental disarmament race."

Canada's provider-state ought to have been put through this change of life far earlier – in 1973-74 when the deficits first began, in 1983-84 when the collapse of oil prices ended Trudeau's last attempt to sustain the old order by exploiting surplus resource revenues, or through the rest of the 1980s when the Mulroney government failed to use a prolonged economic boom to lever us out of the "debt trap" that still has us in its grip. (Mulroney's failure highlights one characteristic of yesterday's spending splurge. Despite the conventional wisdom, those most guilty of fiscal improvidence were far more often conservative politicians than liberal democratic ones: in the United States, Ronald Reagan, George Bush, the savings and loan fiasco, and Orange County's fiscal chaos; here, along with Mulroney, Saskatchewan Premier Grant Devine and the pre-Ralph Klein Conservatives who bloated Alberta's provincial per capita spending into the highest in the country.)

All that really matters is what will happen now. Our provider-state is being hollowed out. Social programs and payments will be cut back and parcelled out among the provinces by way of "block grants." Nation-defining institutions like the CNR, the St. Lawrence Seaway, and probably the Canadian Wheat Board will join Air Canada and Petro-Canada in being privatized so that, by definition, their interests will no longer be the national interest.

Simultaneously, the CBC will be reconfigured into a supplementary network rather than the national one.

Our provider-state isn't going to vanish. An entire new generation of young people and middle-aged self-employed are learning how to provide for themselves so that they no longer need the kind of state that's been around for half a century. As for government itself, downsizing can mean rightsizing. A prolonged global boom may lever us out of the debt trap with no more than a severe shaking-up. Political fads change – today's obsession with deficit reduction as successor to yesterday's alarmism about global warming. Polls show that support for deep spending cuts is quite shallow; also that public support for tax cuts, as opposed to its strong opposition to tax increases, is highly ambivalent (interestingly, public opinion is almost as ambivalent in the United States).

The Canadian state, though, will never again be there for us in the way it has been throughout the lifetimes of almost all Canadians now alive. Its fundamental justifying premises, of managing the national economy and protecting citizens against internal as well as external socio-economic forces, have – largely – vanished.

In his omniscient way, Keynes had foreseen the problem with Keynesianism. "Ideas, knowledge, art, hospitality, travel, these are the things that should of their nature be international," he wrote in 1933. "But let goods be homespun wherever it is reasonable and convenient, and above all let finance be primarily national." For Keynesianism to work, each national economy had to be national rather than a borderless part of a global economy.

Effectively, the Keynesian era ended in 1981-82 when France's newly elected socialist president, François Mitterrand, tried to fulfil his campaign pledge to mop up unemployment by traditional spending programs. (The initial, free-spending policies of

Bob Rae's New Democrat government in Ontario were a last echo of that ideology.) The francs poured out into the economy all right; far too many sloshed straight out again, shrunken in value, into the rest of the world. The market, already global in its financial dimensions, was too powerful for even a strong government in a strong nation.

Mitterrand had the courage to admit failure and the wisdom to find an alternative. Unable to manage the French economy alone any longer, he set out in tandem with Germany to manage the far larger one of the then European Community, turning it into a regional island within the global economy that would be both sizeable enough to be largely self-sustaining (particularly when linked to Europe's "hinterland" of Africa and the Middle East; and, post-1989, also of Eastern Europe) and yet small enough to be managed by strong national leaders, like himself and Germany's Helmut Kohl.

With extraordinary speed, the European Community cured itself of "Euro-sclerosis." First came an agreement, deftly negotiated past a doubting Margaret Thatcher, to replace consensus decision-making – giving each member-state a veto – with limited majority voting. Then came the Single European Act of 1985, to create "an area without frontiers" by allowing the free passage of all goods, services, capital, and workers, and to end national discrimination in the awarding of public contracts. This exceptionally ambitious program, which required each of the twelve member-states to enact 282 separate pieces of legislation, was completed on schedule by the end of 1991. Separately, community life was pumped into the community by devices such as a common passport, the universal use of the twelve-starred flag, and, in 1994, an agreement to dismantle internal customs and immigration barriers (still rejected by Britain).

The real birth of the new Europe occurred in the small Dutch town of Maastricht in February 1992. In a glittering ceremony, the twelve leaders, still Kohl and Mitterrand but with John Major replacing Thatcher, signed a treaty to create a European Union (EU). Its centrepiece was a single European currency to be regulated by a new European Central Bank. The leaders also committed themselves to developing common foreign and defence policies. A "United States of Europe" was being born, proclaimed Kohl.

This was a reach much too far. A headline in the tabloid *Die Bild* alerted the German public, for the first time, to the fact that a common Ecu, or whatever the new currency would be called, would mean the end of the deutschemark, that symbol and reality of all their postwar economic and democratic achievements. German public support for European union has never recovered. In Denmark and France, the Maastricht Treaty was approved in national referendums by only the narrowest of margins. The British, as always, needed no encouragement to be sceptical about anything happening on the continent. Soon afterwards, all the pretensions to a pan-European foreign policy were exposed humiliatingly in Bosnia.

How the EU's future will unfold, how for example it will digest its ever-expanding membership – potentially to more than twenty once East European applicants are accepted – lies far beyond the scope of this book. The EU matters instead as by far the most developed model of what can be done to create a sub-global regional replacement for nation-states. Every bit as much, the EU illustrates the limits to which any regional association can replace nation-states.

People's loyalties are as focused as ever on the political institutions – Britain's Westminster, Denmark's Folketing – and the cultures and histories of their old ethnically defined nation-states. It's for the sake of their imagined communities that they are inspired to write poetry and songs, cheer their athletic teams, get damp-eyed when the troops march by and when the anthem is played; no one will ever sacrifice their lives for the sake of an international agency or a regional trade association (as Thatcher, rudely but quite accurately, has pointed out).

The critical point is that democratic legitimacy resides in and is strictly limited to the old nation-states. So does accountability. That key component of democratic legitimacy is found neither in international bureaucracies nor transnational corporations. Few Europeans thus know or care who their Euro-MP is. The conundrum is that it is only supranational associations like these that now possess the power to intervene to protect the citizens of their member-states against the undemocratic anarchy of the global economy. The old system is obsolete; the new one is not yet rooted in real life. Most probably, it will always remain an artificial transplant.

The issue is belonging. Nation-states continue to command loyalty because people want to belong to them. How long, though, can this loyalty be sustained once it becomes clear that nation-state governments no longer possess the authority and power to reciprocate loyalty?

For Canada, this conundrum is more difficult to resolve than for almost any other nation-state. We aren't rooted in ethnicity. Our history no longer engages us. Almost all of our protective external walls have crumbled.

In addition, and more directly than in any other country except the United States and perhaps Britain, Canadians are having to confront a new internal political contradiction. A major intellectual and political challenge is being made now to the defining justification of modern nation-states – that these should protect their citizens socially and economically by, among other things, redistributing wealth, some part of it, from those who have it to those who lack it. This challenge cuts to the core of our character as a state-nation.

The John the Baptist and the Joan of Arc of the neo-conservative, free-market cause is Margaret Thatcher. Newt Gingrich and the new Republicans are her children; earlier, she was Godmother to Ronald Reagan. In Canada, she is the heroine of Reform's

Preston Manning, Alberta's Ralph Klein, and Ontario's Mike Harris. In addition, neo-conservatives, or proto-Thatcherites, have been breeding like zebra mussels at major media outlets, such as the editorial board of the *Globe and Mail* (and its *Report on Business*), at *The Financial Post*, and at *Saturday Night* magazine, also at influential think-tanks like the Fraser Institute and the C. D. Howe Institute. An outpost of the movement, the Canadian Donner Foundation, has funded the creation of a Halifax equivalent of Vancouver's Fraser Institute, the Atlantic Institute of Market Studies. The single most influential Canadian neo-conservative, certainly the most vocal, is Conrad Black, owner of *Saturday Night* and part-owner of the Southam newspaper chain, as well as extensive media properties in Britain and the United States.

The point-of-sale slogan of the neo-conservatives is freedom of choice. One of the ablest of the group, *Globe and Mail* columnist Andrew Coyne, has argued for the abolition of all government assistance to the arts on the grounds that "Either we trust the audiences' choices or we do not. . . . As much as the artists, the willing paying audience is present at the creation."

Merely by daring to say the unsayable, neo-conservatives have energized Canada's political debate. The public's awareness of the seriousness of the debt and deficit problem is primarily their achievement. They have waged a spirited counterattack against political correctness and the excesses of "identity politics." They have made liberals and social democrats sound like conservatives clinging to yesterday's verities even as the world changes around them.

Ideology, though, has narrowed the neo-cons' vision like the visor of an armoured knight. They seldom look sideways, at context, at nuance, and never, ever, do they look ahead to consider what a society regulated by the single rule of freedom of choice would actually be like. Most curiously, neo-conservatives possess the same self-righteousness certitudes of those early postwar interventionist socialists like Britain's Stafford Cripps and our own Stanley Knowles. They pursue their goal of a society in which all will be unequal with the same moral fervour with which socialists once pursued their New Jerusalem of a society in which all would be equal. To tighten the connections between the opposite ends of the political spectrum, neo-conservatives are as keen on social engineering as socialists, let alone liberals, ever were. They want to use public policy to "cure" welfare dependants and irresponsible single mothers. Without ever admitting it, neo-conservatives are closet supporters of the same "nanny state" their hero Thatcher so often denounced.

Any society structured on the principle of deliberately instigated inequalities is certain, sooner or later, to become as unlivable in, and as unworkable, as societies structured on the "real socialism" principle of enforced equality. This cardinal issue of our times will be discussed in greater length in Chapter Five. It's enough to say here that from the perspective of the nation-state, the effect of this creed is to turn citizens into consumers. We are no longer sovereign citizens of a collective community; we are consumers looking after ourselves while residing in it. Only profit and loss matter. All the rest is bureaucracy, or special-interest groups, or sentimentalism.

Neo-conservatism portrays itself as an attack on government. Instead, it is an attack on community. Thatcher once compressed all her beliefs into a single vivid phrase: "There is no such thing as society; there are only individuals and their families."

In a society that isn't a society at all but an agglomeration of atomized individuals, there can be no mutual interdependence. This is the exact objective of the neo-conservative agenda. The illustration is the incessant clamour for reduced taxes. This demand serves two purposes: to liberate individuals to function as self-reliant self-providers; and to reduce the revenues available to government to implement their collective responsibilities (whether real or self-invented). The first is the rhetoric; the second is the reality. Emasculating governments ensures they can no longer prevent the widening of income inequalities. In turn, the more unequal everyone becomes, the harder each will have to strive and the less time and energy they will have to care about others. At the end will arrive the neo-conservative New Jerusalem in which everyone performs as a consumer and no one as a citizen, above all, a society in which no one is dependent upon anyone else for anything.

Every so often, neo-conservatives are honest enough to admit their ultimate objectives. In the recently published *Saturn's Children*, British MP Alan Duncan and economist Dominic Hobson declare that their goal is to "liquidate the liberal-democratic state." In particular, they list as targets for abolition "the social worker, the traffic warden, the ubiquitous 'counsellor,' the hygiene policeman, the health and safety inspector, the borough surveyor, . . . the health warning, the sex education booklet, the helmet laws, and the motorway camera." (Intriguingly, photo-radar was one of the first targets of Ontario's neo-conservative Conservative government.)

A refusal to pay taxes – "the economic expression of the state" as they've been called – represents the ultimate rejection of the national community and its replacement by – more exactly acceptance of – the global marketplace. In California in June 1995, citizens pursued this logic to its limit, rejecting a referendum asking for approval to increase their taxes by an average of $50 a year so that the state could repay debts caused by earlier shortfalls in revenues.

No taxes, no government. No government, no citizens – "civic" ones as opposed to ethnic ones. Only the marketplace, only consumers.

No society in the world will be more affected by this market-driven rejection of government than the state-nation of Canada.

Without a common ethnic identity, without much remembered (or imagined) history, without external walls, the Canadian community either exists as a political entity within which all who live here act as citizens, involving themselves with others in "a not too-strict account of how much the [tax] bargain is worth," in Michael Ignatieff's phrase, or there is no particular reason for the Canadian community to continue to exist at all.

The Canadian tradition and sensibility will ensure that our state won't unravel nearly as fast as will happen in the United States if the agenda of Newt Gingrich and the new Republicans – massive spending cuts; radical devolution to states and individuals; a flat-rate income tax to ensure that post-tax incomes remain as unequal as possible – is actually implemented. (In Britain, some neo-conservatives want government spending as a proportion of the GNP to be reduced to 20 per cent, or to its 1930s levels.)

Nevertheless, in a speech in May 1995, Deputy Minister of Finance David Dodge worried about the burden of taxes being born by Canadians with high incomes: Individuals making $70,000 a year, Dodge pointed out, paid $7,000 more in taxes than their American counterparts, and those at $200,000 proportionately even more. As Bob Rae warned during his losing election campaign, "You cannot have European-style services with American-style taxes." (At 36.6 per cent of the GNP, Canada's tax take is, in fact, slightly lower than the 38.3 per cent average of all developed countries; as the only comparison that counts, certainly to neo-conservatives, it is decisively larger than the 29.5 per cent take in the United States.)

The real question is whether, without Canadian-style services, even after these have been reformed and restructured as they must be, Canadians can still have Canada.

Many peoples have survived the vanishing of their nation-state. The French did it through four years during the Second World War, the Poles through two centuries of partition, the Jews through two millennia in the Diaspora. How though, do the people of a state-nation anchor their sense of belonging after their defining state has hollowed out and become marginal to their daily lives and concerns?

The next three chapters of this section will address one of the key reasons for this hollowing-out – the vanishing of the external walls that once marked where our nation-state began and ended. The succeeding chapters will attempt to describe the socio-economic effects of this phenomenon upon our community as a whole.

2

Associating with the Yanks

"No small nation can depend for its existence upon the loyalty of its capitalists."

— George Grant, *Lament for a Nation*, 1965

On January 2, 1989, Prime Minister Brian Mulroney and President Ronald Reagan enacted the Canada–United States Free Trade Agreement (FTA) into law by signing the document, more or less simultaneously, the one in his office at the Langevin Building in Ottawa, the other at his ranch in Santa Barbara, California.

This piece of paper constitutes the single most important change in Canadian economic policy since John A. Macdonald's National Policy of 1879. Revised a bit here and there over time but never fundamentally altered, that century-old doctrine's purpose was, in Macdonald's words, to ensure that by means of tariff walls "every appliance of civilization should be manufactured within our boundaries" instead of these being imported from Britain and the United States, thereby leaving us forever "hewers of wood and drawers of water." The FTA's purpose was the exact opposite: By being forced to compete directly with one of the world's most efficient economies, Canadian businesses would have no choice but to become productive enough to sell not just to Canada but to the United States, and then the world.

As Karl Marx was the first to appreciate, economics is about far more than economics. In train behind the FTA came transformational political and social changes. The implications of these second-order consequences of the FTA can be best described as the economic equivalent of our having enacted the Meech Lake Accord and the Charter of Rights and Freedoms *combined*.

The solution to the conundrum George Grant raised about the doubtful loyalty to a small country of its capitalists has been to turn all Canadians into capitalists. The FTA has transformed us, irrevocably, from a protected economy into a free-market economy. It has removed almost all of the walls that once shielded us from the economic superpower next door. Instead, in our new order, our capitalists, businesspeople, and entrepreneurs have become our economic walls, or, better, our springboards, because the further they are able to leap outwards with their goods and services, the more resilient the underpinnings of our nation-state itself.

One qualifier limits the FTA's transformational importance. Much that has happened to us as a result of it would have happened anyway because, since its enactment, the global economy has washed over us, transforming all nation-states as well as our own.

When Mulroney rose in the House of Commons on a sunny afternoon in September 1985 to announce that his government would soon open trade negotiations with Washington, he gave no hint that he understood any of these apocalyptic political and psychological implications. Even as to the economic implications, he had little to say. He was out to achieve what he called, variously, "enhanced trade," "freer trade," and "secure access." Even the actual phrase "free trade" was absent from Mulroney's statement. His lack of candour was understandable: On the one previous occasion Canadians had been asked what they thought about continental free trade, in 1911, they had turned massively away from even the immensely popular Wilfrid Laurier.

Political tactics aside, Mulroney was dead right to minimize the free-trade implications of the FTA. Whether fully free or only "freer" or "enhanced," trade was in fact the least important aspect of the project. Freeing up cross-border trade was little more than a come-on: Canadians had all learned in school and were told constantly by their economic experts that free trade was a good thing, certain to benefit everyone in the long run, despite some "transitional adjustments."

The real reason trade mattered so little to the FTA deal was because trade between Canada and the United States already flowed freely across the border, if not yet freely in legal form. Even before the FTA's enactment, the United States accounted for three-quarters of all our exports; indeed, principally because of the Auto Pact, the United States was the only market to which we sold anything in quantity except logs, rocks, and grain. Of these pre-FTA exports, and of our imports from the United States, more than 90 per cent crossed the border after paying customs duties of less than 5 per cent – too trivial a cost of doing business to deter many businesses.

Pre-FTA, cross-border trade was freer than between any two member-states of the then European Common Market (their continuing protective "walls" being those of language and culture). Very simply, Canadians and Americans traded a great deal with each other because we were so close and so alike. Our common language, personal tastes, and popular culture meant that salespeople could begin their bargaining by talking about the movies, TV shows, or World Series games they'd just watched. With a few variations, our commercial laws and business practices and rules were the same. So were the technologies we used, and the corporate structures, and the financial systems. Lastly, there was the massive cross-border corporation ownership: The vast American investment here was known in obsessive detail by Canadians; less well recognized was that, by the mid-1980s, Canadian investments in the United States had reached up to

$40 billion, second only to the British, even if preponderantly, and unexcitingly, in real estate. Often, cross-border trade amounted to internal dealings within the same corporation.

Not that the two economies were by any means one then. In a fascinating study based upon the "gravity model" (essentially, it assumes that people near each other do a lot of trade with each other whatever their nationalities), and published in May 1995, economists John McCallum of the Royal Bank and John Helliwell of the University of British Columbia found, to their surprise, that while 90 per cent of Canadian extra-provincial trade "ought" to have been north–south and only 10 per cent east–west, in fact more than half went to other provinces. "The Canadian economic union has been a powerful generator of trade," they concluded. It was only after FTA's enactment that there was a "surge in Canada–U.S. trade . . . and an absolute drop in east–west trade."

This "surge" was a bit like the moment when a solution crystallizes. The year-by-year diminution in cross-border tariff levels – legitimized politically as part of successive international agreements under the General Agreement on Tariffs and Trade (GATT) – and the steady rise in interconnectedness – commercial, cultural, personal – had already created most of the preconditions for Canadian trade to undergo a transformational shift.

Certainly, the FTA further loosened cross-border trade to a significant degree. All remaining tariffs were to be abolished within ten years. Businesspeople and professionals would be able to border-hop much more easily on short-term contracts and assignments. Both sides agreed to draw up matching codes to limit export subsidies. There were a lot of complicated "rules of origin" to deal with items that could now cross the border duty-free but of which bits and pieces had been made in other countries. There were some innovative new techniques for "disputes settlement," or rules for figuring out of who could do what, legally, to protect their producers against "unfair" imports.

All of this was useful. Inherently, though, it was little more consequential than the 1964 Canada–U.S. Auto Pact, which by creating a single producer and consumer market for the most important of all commercial products had locked Canada's industrial heartland of Ontario into the United States' industrial empire. It's just one of life's ironies that the Auto Pact should have been negotiated by the godfather of Canadian nationalism, Walter Gordon, and that one of the strongest opponents of the FTA should have been one of its greatest beneficiaries, Bob White, head of the Canadian Autoworkers.

Only the economic and cultural nationalists spotted the deeper implications within this kind of housekeeping detail. Their great failing, though, was never to be able to suggest a credible alternative way to restructure a Canadian economy that by the mid-1980s was clearly in decline (rising deficits; falling productivity; a continuous increase in the underlying rate of unemployment). Even in hindsight, knowing what would happen once our cross-border walls came down, it's hard to know what else could have been done. Looking back from today at the period when the irrevocable choices had to be made, though, it's striking how little foresight existed then.

Let me intrude a personal note. In a book published in 1985, *The 49th Paradox*, I broke with my nationalist sentiments, as well as those of my employer, the *Toronto Star*, to argue that free trade was the best, and only, way to go. Our resource boom was over, I argued: "From now on, Canadians will have to live by their wits." I arrived at the pro-free-trade position even while accepting that "free trade will almost certainly evolve into economic union." In hindsight, my own foresight was pretty limited.

The least useful place to look for insights into the wider implications of the FTA is in any of the speeches made about it by Brian Mulroney, or by any of his ministers or officials, or by supporters of the pact, such as the Business Council on National Issues.

It's necessary to turn first to an American politician, then to linger over an offhand remark made long ago by a Canadian economist (by coincidence, born in the United States).

The politician is Ronald Reagan. He once described the FTA – more likely, read out a line on a cue card composed by an aide – as "An economic constitution for North America."

The insight was brilliant. During his term in office, Mulroney was accused constantly of implementing a "corporate agenda" and of importing the doctrines of Thatcher and Reagan. In fact, Mulroney's failure to do anything about the never-ending budget deficits put a strict limit upon how far he could go in the direction of true free-market economics.

Mulroney, though, isn't so much the boy from Baie Comeau as the man from Iron Ore of Canada and the Hanna Mining Corporation. In retirement, he's moved smoothly and profitably back into the corporate boardrooms – almost ending up in a high-backed chair at American Express. In-between, while in office, he was openly scornful of the kind of officials who by then had run Ottawa and the country for a half-century. His kind were the corporate lobbyists.

Above all, Mulroney is a deal-maker. As with his "rolling the dice" tactics during the Meech Lake negotiations, it's impossible to know whether he cared only for making the FTA deal itself rather than for whatever it might actually have contained. In any event, Mulroney this time rolled the dice with considerable skill. He achieved his objective of implanting the corporate agenda into Canada by following the only political route that could have taken him there: That route was *outside* Canada. By negotiating an international free-trade treaty that sanctified these policies as a binding legal commitment, Mulroney was able to import back into Canada the corporate agenda and the rules and practices of free-market economics. These came to Canada like a gaudily coloured tail attached to the FTA kite.

As an "economic constitution," the implications of the FTA indeed bear comparison with those of the Charter of Rights and Freedoms. By opening Canada's economy to Americans, Mulroney ensured that it would become like America's. Post-FTA, Canada's guiding economic rule has become the American one of the free market. Many government policies are being decided now by the urgent need to reduce their deficits; just as many are being determined by the equally urgent need to create a market economy as efficient as those with which Canadian businesses are now competing directly. Hence all the privatization and deregulation, the downsizing of governments and public services, and the acceptance of the necessity of reducing taxes, especially those that inconvenience corporations (a major reason for reforming unemployment insurance and, after it, the Canada Pension Plan is to halt the increase in payroll taxes).

The FTA's single most important contribution to free-market economics was to create a continental, hands-off market for energy: Never again a National Energy Program. It also provided the political justification for earlier moves towards free-market economics, like defanging the Foreign Investment Review Agency, and the 1987 revision of the Bank Act that opened up Canada's market to foreign chartered banks, and vice-versa, and allowed banks to compete for the first time in related financial services like stockbroking.

The truth is that had Trudeau stayed on, and won, he probably would have followed pretty much the same path: In its 1985 report, the Royal Commission on Canada's Economic Future, created by Trudeau and chaired by his former cabinet colleague Donald Macdonald, recommended a "leap of faith" into continental free trade.

Yet the fact remains that when Mulroney, supported by the entire business community, convinced Canadians to vote for free trade in the federal election of November 1988, neither he nor the business leaders nor any economic experts told the public that what they were really voting for was a new "economic constitution" with profound political and social consequences.

Much earlier, one individual had issued a warning. Back in 1984, Carl Beigie, now a professor of economics at McGill University, then head of business-oriented think-tank the C. D. Howe Institute, mused out loud about what a free-trade pact might really mean. During an interview with me, he remarked that a continental pact could amount to "sovereignty-association between Canada and the United States."

As a supporter of free trade, and no doubt also because he was reluctant to stir up provocative thoughts about Quebec's proposals for a "sovereignty-association" that other Canadians had so consistently rejected, Beigie tossed out his comment diffidently, almost jokingly. I used it in a column, but made no great to-do about it. I've often kicked myself for failing to follow it through. Even today, the notion that we've backed into a sovereignty-association agreement with the United States hasn't entered the popular vocabulary, no doubt because Canadians resist accepting for themselves a concept they continue to refuse to grant to Quebeckers.

This is the Meech Lake aspect of the FTA. Even if unintentionally and unknowingly, we've associated ourselves with the Yanks in the most intimate of all possible arrangements short of outright political union.

We're as sovereign in international law as we ever were. But economic intimacy constrains political independence, a distinction that Parti Québécois Premier Jacques Parizeau understands full well, which is why he resisted for so long Bloc Québécois Leader Lucien Bouchard's call for a referendum on sovereignty *and* association.

The trend-line of our "association" is bound to affect the trend-line of our "sovereignty." The European Union, for example, as it approaches its goal of a single common currency and single central bank, is light years away from the limited common market its members originally committed themselves to. One of the long-range possibilities for new interconnections within our continent is a customs union to standardize external tariffs and thereby end the wrangling over "rules of origin" affecting goods imported to either country and then re-exported to the other. Another is expanded cross-border movement of labour – along the lines of the arrangements within the EU – not least because the current agreement discriminates in favour of capital over labour. Already, a joint task force of officials is examining ways to quicken cross-border passages, as by means of a "fast lane" to allow regular travellers to bypass the normal border checks and for customs and for immigration officials of both countries to take turns scrutinizing incoming as well as outgoing baggage and travellers.

Linkages like these are all either technical or of obvious practical value. Two other possibilities would bring home to Canadians just how intimately we are now associated with the Yanks. The first would involve approval for major sales of water, from British Columbia to California, say, that are currently exempted from the commercial rules that apply to exports of oil, gas, and hydro power. Selling water, no matter that we have a surplus of it and that it's a renewable resource, would touch the nerve within the Canadian psyche that political scientist Abraham Rotstein defines as "territorial nationalism." As Rotstein writes in *The Precarious Homestead*, "In the inner recesses of the Canadian self-image, there remains the indelible imprint of the pioneer struggle with the land." This sense of stewardship over a fragile landscape explains the enthusiastic public support for the Arctic environmental regulations that followed the 1969 passage of the U.S. supertanker *Manhattan*, for the establishment of the two-hundred-mile fishing limit, and for Brian Tobin's seizure of the *Estai* to protect the stocks of the near-uneatable turbot. How Canadians might react to a major water-sale proposal in a few years, when such a project would generate badly needed jobs and revenues for governments, would be a defining test.

Equally defining would be the public's reaction to a possible interlinking of the two currencies. In such a system, the movements of the two dollars in relation to each other might be limited in the manner of the multiple currencies within the European Exchange Rate Mechanism (itself a precursor to the planned European single currency). In 1991, former Federal Reserve Bank chairman Paul Volker told a conference in Kansas City, "If we all came back here five years from now, I would not be at all surprised to find a fixed exchange rate between the U.S. dollar, the peso, and the Canadian dollar." One part of Volker's prediction has been overtaken by the meltdown of the Mexican peso. As for the other part, at least one academic has gone further than Volker. At a conference on cross-border trade organized by the University of Toronto's Centre for International Studies in May 1995, George von Furstenberg, an American economist and visiting professor at the U of T, proposed an all-out monetary union. Von Furstenberg argued that a new North American Central Bank, similar to that planned for Europe, and in which Canada could secure minority membership, would give the country more effective control over its currency than that now exercised by the nominally autonomous Bank of Canada.

At that same conference, Tom d'Aquino, head of the Ottawa-based Business Council on National Issues, declared, "We are going to have to face some tough political questions over the next decade," citing, as an example, the "lack of an institutional infrastructure" to deal with the growing integration of the two economies. Gary Hufbauer of Washington's Institute for International Economics argued that, similar to the Schengen agreement within the EU, all border inspections should be ended "as a symbol of the integration we have arrived at." All participants at the conference agreed that the political pressures in the United States to cut government social programs and to cut taxes would create powerful echo effects north of the border. Former ambassador to the United States Allan Gotlieb suggested that the only way Canadians could have real influence over the American economic decisions that are now so vital to it was by political union. This wouldn't happen, Gotlieb added, because the United States has no interest in it now.

Among Canadian opinion-leaders and politicians, the possible effects of the rapidly evolving state of our association with the United States are being dealt with by denial. The subject has become a "non-subject," in much the same way that during the various crises of national unity any discussion of the possible benefits to *both* Canada and Quebec of some form or other of sovereignty-association has always been treated as unmentionable, indeed treasonable.

The truth is, American diplomat George Ball was quite right to predict, two decades before it happened, that free trade would bring in its wake "a progressively expanding area of political cohesion."

To magnify our dilemma, our national interest now resides in our achieving the closest possible cross-border economic intimacy. Easy access to the United States has become our "comparative advantage" over all other countries trying to sell there. The easier that access becomes – by labour mobility, a customs union, new monetary arrangements – the greater our advantage over our competitors. The cost of these benefits, though, is the progressive diminution of our political sovereignty, if not in law then in real-life fact.

To borrow Trudeau's famous metaphor, we're now in bed with the elephant. We can no longer act surprised if every now and then it rolls over on us. What we can still do, though, is figure out how best to preserve what's left of our national purity.

3

À *la Carte* Americans

"Economic interdependence transcends trade barriers. It goes to the heart of our national values and the way we structure our political ideas."

— Pierre Trudeau, in his last official speech as prime minister, to the American Publishers Association in Montreal, May 1984

In his column of November 18, 1993, the *Globe and Mail*'s Michael Vxalpy delivered himself of a splendid diatribe against Canadian Pacific Ltd. for having added the stars and stripes to the maple leaf in its corporate logo. Valpy lamented the diminishing of the National Dream, quoting Pierre Berton describing how the CPR had tied us together across "a bleak Pre-Cambrian desert, an angry ocean of plumed mountains, a chill wasteland of muskeg" and the description by Agnes Macdonald, wife of the first prime minister, of a ride through the Rockies on the cowcatcher of a locomotive as "lovely, quite lovely." Valpy himself denounced CP executives for "com[ing] up with the idea of pretending their company has no national home."

The newspaper printed just two letters of protest from readers. Canadian Pacific spokesman Paul Thurston commented coolly that it was necessary to be practical: "We do 25 per cent of our business in the United States." That was it. A cry of nationalist angst had been uttered in a vacuum.

One of the great unanticipated consequences of the FTA has

been to change Canadians' attitudes towards Americans. Even more, it has changed Canadians' attitudes towards themselves. As playwright John Gray writes in *Lost in North America*, "More and more, America is going to become the here and now from which we have been trained for generations to flee."

Threatened now is a chain of Canadian consciousness, an instinct for being distinctive, that begins with the Loyalists and their determination to build here "a better America" and continues on through Canadians' decision to have No Truck or Trade with the Yankees in the 1911 free-trade election. After the First World War and the triumph at Vimy, this urge to remain separate expressed itself in the Canadian Movement of the 1920s and 1930s that captured a share of the airwaves – "It's the state or the States" – by way of creating the CBC. After another world war and the nation's detachment from its original umbilical cord, the emphasis shifted to searching for a distinctive place for ourselves within the continent. Louis St. Laurent's Liberals were defeated for giving the contract for the TransCanada Pipeline to an American company. John Diefenbaker took up the cause with his "Northern Vision" of 1957-58; also, by the decision to maintain diplomatic relations with Cuba that precipitated Canada's first serious foreign-policy disagreement with the United States. During the late 1960s – not least because Expo 67 had proven that we could produce more than wheat and hockey players – came the flowering of the twin movements of economic nationalism and cultural nationalism that, even if they wielded more political influence than actual power, dominated English-Canadian public debate right through to the end of the 1980s.

As is true everywhere, these nationalist movements were primarily élite movements. Many ordinary Canadians viewed them with bafflement. They liked individual Americans and admired the United States. To most Canadians, TV was American TV, films were American films, and the same applied to books, magazines, music, entertainment, clothes, food, housing, and technology. For millions, "MY CANADA INCLUDES FLORIDA" as a *Maclean's* cover put it brilliantly: They went south for sun, and also for the metropolitan experience, whether in the theatres of Manhattan or at Disney World. They emigrated to achieve the heights in their profession or trade, from business to the arts to science to being TV anchors (a Canadian specialty). While many thousands of Americans came here to avoid the Vietnam War, forty thousand Canadians went south to fight in it. More than four hundred thousand Canadians now live in the United States; some three million live there part time.

No élite, though, can pursue causes unless the public at large shares its underlying anxieties and sentiments – Quebec nationalists as a case example. On several occasions during the 1970s and 1980s, polls showed majority public support for measures to increase Canadian cultural content and ownership of corporations; the National Energy Policy was immensely popular – outside of Alberta.

Shelves of books have been written about the cross-border national differences. One way to cut through all of them is to say that Canada represents the feminine principle in North America. The Americans had the Vietnam War and riots in Watts and Harlem; we had medicare and peacekeeping. Today, they have the homeless and assault weapons; we have social programs and gun registration.

As if it were a contest between the genders, an intense cross-border competitiveness has developed, seldom stated out loud on the Canadian side because the contest is so obviously unequal, and unrecognized on the American side except by a few astute observers.

One strand of that competitiveness has been the search for ways of being, at the very least, "not-American" and, at best, as some Canadian commentators have put it, "a distinctive kind of North American."

On a matter as central to their psyche as this, Canadians, being Canadians, tend to discount their own seers. American commentators may have more credibility. Stephen Blank, director of Canadian affairs for the New York-based Americas Society, observes, "You have, although you refuse to admit it and would rather not be told it, a civilizing mission in North America." In his book *The Wrath of Nations*, William Pfaff, the columnist for the *International Herald-Tribune*, writes, "It sometimes seems that citizens of the United States believe more in Canada's necessity (as a non-United States America; evidence of alternative possibility; demonstration of non-inevitability – even of refuge) than do Canadians themselves." Pfaff adds, "Quebec is a nation. But it is unclear that English-speaking Canada really is – which is a pity."

The most eloquent comment has been made by British writer Jan Morris, who got to know the country well in the late 1980s while researching a series of articles profiling Canadian cities from Vancouver to St. John's for *Saturday Night*. In March 1990, shortly before the Meech Lake fiasco when the country's rupturing seemed probable, Morris wrote an essay about Canada for the *Independent* newspaper: "It is plain nonsense to say, as foolish Canadians often do, that there is already no real difference between English Canada and the United States. There is almost nowhere in Canada, even in the neo-Manhattan of Toronto, where I feel for a moment that I am on American soil. It is not merely that the terrain is different. It is a much deeper difference in manners, in attitudes, and, I think, in values."

Morris was quite right to condemn as "foolish" those who believe no cross-border differences exist just because the borders themselves have largely vanished. They are as palpable as those between the Irish and the British, or among the British, or between the Scots and the English, even though, as do all North

Americans, they also speak the same language, wear the same clothes, eat (pretty much) the same foods, share the same popular culture, and watch the same television and films (mostly American).

This cross-border difference isn't a regional one, as between Texas and California say, or between Alberta and British Columbia. It's national because, despite all their internal regional differences, all Canadians are different from Americans in the same way.

Americans believe in competitiveness and in the marketplace, and have done exceedingly well out of both. We believe – within sensible limits – in collectivism and egalitarianism; out of these we have created a society that Morris described as "all in all, on the whole, the most admirable on earth," the UN having added its Housekeeping Seal of Approval to that judgement.

That makes us sound unbearably admirable. Far too often, Canada's distinctive consciousness expresses itself in carping, whining, and fear of – worse, envy of – individual success. Unquestionably, we're often parochial and passive. Yet tolerance, civility, and caring and sharing are, all in all, pretty admirable national traits. They are why we aren't Americans. Even while admiring Americans intensely and being drawn constantly towards the magnetic dynamism of that country, they are the reason why Canadians have, stubbornly, determinedly, at times despairingly, spent two hundred years not being Americans and will go on forever searching for ways to be distinctively Canadian. Rather than "not-American," our collective destiny, from which we cannot escape, is to be Canadian.

The other strand of cross-border competitiveness has been plain and simple anti-Americanism. A sizeable number of intellectuals, artists, and members of the political élite have harboured this attitude, even while denying it. Since expressing it openly would have been uncool and tacky, it's usually been expressed indirectly, as in comments about the numbers of medically uninsured south of the border, or about the extent of the violence there. Some of this was smugness, some of it was defensive (they are richer; they have cruise missiles). Some of it was simple patriotism.

Those two strands came together in opposition to the FTA. It was determined and impassioned, and although mustered up by a coalition of unmoneyed amateurs – artists, intellectuals, unionists, church groups, anti-poverty groups, feminists, environmentalists – it was often exceedingly skilled. (In their retrospective book, *Decision at Midnight*, three bureaucratic free-trade negotiators complain repeatedly about the influence upon public opinion of "glitterati" like writers Margaret Atwood and John Ralston Saul.)

The anti-free traders secured an exemption for cultural industries. They forced the draft treaty to be amended to make it clear that Canada was not committed to exports of water on the same strictly commercial basis as those of oil, gas, and hydro power. They extracted from Mulroney a pledge to introduce an "adjustment" program to help workers who'd be hard hit (he never implemented it). They even came within reach of winning.

For one incredible moment, during a televised debate with Mulroney in the middle of the 1988 election, Liberal Leader John Turner rose above his usual strangulated rhetoric to project the intensity of his patriotic feelings. Briefly, the polls turned around. Then the money poured in from the corporations. The ad blitz and the widespread doubts about Turner's capacity to lead the country were enough to turn the polls back around, and to give Mulroney a majority.

Not long after the election, opposition to the FTA actually increased. In 1990, the long "casino" boom fuelled by speculation and credit came to a shuddering halt. Unemployment and personal and corporation bankruptcies soared; real estate values crashed. Words like downsizing and restructuring entered the public vocabulary.

Little of this was attributable directly to free trade. Mostly, it was caused by a global downturn, magnified here by the tight money policy of the Bank of Canada as it zealously used high interest rates to suppress an inflationary threat that didn't exist. It was true, though, that the instant the FTA was signed, foreign companies with branch plants here stopped pretending to be "good corporate citizens" by making gestures to the locals like putting a few of them on their boards or issuing minority shares on Canadian stock exchanges. To rationalize their continental operations, a clutch of foreign-owned companies, including Inglis, Bendix, Consumers Glass, Burlington Carpets, Outboard Marine, Campbell Soup, and Gillette, closed branch plants here and expanded production at their plants in the south. In 1991, Varity, one of Canada's historic companies as Massey-Ferguson, closed its headquarters in Toronto and reopened it in Buffalo. During the first three years of free trade, at least three hundred thousand manufacturing jobs, close to one in five of the total, either moved south or vanished permanently.

Scared for themselves and for their children in a way that no generation had been in more than half a century, Canadians exorcised their anxiety by lashing out at scapegoats. One was free trade. The other – by far the preferred one – was Mulroney. His personal popularity dropped to an all-time low.

Canadians have yet to forget or to forgive Mulroney. Most probably they never will. Early in this decade, though, Canadians began to forget about free trade. They began, that is, to accept it as a fact of life. Having accepted it, people gradually welcomed it. By some kind of revision-by-osmosis, more and more people came to regard free trade as a positive development. That we had taken the ultimate dare of opening ourselves wide to the Yankee traders and had survived was a major factor. As significant was the growing recognition that many of our problems were self-inflicted – like the debt and deficit. The view began to take hold that free trade had actually improved Canada's prospects by bringing us into intimate contact with the world's largest, richest, and most creative country, even if also one of the most socially polarized and violent.

So our image of Americans changed. In our collective mirror, so did our self-image. Being Canadian began to mean being a kind of *à la carte* American. For some, being Canadian became a handy way of being American without actually having to live in the United States.

The quickest way anyone can insult a Canadian encountered abroad is to say, "American?" The denial comes instantly, and is always uttered with defiant pride. The notion that Canadians have become *à la carte* Americans thus demands an explanation.

Not a scrap of evidence exists that Canadians want to become Americans. In April 1995, a survey by Decima Research for the Canadian Council of Christians and Jews found that just 3 per cent polled favoured "union with the United States." This was down from a 5 per cent tally measured by an Angus Reid survey in 1991. It's entirely probable that fewer Canadians want to become Americans than do the citizens of almost any other country in the world. Given the margins of statistical error, it's possible that *no* Canadians want to become Americans. (Interestingly, the reverse isn't true: While a 1989 Decima poll recorded 86 per cent opposition to continental union among Canadians, it found that 56 per cent of Americans fancied the idea.)

If anything, references in casual conversations to the numbers of homeless and lack of gun control there in comparison to the relative absence of outright social tensions here occur much more often than before. When Preston Manning met with House Speaker Newt Gingrich in Washington in the early spring of 1995, he went out of his way – "We in no way, shape, or form are in favour of an American-style health-care system" – to emphasize (quite correctly) how unlike the Reformers were to the new Republicans, despite some ideological similarities.

One of Prime Minister Jean Chrétien's shrewdest political moves has been to put a distance between himself and Washington. Perhaps Mulroney's worst political blunder was to sing "When Irish Eyes Are Smiling" with Ronald Reagan at the Shamrock Summit right after having declared that "Good relations, super relations, with the United States will be the cornerstone of our foreign policy." Ever afterwards, Canadians doubted his Canadianism. With good reason: Mulroney sent his children to Harvard and Hotchkiss, holidayed regularly in Florida and Maine, shopped in New York (or, more exactly, Mila Mulroney shopped there), and was entranced by the intimacy of his relations with Reagan and George Bush and his close acquaintanceship with cabinet ministers, senators, and corporate leaders.

Chrétien did the exact opposite – because it was good politics but also because he believed in keeping his, and Canada's, distance. He disagreed with Washington over issues like Cuba and Bosnia. He delayed his first bilateral meeting with President Bill Clinton for almost a year and a half. Formally, the government's foreign-policy paper of January 1995 declared, "Differences of view do arise in such a multi-faceted relationship (as the Canada–U.S. one). They are differences between sovereign-partners, acting as equals."

Canadians were delighted. Personally, though, we moved closer to Americans and to the United States than ever before in our history.

The change was signalled politically during the 1993 election. FTA's successor, the North American Free Trade Agreement (NAFTA), aroused no public interest at all. The old nationalist warrior Mel Hurtig did conjure up a Nationalist Party into existence: It won just three hundred thousand votes, then collapsed amid recriminations about lost funds and administrative chaos. The new Chrétien government went through the motions of fulfilling its campaign promise to "renegotiate" NAFTA, then dropped the topic. Few complained.

All that ever matters is how people themselves actually behave. Soon after free trade had been enacted, Canadians began crossing the border in quest of bargains. In 1991, the number of day trips topped fifty-nine million, or more than two by each Canadian man, woman, and child. In Buffalo, below Toronto, and in Plattsburgh, below Montreal, one-quarter of all retail sales were accounted for by cross-border shoppers. North Dakota piled up $300 million in sales to Manitobans. When, from 1993 on, the decline in the value of the dollar erased much of the value of cross-border shopping, the hottest stores in Canada became the new American superstores that had hopped across the dismantled border – Wal-Mart, Price Club, Business Depot, Home Depot. (In fact, sales at some of these stores quickly cooled off.) The new GST provided people with a justification – "we're not giving Mulroney our money" – for their southern shopping sprees. The fact remained that a large number of Canadians now regarded it as normal to spend money they had earned here outside of the country, even though if spent here it would have generated tax revenues to help pay for their social services.

Attitudes about sports matter at least as much because sports take up the time of more Canadians than any other social activity. In the mid-1970s, plans by Toronto TV tycoon John Bassett, Jr., to bring a National Football League (NFL) club to Toronto pro-voked questions in the Commons and a threat of court action by Minister for Health and Sports Marc Lalonde. By the mid-1990s, the only sports that mattered to Canadians were American sports – precisely because these were American and so were the real thing. In Toronto, it's the Blue Jays, with the Raptors of the National Basketball League due to follow soon (conspicuously a rootless name, unlike the Maple Leafs, the Canadiens, the Vancouver Canucks). In Vancouver, another National Basketball franchise, the Grizzlies, was announced; soon afterwards, an American busi-nessman bought both the Grizzlies and the Canucks. Hockey remains the quintessential Canadian sport, the great assimilator of the children of immigrants, our own undimmed dream factory. The National Hockey League, though, long ago moved its head office from Montreal to New York, non-Canadian players now make up one-third of the league's roster, and at least two teams, the Quebec City Nordiques and the Winnipeg Jets, are due to move south. To complete the Americanization of Canadian athletics, a group of Toronto businessmen are planning to bring an NFL franchise to the city by 1998.

Up until the end of the 1970s, *the* national sporting event was the Canadian Football League's annual Grey Cup. The CFL is now in full transition towards becoming a cross-border hybrid (one-third of its teams are American); sooner or later, it's going to be renamed the Continental Football League. That the 1994 Grey Cup was played between the B.C. Lions and Baltimore makes Canada the only country in the world without any professional sports league or division of its own. It also means that the quintessential Canadian activity of West battling East has no focus now, indeed is likely to be replaced by two American clubs battling it out in the CFL finals.

Besides watching sports, our principal social activity is watching television. The public's new attitude about television was revealed during the great "cable-TV rebellion" of January 1995. To fulfil a CRTC directive, and to earn themselves easy profits, cable-TV companies like Rogers presented subscribers with the choice of either automatically receiving seven new Canadian channels at an additional cost of four dollars a month, or of facing the loss of several popular American channels, CNN, TSN, Arts and Entertainment. The rebellion was provoked specifically by the cable companies' manipulative "negative option" marketing scheme. It's an open question, though, whether as much populist outrage would have been stirred up had the offer involved the addition of seven American channels. As a measure of the public's contemporary viewing preferences, CBC-TV's share of the (English-speaking) national audience has slipped to 14 per cent from 20 per cent a decade ago. Impending spending cuts will further contract the quality of CBC programming, and therefore its audience. What was once *the* national network will probably dwindle down to a supplementary network, like PBS or TVOntario. Where Canadians are now going for their sports and their TV, their businesspeople have already long since gone. For Canadian Pacific Ltd. not to have wrapped itself in the stars and stripes as well as the maple leaf would have been, by late 1993, almost unusual. The head of Canada's national airline, Air Canada, is an American; so, once even less imaginable, is the publisher of Canada's "national newspaper," the *Globe and Mail*. In recent years, Americans have headed many major Canadian corporations: Ford Canada, Xerox Canada, Bank of Montreal, Honeywell Canada, General Electric Canada, Mobil Canada, and Maple Leaf Foods. Although Northern Telecom is still majority Canadian-owned, it is at least as much an American company now as a Canadian one, with dual head offices in Mississauga, Ontario, and in McLean, Virginia.

One reason why it's normal now for Americans to come here is that we are there now. In a study for the Americas Society, Stephen Blank writes of the "new economic architecture of North America." Essentially, two buildings have been renovated into one. Xerox Canada, for example, now ships almost all of its products to Canadian customers directly from U.S. sites; General Motors has moved its purchasing office for the Canadian market from Toronto to Detroit; Consolidated Bathurst, as soon as it was bought up by the Stone Corporation of Chicago, trimmed its Canadian head office from a staff of four hundred to one hundred and moved the Canadian CEO and chief financial officer south. In the new order, writes Blank, American-owned plants in Canada function as nodes within "continental production, sourcing and marketing networks." Several – Hewlett-Packard Canada, Kodak Canada – have gained "world product mandates" to produce particular lines for the global market. One unexpected result, argues

Blank, has been "greater differentiation" between the Canadian and American economies. This is to say that companies use their plants on each side of the border to produce whatever it is they are best at. The crucial cross-border difference is of course that the Canadians do this on behalf of their American employers.

For almost all practical purposes, the Canadian national market no longer exists. In its place are five subregional markets, each extensions of the counterpart regional markets within the continental economy (which in turn now extends into Mexico). The most developed of these subcontinental markets, Cascadia, embraces Alaska, British Columbia, Washington, Oregon, and northern California. Even Ontario, the national industrial heartland, now exports only 13 per cent of its total economic output to the other provinces.

As go trade, sports, and TV, so go ideas. In sending his children southwards, Mulroney was only following the crowd. Some twenty thousand Canadians are now studying at American schools, colleges, and universities. Once fees (now only half those at American public equivalents) are increased at universities here, as is bound to happen because of budgetary constraints, the number of young Canadians spending their formative years in another culture will increase considerably. Many of these will be our best and brightest: In one recent year, one-third of the graduating class of Upper Canada College went on to American universities.

Often, the FTA's impact has been symbolic rather than substantive. It has legitimized the idea that being a Canadian includes being an *à la carte* American, maybe even being a non-resident American. Many of the cultural nationalists who once fiercely opposed free trade travelled south soon afterwards in search of agents, publishers, and gallery outlets. The apotheosis of this new realism about the change in our national nature happened in June 1995, when the RCMP announced that it had sold exclusive merchandising rights to the Walt Disney organization, for $2.5 million over five years. Perhaps the most telling aspect of the deal was that the minister who approved it, Solicitor General Herb Gray, had once been the most ardent of the economic nationalists in Parliament. Even the *Globe and Mail*, house-organ of the neo-conservatives, was moved to protest: "We support open borders. . . . But Canada's symbols are not commodities." As it turns out, they are: The newspaper's complaint had no more effect than that by its columnist Valpy against Canadian Pacific Ltd.

Much of this attitudinal change had been in train long before the FTA. First under Trudeau, incomparably more under Mulroney, the prime ministership acquired a presidential aura (Jean Chrétien has since muted this by his populist style.) The enactment of the 1982 Charter of Rights and Freedoms Americanized Canada's political system significantly, shifting authority away from Parliament and the legislatures towards the courts, and so towards the United States' "division of powers" system. It has also turned Canadians into litigious rights-seekers on the American model.

The new legitimizing of the American way of doing things can be seen most strongly in the current ascendancy of neo-conservative ideologues in Canada's media, as noted in Chapter One. That a number are American themselves or studied south of the border is neither here nor there. The significant change is that for the first time in Canadian history a clutch of distinctively American political ideas are being injected into the Canadian bloodstream; there, they are adulterating our own distinctive sense of *civitas*, or civic-mindedness.

Neo-conservatism exercises the magnetic power of a clear, simple idea, and an agenda and a plan for implementing it. Its allure is magnified by the absence of confidently expressed alternatives, other than of a clinging to the past by liberal democrats. Today, one in two Canadians is represented politically by neo-conservatives or right-wing populists, whether by Reform MPS or the Klein and Harris governments.

In parallel, the American political idea of opposition to paying taxes has been imported here. Launched more than a decade ago in California, and sparked here by opposition to "Mulroney's GST," the anti-tax movement is now in full flight. Prior to Paul Martin's February 1995 budget, when reports of possible tax increases were leaked to the press to test the public's mood, Jason Kenney's Canadian Taxpayers Foundation mustered up and delivered to Parliament Hill 230,000 letters that helped significantly to convince Chrétien and Martin to achieve their deficit reduction targets entirely by spending cuts. While Harris's promise to reduce provincial income taxes by 30 per cent was probably marginal to his victory, it is nevertheless a key part of the platform he intends to implement – one that he gave Ontarians more than fair warning about by releasing his Common Sense Revolution agenda a full year before the election.

In essence, the neo-conservatives want to remake Canada into a mini-version of contemporary America – the same individualism in place of collectivism, the same minimal government, the same supremacy of the market and consumerism. For Americans, these ideas make a good deal of sense: Americans are individualist, have always been sceptical about government, and have always believed that each person should be free to pursue "life, liberty and happiness" in their own way.

Even for Americans, though, the dogma that individuals there can make it to the top and have only themselves to blame if they fail has always been something of a con for co-opting dissent. In practical fact, few sons or daughters of American investment bankers drop down the scale to become truckers, say, and few truckers ever clamber up it far enough to head investment banks. There's more social mobility in the United States, but despite the rhetoric not a great deal more – few contemporary Rockefellers are indigent – than in much of "Olde Worlde" Europe. In his animal-like way, Timothy McVeigh, the alleged Oklahoma City bomber, understood instinctively that the low cards dealt him at birth were all he'd ever have.

Whether Americans can sustain their particular version of the social contract – make a bundle on your own; go bankrupt on your own – now that its essential lubricating fuel of endless economic growth appears to have run dry is an open question. That's their problem. Canadians' contemporary problem is that while we are in the free market now, we are not, naturally, fully of it.

By doing everything the neo-conservatives clamour for – cut taxes, cut spending, eliminate the deficit, deregulate, privatize, downsize, restructure, encourage income inequalities in order to *encourager les autres* – Canadians may indeed be able to prevent the cross-border gap in living standards, of about 20 per cent, from widening. That's about as far as were are likely to go, no matter how deeply we may stride into the neo-conservatives' promised land. As a peripheral northern region of the continent (more exactly, five peripheral subregions), the economic and geographic logic of the marketplace will inevitably always marginalize us.

The inexorable outcome of neo-conservatism thus will be to make Canadians into poorer Americans rather than distinctive North Americans.

The alternative of remaining distinctively Canadian means maintaining our distinctive social contract: limiting the numbers of the poor amongst us even at the cost of limiting the numbers of the rich.

Much in the neo-conservative agenda is valid. Deficits do have to be reduced; governments are overdue to be reinvented, individuals need to be – have no choice but to be – more self-reliant. The distinction is in the objective. The Reform Party illustrates that distinction. Preston Manning's distancing of himself from the new Republicans while in Washington wasn't just tactical: It was visceral. As its title suggests, the party's objective is reform, not revolution or deconstruction. The motive for Reform's calls for spending cuts has been to make our social programs sustainable, for its direct democracy proposals to reconnect our governing system to the people, for reform of multiculturalism and immigration to make all Canadians again feel they are part of an integrated community. Martin's February budget illustrates the same distinction. Unlike the Republicans, Martin did not conjoin tax cuts together with spending cuts in his deficit-reduction package: His purpose was fiscal reform rather than social engineering by way of magnifying income inequalities.

Beyond argument, the Canada of tomorrow is going to have to be decisively different from the Canada of yesterday. There simply isn't any more money. Our resource surplus is long gone. No barriers remain between our economy and the global one. Canadians themselves are self-reliant, and survivalist in ways they haven't been in decades.

The distinction is between living in a community as citizens and residing in it as consumers. It's between unregulated individualism and *civitas*. Distinctive Canadian aptitudes do exist. We possess a special skill at public enterprise, which we regularly demonstrate by the excellence of our peacekeepers and by the unusual competence with which we stage public events, from Expo to the Olympics to G-7 gatherings. Many – most probably all – of our public institutions do need to be "reinvented." But if most are privatized, or are commercialized as the current vogue phrase goes, few foundations will be left upon which to exercise our skills at public enterprise, or to use these institutions as the sustaining nervous system of a community.

Taxes mark the real dividing-line between democratic citizenship and neo-conservative consumerism. The great social challenge presented by taxes is that they are taken from each of us to be spent on people whom we do not know, while they at the same time are paying taxes of which part may be spent on strangers like us. Taxes are the most visible, and painful, of our societal "recip-rocal obligations," to use the phrase of historian Christopher Lasch. Debates about the scale and nature of taxes is one thing, and a wholly proper one. Questioning taxes themselves, as is now the dominant creed in the United States, and echoed by neo-conservatives here, is to question the nature and value of the national community itself.

According to the polls, 97 per cent of Canadians want to continue to be Canadian, whether to fulfil their "civilizing mission in North America" described by Stephen Blank, or to perform "as alternative possibility" as suggested by William Pfaff, or simply to continue to live in a community that is relatively safe, non-violent, and decidedly orderly. To do all this we certainly need to rethink and reinvent to suit today's circumstances, our own defining creed of "good government." Without government itself, though, we will neither have "peace [and] order," nor eventually, Canada itself.

Allan Gotlieb's comment, quoted in Chapter Three, that in order to have real influence over U.S. trade and other decisions that affect us vitally would require a political union that Americans now have no interest in extending, is an apt one. Our admission to the union would impose immense regional and political complications upon Americans – too many additional northerners; far too many extra Democrats. More to the point, the FTA has changed the traditional political equation. The United States already has all the financial, commercial, and industrial access northwards that it needs; it has no residual interest in offering us political access in exchange. Thus the paradoxical consequence of the FTA has been to remove the "alternative national option" we've spent our entire history rejecting even while drawn magnetically towards it.

We're on our own now. Either we make our community work our way or we let it fade away with a whimper.

4

Into the Wide World

"The culture of business is becoming global culture itself."
— Derrick de Kerckhove, *The Skin of Culture*, 1995

Although the FTA has long since been superseded by NAFTA, it merits one last backwards glance. It pushed the Canadian economy out from a backwater into the broad waters of the continental economy; no sooner had we embarked on that journey, though, than we found ourselves in the middle of the immense and turbulent ocean of the global economy.

As Brian Mulroney kept saying, the FTA's core justification was to "protect us against American protectionism." This objective was eminently sensible. At that time – the late 1980s – the U.S. economy and its industries were in retreat. At the same time as Ronald Reagan was telling Americans to "stand tall again," the auto plants, steel foundries, and machine shops of the new "Rust Belt" were sending their blue-collar workers trudging home. The Japanese, besides selling Americans everything from VCRs and autos to computers, were now buying up the best of America, from Hollywood studios to Manhattan office towers. This was the era of Michael Crichton's chronicling of an implacably predatory Japan in *Rising Sun* and of historian Paul Kennedy's warning that the United States was about to suffer the same "imperial over-reach" that had brought down the empires of Holland, Spain, France, and Britain.

The FTA, went the analysis, would get us across the drawbridge before the Americans pulled it up to protect themselves against the Japanese, the Little Dragons of Southeast Asia, and the suddenly revived Europe as it gave its corporations economies of scale by giving up on internal trade barriers. A cross-border trade deal would protect us against being sideswiped, even unintentionally, by a U.S. retreat into the protectionism of Fortress America.

The theory was sound. Reality pushed it to the margins. From 1990 on, in one of those spasms of national stable-cleansing that is so quintessentially American, the United States put itself and its economy through the wringer. The techniques – restructuring, re-engineering, de-layering, downsizing – were brutal; some of the more benign of the new techniques, such as just-in-time inventory management, were copied from the Japanese. Yet the task was done. Suddenly, American corporations began venturing out into the world. Since 1990, Procter & Gamble has increased the share of its total sales accounted for by exports from 29 per cent to 51 per cent, and General Electric from 22 per cent to 40 per cent. During the same timespan, Caterpillar reduced the assembly time for a tractor from twenty-five days to six. The world's leading high-tech electronic companies are now Intel and Microsoft. In software programs, in multimedia, in electronic entertainment, the United States is easily the world's leader, even in some automobiles, such as the minivan. Personal computers are now a distinctively American product; so, predominantly, are semi-conductors. Japan is no longer Number One: It's a horrendously expensive place to do business; its workforce is ageing; its R&D has tailed off; its financial sector is shaky. The United States has beaten Japan, and Europe, in the race to develop high-definition TV. As well, since the signing of NAFTA, the principal noise along the Rio Grande has not been the "giant sucking sound" of factories and jobs moving there, in failed presidential candidate Ross Perot's alarmist warning, but the sound of American articulated trucks moving south – at least, until the peso dropped.

Certainly, the United States has lots of economic problems. It has fewer, though, than most countries. Its rate of unemployment is one of the lowest in the West; it's creating more new jobs than Europe and Japan combined. The biggest change has been in attitude. The "Gingrich revolution" may or may not make sense; it does bespeak a political and economic boldness no other industrial country has had the self-confidence to attempt. Americans feel cockier about competing because they *are* now competing. From a lowly 6 per cent of GNP in 1972, the role of exports in the United States' total output has almost doubled, to 11 per cent. That's still a lot lower than Germany, Britain, Japan, and Canada (29 per cent). But the United States is achieving one of the fastest relative increases in exports; in the vital "emerging markets" of the Pacific Rim, it's now beating out Europe, if not yet Japan.

Thus a major part of the U.S. protectionism that we went into the FTA to protect ourselves against has vanished. True, the United States is more than ready to use its raw power to benefit its producers in ways that small nations, like Canada, cannot do – pressuring China to observe copyright laws on CD-ROMs and videos or threatening stiff tariff duties on Japanese luxury cars to ease open the Japan market to foreign cars. Mostly, though, the United States is now steaming along in the global ocean. Like a pilot boat hawsered to a supertanker, we have to do the same.

Before looking at how we're coping, it's worth scanning some of the aspects of the "global economy" phenomenon, which has become the great change agent – and cliché – of our times.

The first useful comment to be made about the global economy is that it doesn't really have a lot to do with economics. It has to do with finance. From FTA to NAFTA to the new international GATT deal, all trade pacts are now much less about liberalizing trade than about liberalizing money to go wherever it wants to go by making investors feel as secure abroad as they are at home. It's these financial decisions that determine what gets made where and sold to whom, at what price, in what currency. The really decisive aspect is that these are non-national decisions. During the three decades of 1964 to 1992, lending and borrowing across national boundaries increased at an incredible compound rate of 23 per cent a year.

The origins of today's footloose global financial system can be traced back almost a quarter-century. In the early 1970s, runaway U.S. inflation (precipitated by President Lyndon Johnson's attempt to combine the guns in Vietnam with the butter of his Great Society spending programs) brought down the Bretton Woods international financial system. This arrangement, dating back to 1944, and monitored by the International Monetary Fund, ensured that all countries maintained their currencies at fixed rates (except when devaluing or revaluing them to new fixed levels). Once currency values began to float, everyone wanted to keep their money mobile. From just $3 billion in 1960, the so-called Euro-currency pool – most of it in actual dollars and all of it unregulated – increased to $1 trillion by 1980. (Recycled petro-dollars were a major new source of footloose funds.) To promote financial mobility – and to attract it to the City of London – Margaret Thatcher, in perhaps the single most daring economic decision of her career, ended all exchange controls in 1979; all other European countries followed eventually. As for Canada, foreign trading in Canadian stocks, bonds, and currency jumped from $50 billion in 1982 to just under $2 trillion in 1994. Today, any hard currency can move to and from anywhere to anywhere at will, regardless of the will of the national government. This was demonstrated in 1992 when both Britain and Italy were forced out of the European Exchange Rate Mechanism by speculators bidding down their currencies; the same run was taken, much more brutally, against Mexico in the winter of 1994-95.

In his book *States and the Re-Emergence of Global Finance*, University of Toronto political scientist Eric Helleiner analyses these events and concludes that a major contributing cause was the deliberate policy of several nation-states, most particularly the United States and Britain, to use international financial liberalization as a way to discipline their domestic economies. If Helleiner's analysis is correct, nation-states must still possess the power to redo much of what they once undid. The protests by national leaders that they are impotent against the power of global finance – as were made at the G-7 meeting in Halifax in June 1995 – are at the very least exaggerated. Lack of nerve in the face of the mysteries of money may well be the real cause of their impotence.

The most dramatic aspect of today's global financial market is the trillion-plus worth of dollars, yen, deutschemarks, pounds sterling, francs, and the rest zipping around in the ether *every day* as currency traders and bond dealers chase fractional changes in interest rates and relative currency values. (One Canadian bank once tracked the movement of some Third World debt it was holding: It recorded eight purchases and sales of the same $20 million within a twenty-four-hour period.)

These traders and dealers, mostly male, mostly in their twenties and thirties, mostly wearing wide suspenders, have been called "stateless legislators." They, and their scorekeepers like Moody's Investors Service of New York, now determine national currency values and therefore domestic interest rates at least as much as national governments and national central banks. In a speech in April 1995, Tom d'Aquino, of the Business Council on National Issues, criticized proposals by Nobel economics laureate James Tobin for nation-state taxes on international financial transactions. "We should be wary of such appeals," said d'Aquino.

Financial globalization would eventually benefit everyone. As an interim benefit, "Governments will no longer be able to spend and tax at will. The punishment for spendthrifts will be certain and costly," d'Aquino noted approvingly. (He didn't bother to add that in the absence of tax revenues, the heaviest costs would fall upon those dependent upon governmental social programs.)

Just as governments have to dance to the tunes of the currency traders, so must they bob and bow before the transnational corporations. These make the decisions about what to produce where, and whom to sell it to. Indeed, the less national transnational corporations become – the prefix "trans" conveys their contemporary character far better than the old one of "multi," which meant that they operated a number of *nationally based* branch plants – the more efficiently they can function globally. As an encouragement to growth, the larger transnational corporations become, the more stateless, and less regulated, they become. The ideal transnational corporation is self-sufficient, liberated from national governments, and in most respects, from its own workers.

According to the UN, transnational corporations account for one-quarter of the entire global output, and for one-third of all the world's exports by way of internal transactions between these corporations and their 170,000 subsidiaries. As an example, Canada's Northern Telecom operates plants employing 33,000 people in forty countries. The sales of the foreign subsidiaries of U.S.-owned transnationals are now more than twice the United States' total exports.

Transnational corporations provide the motor fuel for the global economy by way of foreign direct investment (FDI). During the half-decade of 1987 to 1992, FDI doubled from $1 trillion to $2 trillion. More than 90 per cent of all the moneys channelled into developing countries is now private investment rather than public foreign aid.

Another useful point to be made about the nature of the global economy is that within it the most important asset is now neither goods nor services nor even money. It is knowledge itself.

Knowledge has become the true global currency. It can neither be taxed nor be halted at any border. It can be transported anywhere, effortlessly, on a floppy disk or in someone's head. Along with its operating partner, information, knowledge determines almost everything else that happens. It has displaced the traditional capital assets of land and equipment, not to mention labour.

The shrewdest comments about the role of knowledge in the global economy have been made by American management guru Peter Drucker. "There is no domestic knowledge or international knowledge. There is only knowledge," Drucker writes in an article in the November 1994 *Atlantic Monthly*. He also mints the insight: "There are no poor countries; only ignorant countries." Together with U.S. Labour Secretary Robert Reich, Drucker identifies education, and training and apprenticeship, as the single certain response that nation-states can make to help their citizens cope with the global economy.

Knowledge's other partner is of course communications. Anyone can talk now to anyone else, and send and receive data from anywhere to anywhere. Nothing makes the global economy more of a piece than the fact that 80 per cent of all the data stored in computer data banks is in English, except perhaps for the fact that CNN is received in 110 countries, or that the empire of media colossus Rupert Murdoch now encircles the globe, or that dissidents in Tiananmen Square and rebels in Chiapas were able to send out faxes to the world's media even as the tanks were rolling down upon them.

A last useful comment to be made about the global economy is that it isn't really global. Certainly, it's that potentially: The Cold War's end has removed all political barriers to its growth, soon even in Cuba and perhaps in North Korea. What really exists, though, is a *Westernized* global economy.

One of the great socio-political developments of our times is the ascendancy of Western economics everywhere. North American and European economic systems, management techniques, and technology, and laws and conventions about everything from bankruptcy laws to stock market regulations to commercial law, are now the international standard. Western companies, for example, have introduced life insurance to China and mutual funds to Thailand. Hence the shrewdness of de Kerckhove's comment: "The culture of business is becoming global culture itself." Hence the globally homogeneous quality of hotels, air terminals and passenger planes, plants, office and apartment buildings, telecommunications and computer systems, automobiles, movies, music, restaurants, fast foods, clothes. Local culture is now either staged for tourists, or is private.

Where the Western economy hasn't yet reached – much of Africa and the Middle East, parts of Asia and Latin America – there is, effectively, no economy at all. Moreover, it is the West, most especially North America, that has provided the market for developing countries to become developed ones, first Japan, then the Little Dragons, and today Malaysia, Thailand, parts of China, parts of Indonesia and India at least potentially, and, iffily for the time being, Mexico. As an illustration of Western dominance (more specifically of U.S. dominance), Mexico has had to rewrite the rules of its own economy – a governmental commitment to privatization and to putting up a major share of its oil revenues as collateral – in exchange for Washington's advancing a $20-billion loan to halt the meltdown of the peso. No developing country can escape this kind of pressure. Worry over rising complaints by foreign investors about the commercial lawlessness there has forced China to crack down on corruption, including by its own public agencies.

The quickest way for developing countries to create Westernized economies is to create "special export zones." There are now several hundred of these zones where foreign investors pay no taxes, are exempt from most local laws about the environment, health, and safety, and can exploit cheap local labour to make finished products for export from bits and pieces imported from other duty-free zones. In the largest, the *maquilladora* zone along the Rio Grande, half a million people work in eighteen hundred factories for an average wage of $U.S.2.40 an hour. In China, India, Vietnam, and Indonesia, the average wage is fifty cents an hour. In the United States, it's $16.00 and in Germany, it's $25.00. One reason why American high-tech companies are setting up research labs in Russia is that the pay for superbly trained Russian physicists is $100.00 a week.

Eventually, much of the globe should join the global economy. A middle class is emerging in China and India, numbering in each case about one hundred million. Some of the world's most efficient software companies are in Bangalore, India. A number of U.S. immigrants are returning to China, India, and Vietnam, because the prospects there are so much more promising; similarly from Canada to Hong Kong.

By the year 2010, according to the World Bank, all but six of the fifteen largest economies in the world will be developing nations; Canada, now thirteenth, will drop off the list. By the year 2020, Malaysia is forecast to achieve a standard of living equal to the European average. Sooner or later, this shift in economic power will be reflected in shifts in political power as measured by membership in the UN's Security Council and of the G-7 (either its size will increase or we'll be dropped from this inner circle).

In lockstep, as economic and political power shifts, so will cultural influence. Increasingly the cultural values of newly developed countries, especially those of the successful but authoritarian states in East Asia, will extend backwards into the developed industrial countries. Singapore's lecturing of Western countries about the superiority of its tightly regulated version of human rights is a foretaste of what's to come.

Much that should happen may not happen. Because they are rigid, the authoritarian regimes in most underdeveloped countries are fragile. All bets are off, up to the possibility of civil war, during the post-post Deng Xiaoping era in China. The same applies to Russia. Even a "soft authoritarian" state like Singapore is finding it hard to cope with the rising expectations unleashed by affluence. A contemporary worry of Singapore's regime is how to censor the Internet. In most developing countries, especially China, the gaps in wealth are outrageous, and the exploitation of workers far worse than anything perpetrated by pre-Communist capitalists. Environmental degradation is widespread and agricultural output is declining as peasants move to the cities and as prime land is ripped up for everything from factories to golf courses.

The West's response has been to look the other way. Occasionally, proposals have been made to add rules about child labour and environmental degradation to global-trade pacts. These have always been withdrawn in the face of accusations of "neo-colonialism." The more urgent motive has been that the West is now dependent upon the global economy. During the next decade, half of all commercial airliner sales will be made within the Pacific Rim; total infrastructure spending in Asia in the next half-decade will top $U.S.600 billion. Foreign Minister André Ouellet's denunciation of attempts to influence human rights conditions in these prime markets as "Boy Scout[ish]" illustrates the prevailing Western attitude. It represents a radical break with our own tradition, though, indeed a decisive departure from the policy of the preceding Mulroney government of making observance of human rights a condition of foreign aid. To put it straightforwardly, looking for exports means looking the other way.

Periodically, demands are made to loosen the knot between West and East, more exactly between North and South. "What has got forgotten is that the purpose of an economy is social stability," James Goldsmith, financial speculator turned environmentally minded French Euro-MP, writes in his recent book, *The Trap*. Goldsmith warns that global free trade will "impoverish and destabilize the industrialized world while at the same time cruelly ravaging the third world." It will create high unemployment in the West while destroying the agriculture and the environment of developing countries, he argues.

Unquestionably, Goldsmith is onto something. On the one hand, unemployment in Europe, and in Canada (although not in the United States), is stuck seemingly permanently at a socially destructive 10 per cent. On the other hand, China's agriculture is collapsing to the point where by 2030 it will need to import one-half of all the grain now being exported throughout the entire world. Unless regulated, global capitalism is indeed set to impoverish a good deal of the industrialized world and to "ravage" much of the Third World.

To find a way out is going to take a new Keynes. This, precisely, is the point. Global free trade and the free market have become today's Keynesianism, a magic solution to economic growth accepted by all governments and all economists as the best, indeed the *only* solution in exactly the same way they all once believed uncritically in Keynesian pump-priming. They were wrong then, if only in the long run. They may well be wrong again – absent a coincidental, prolonged global boom mirroring that of the early postwar years. But not until the industrialized world has been socially destabilized by permanent high unemployment and widening income gaps will today's conventional wisdom be challenged seriously. At which point, a ferocious political backlash will occur.

As for Canada, the only certainty is that as a small nation, we're going to have to survive, and do our best to thrive, amid the free market and free trade for quite a few years yet.

Given that we're out on the broad sea, we have no choice but to chart our course as best we can. Encouragingly, some signs exist that we're getting the hang of it. In late 1994, Prime Minister Jean Chrétien led a highly publicized Team Canada group of premiers and corporate leaders to China, and on to Vietnam and Indonesia, and returned with an even more highly publicized $12 billion worth of export contracts. That many of these deals later unravelled, as always happens in China, didn't diminish the drama of the enterprise. Later, Chrétien headed a successful mission to Latin America.

These initiatives demonstrated how significantly our national attitudes have changed. Once, Canadian businesses aimed to sell in mass to the protected domestic market. Now, they aim to sell to niches of the global market. Today, even though the United States still matters by far the most to us (indeed, since the FTA its share of our exports has increased to more than 80 per cent) while in the rest of the world, except for Hong Kong where fifty thousand Canadians are the single-largest foreign community, we are still scarcely visible, at least some of our businesses are now venturing out into the wide world. As an example, a Canadian industrial exhibition in Mexico City in the summer of 1994 attracted more than four hundred exhibitors.

If anything, government attitudes have changed even more radically. The Mulroney government moved into NAFTA edgily and late. By contrast, the Chrétien government, no matter the Liberals' past opposition to free trade, is reaching out everywhere. Canada has championed the addition of Chile to NAFTA, to turn it into what Chrétien calls "the four amigos." In July 1994, we were one of the strongest advocates of an Asia-Pacific free-trade arrangement on which agreement in principle was given by the twenty-two members of APEC at their summit in Indonesia. In

Paris the following December, Chrétien tossed out the idea for what would be the granddaddy of all pacts, encompassing Europe and North America. Later, International Trade Minister Roy MacLaren followed up by making the rounds of the European Union's headquarters in Brussels; in fact, his reception was lukewarm. Canada has been one of the strongest supporters of the global trade liberalization deal negotiated under GATT, and is a firm backer of that body's successor, the World Trade Organization. Separately, MacLaren has also been pursuing free-trade deals with Israel and Jordan, and has talked about possible ones with Australia and South Korea.

As always with us, it's a balancing act. In trade terms, only the United States really matters to us – as yet. In economic terms, therefore, we are trying to transfer our traditional multilateral diplomacy at organizations like the UN and NATO by using all these regional free-trade pacts to give ourselves a bit of manoeuvring room so that we can keep ourselves at a political distance from the United States. Having gone global for the sake of economic survival, we now have to do the same thing for the sake of political survival.

It won't be easy. Despite all the business club rhetoric about Canada as a trading nation, we've traditionally performed more like a nation of head-waiters taking orders for commodities. In *Fortune's* list of the top five hundred international industrial companies, Canada ranks only in twelfth place, with just six firms making the list. (In service corporations, including banks, though, we do better: Here, we rank sixth, with seventeen firms on the list.)

Nor will the political part of the balancing act be easy to bring off. In January 1995, a foreign-policy statement by the Chrétien government that described Canada and the United States as "sovereign partners acting as equals" also talked about the need to "secure and enhance our economic partnership with the U.S." As remarked earlier, the hard truth is that easy access to the huge

U.S. market is our "comparative advantage" over all other nations. It's therefore in our self-interest to make that access ever easier and more comprehensive.

There's also the fact that to make our way in the global world we have little choice but to become more like much of the rest of the world. To exaggerate, but not by that much: In order to compete successfully with a South Korea, say, our wages, social systems, and taxation schedules cannot be too different from those of South Korea, even after allowing for our built-in advantages of political stability, resources, installed infrastructure, the creativity generated by our multicultural population, and, far from last, our easy access to the U.S. market.

Two comments illustrate how tightly the global straightjacket now envelops us. Peter Drucker has developed the useful notion of "the maximum wage." He argues that workers in developed countries can push their wages up only so far now, or improve their working conditions only so much, before their employer will respond by shifting production to a developing country. Queen's University economist Thomas Courchene has made the same point in a different way. In his 1994 report, *Social Canada in the Millennium*, for the C. D. Howe Institute, Courchene warns that either we adopt radical but "made-in-Canada" social policy reforms or "we will likely end up with a made-in-international-capital-markets social policy." Lastly, there are the constraints imposed upon us by those "stateless legislators" in their wide suspenders.

The great unanswered question about the new Keynesianism of free trade and free markets is whether it will ever create enough jobs or will only create large numbers of McJobs surrounding the core jobs of the technically skilled, internationalist "knowledge workers." This issue of the potential economic polarization of our community is the topic of the next two chapters. There, a comparison is made between the magnitude of this challenge and that posed to us by the Depression. One difference over time is that in addition to the looming economic fracturing of our community, we are also far more fractured socially and culturally than we were back then.

No certain answers exist to the existential question of whether, amid today's stresses and strains, we will again be able to survive as an integrated community as we did six decades ago. The magnitude of the threat needs to be recognized and to be debated candidly in a way we haven't yet done. To engage in such a national debate we need to understand better what is, or may be, happening to us.

5

The Two New Nations

"The palace is not safe when the cottage is not happy."
— Benjamin Disraeli, *Sybil*, 1848

There is a magnificent anger, a last defiant rage against the dying of the light, to historian Christopher Lasch's essay *The Revolt of the Elites*, written when he was terminally ill and published posthumously early in 1995. Into his prose, this lifelong champion of the necessity of respect for the common sense of common people and of a sense of civic responsibility poured all his eloquence, all of his fury, and a good deal of his despair. He saw the society he loved being sundered, not even by design but by indifference. "The new elites are in revolt against Middle America," wrote Lasch. "Those who covet membership in the new aristocracy of brains tend to congregate on the coasts, turning their backs on the heartland and cultivating ties with the international market in fast-moving money, glamour, fashion and popular culture. It is a question whether they think of themselves as Americans at all. . . . They are at home only in transit, en route to a high-level conference, to the grand opening of a new franchise, to an international film festival, or to an undiscovered resort. Theirs is essentially a tourist's view of the world."

John Kenneth Galbraith said something similar in *The Culture of Contentment*, as did Robert Reich, now U.S. secretary of labour, then a professor at Harvard, in his 1992 book, *The Work of Nations*. Management guru Peter Drucker forecasts an impending "class conflict between knowledge workers and service workers." New York financier Felix Rohatyn warns of the social consequences of the "huge transfer of wealth from lower-skilled middle-class Americans to the owners of capital assets and to the new technological aristocracy."

No commentator has matched the passion unleashed by Lasch about his real concern, expressed in his subtitle: *The Betrayal of Democracy*. "There always has been a privileged class in America, but it has never before been so dangerously isolated," he writes. Because of "the decline of the old-money ethic of civic responsibility, local and regional loyalties are sadly attenuated today." In their place had come the new technological and management élites, "far more cosmopolitan, or at least more restless and migratory, than their predecessors. . . . Their loyalties – if the term itself is not anachronistic in this context – are international rather than regional, national or local. They have more in common with their counterparts in Brussels or Hong Kong than with the masses of Americans." Towards the masses, the new élite felt "no acknowledgement of reciprocal obligation." Instead "they have made themselves independent not only of crumbling industrial cities but of public services in general. . . . In effect, they have removed themselves from the common life. It is not just that they see no point in paying for public services they no longer use. Many of them have ceased to think of themselves as Americans in any important sense, implicated in America's destiny for better or worse."

Lasch has said everything that needs to be said about the transcendent political and social challenge of our times: The "Two Nations" identified a century ago by Benjamin Disraeli are returning to dwell amongst us, one nominally still national but increasingly international in its lifestyles and attitudes; the other, no longer encompassing only Disraeli's poor but a major part of the middle and working class also, all clinging to what's left of the nation-states that once created their class and nurtured it. As Lasch ends his essay, "Whatever its faults, middle-class national-ism provided a common ground, common standards, a common frame of reference without which society dissolves into nothing more than contending factions . . . a war of all against all."

Much that Lasch wrote about his nation applies to our own. Our incomes don't yet diverge anything like as widely as those in the United States. Our social safety nets are much more closely meshed and are fixed at levels far higher off the ground. All Canadians are covered by medicare, while one in eight Americans is protected by neither public nor private health insurance. Triumphalist displays of wealth are still regarded more scornfully here.

Yet we are being dragged through the same economic wringer as Americans. Of its nature, the global economy advantages those who can function globally – the "knowledge workers" or, in Reich's phrase, the "symbolic analysts" – by manipulating con-cepts, images, and information, while disadvantaging those whose skills and education equip them to function only within the old, now permeable, nation-states.

We are being reshaped also by our governments' need to cut their spending in order to cut their deficits. Former senior civil servant Arthur Kroeger has described Finance Minister Paul Martin's February 1995 budget as a "Contac C budget," filled up with time capsules – reductions in social spending, specific cuts like those to Toronto's Harbourfront cultural centre – that take effect over the next year or so. A second round of cuts is certain in the 1996 budget, on and on after that for most of the rest of this century unless there's a global boom. The same contraction is taking place in all provinces, most dramatically in Ontario now.

At the same time as the marketplace is making Canadians more unequal, their state-nation is losing – often is surrendering gladly – its ability to limit these inequalities.

It would be too strong to say that Canadians are entering a post-welfare-state era. Medicare and unemployment insurance will be reduced and reformed, but they will always be with us.

Instead, we may be on the cusp of a post-egalitarian era. A natural sense of the importance of fairness, a taken-for-granted conviction that we should try to achieve rough and ready equality, economically, socially, culturally, *is* Canada though. It's part of our national DNA. It's our substitute for the ethnic identity possessed by almost all other nation-states. That we are both North American, and hence are individualistic and meritocratic, and yet are egalitarian or collectivist is what defines us as a nation-state. In a New World context, those aspirations contradict each other. Somehow, we have woven them into a single whole. Now we may lose it. Holding on to that ethic – that distinctively Canadian sensibility – amid today's polarizing pressures is a national challenge as considerable as the one Canadians confronted during the Depression.

A greater challenge indeed. Back then, the Canadian community had far more sense of cohesion and solidarity than it does today. Expectations – about the possibility of upward mobility, about job security – were far lower, so that becoming suddenly poorer didn't jolt individuals psychologically the way it now does. The alternative communities of extended families, of religious congregations, and the kind of neighbourliness that exists within isolated towns and villages, and sustaining all of these the legacy of Victorian values, were all far more adhesive then. Lastly, because today's national trial by ordeal is less stark and brutal – so far – it may be a more insidious challenge to our collectivity than the Depression was.

One of the earliest insights into what was happening was provided neither by Galbraith nor Reich nor by any other American expert but by an institution, the Economic Council of Canada, that the Mulroney government disbanded on the grounds it had nothing more to tell Canadians that they needed to know. In one of its last reports, issued in 1990 and titled *Good Jobs, Bad Jobs*, the council warned of a "widening disparity in the quality of jobs and in the degree of security these provide for workers."

Since then, these disparities have been widened further by the "jobless recovery" in which job gains are constantly being minimized by the job losses caused by the restructuring and downsizing required so that companies can remain globally competitive. (The steel industry today produces as much steel as a decade ago with half the workforce; knowledgeable observers reckon it will shed as many workers again proportionately over the next decade.) By downsizing, companies solve their own immediate problems at the cost of magnifying, through the increase in unemployment, those of the community at large. For both community and corporations to benefit, these companies would have to develop new products and new export markets. Since 1990, few Canadian companies have done this. They have thus "socialized" their downsizing costs onto the community.

As relevant is the effect of the progressive introduction of labour-displacing computer technology and information systems. Also the knock-on effect of social security cutbacks: These reduce the incomes of the disadvantaged and reduce thereby the job-creating demand for goods and services. Lastly, there's the polarizing effect of the global economy upon the nature of jobs themselves. At the same time as knowledge workers are liberated from the confines of their narrow national economy, the wages of all those still anchored in national economies are being undercut, either directly through the "dumping" of jobs into low-wage Third World economies, or indirectly by Peter Drucker's "maximum wage," or the setting of limits on the

wages employees dare demand lest their employers shift production overseas.

In parallel, many of those with actual full-time jobs are
working ever-longer hours, either to maintain their incomes or to
maintain their jobs by catching their bosses' eye. Other workers,
especially young ones, are thus crowded out. A similar employment contraction will happen if, as is almost certain to happen,
the retirement age is raised to maintain the solvency of the
Canada/Quebec Pension plans.

All of this may represent only our first step into the bleak new
world of what has been called the "post-market" or "post-capital-
ist" economy. In his book *Jobshift*, U.S. economist William Bridges
writes that "what is disappearing today is not just a certain
number of jobs, or jobs in certain industries, or in one country, or
even jobs in the developed world as a whole. What is disappearing is the very thing itself: the job." In Bridges' description, jobs
are "like some species caught in the flow and ebb of evolution,
(that) emerged under one set of conditions and now begin to
vanish under another." He writes of a coming "de-jobbed system"
in which an ever-increasing number of people will never get jobs
at all in the traditional sense but will have to get by on an ever-
changing series of alternating part-time work and short-term
contracts and contingent employment and self-employment –
"portfolio employment" is the approved term.

In his recent book *The End of Work*, American economist
Jeremy Rifkin goes much further: "The road to a near-workless
economy is in sight. . . . Massive unemployment of a kind never
experienced before seems all but inevitable." Already, eight
hundred million people are unemployed or underemployed
around the world; that figure is bound to rise sharply because of
"a technology revolution that is fast replacing human beings with
machines in virtually every sector and industry of the global
economy."

Bridges and Rifkin may be too pessimistic. The Luddites fought the Industrial Revolution – futilely – but while mechanized reapers and spinning jennies took away their jobs, many more new ones were created by other new machines. All kinds of jobs, from aerobics instructors to derivatives specialists to dog walkers, exist today that were unknown a few years ago. As the population ages, major expansion is certain in the health-care and home-care industries. Although the new computer-communications technology is far more widely used in the United States than anywhere else, unemployment there is little more than 5 per cent. Japan has the world's highest rate of implementation of industrial robots but the lowest unemployment rate among developed countries.

Rifkin rebuts this kind of optimism. In the United States, three in four jobs involve the kind of repetitive work that can be replaced by machines or information systems. The average size of reduction of restructured companies is 40 per cent; one such company, the international conglomerate Asea Brown Boveri, has reduced its workforce by fifty thousand employees while increasing its output by 80 per cent. The heaviest cuts are often in middle management: Intel has reduced – "de-layered" – its management ranks from ten people to five; Eastman–Kodak from thirteen to four. Most importantly, the new technology has long since reached beyond routine manufacturing into the service sector. A reduction in current bank employment of one-fifth by the year 2000 (because of cash machines and other new technology) is widely forecast. There are few foreseeable limits to the impact of technology upon the service sector. The "paperless, electronic office" in which executives can function more efficiently than before without any support staff is now in sight. One chilling new phrase is that of the "virtual corporation," composed of a core of highly paid executives with almost all services being contracted out. Robots capable of performing hip replacement operations are being developed in California. More and more companies are screening job applicants by the automatic system Resumix. In April 1995, the *Toronto Star* reported that the Toronto General Hospital planned to switch to an all-automated system of analysers for testing patient samples. The new lab would be patterned on one in St. Louis, Missouri, where 80 workers execute 8,000 sample tests a week; in contrast the Toronto lab employs 420 technicians to do 3,500 tests. As one doctor explained, "These analysers don't take coffee breaks and they never make mistakes."

In his most alarmist passage, Rifkin quotes Nobel economics laureate Wassily Leontief as speculating that computer-communications technology may displace human beings from the production process just as industrial technology once displaced horses from agriculture.

Endangered now are the middle and working classes that represented the great social achievements of the nation-states of the industrial age. With their stake in the system through their secure jobs, these workers achieved the transformation of the proletariat that Marx dreamed of. The consequence was political stability within these nation-states, even if, in Marxist terms, the workers were thereby co-opted into the bourgeois system. It's no coincidence that unions, with their membership confined within national boundaries, are declining at the same time as are nation-states.

This epic social achievement is threatened by demolition. Members of the middle and working classes are undergoing "deep anxiety," in Reich's phrase, about their jobs and income prospects – even more about the prospects for their children – at the same time as they watch the upper middle-class knowledge workers, in computer communications, law, accounting, advertising, marketing, entertainment, electronic media, investment banking, financial services, management consulting, and software programs, soar off into the global stratosphere.

Political tension is inevitable sooner or later. An inchoate sense of having lost out to an invisible enemy – also unreachable because it is global – is the driving force behind much of today's right-wing populism, from Ross Perot and the new Republicans to Reform and Alberta's Ralph Klein and most recently Ontario's Mike Harris. European equivalents include Jean-Marie Le Pen's National Front in France, the Lega Norde in Italy, and the right-wing Republicans in Germany.

Right-wing populism often amounts to a misplaced lashing-out against the only "enemies" who can actually be reached – mainstream politicians, bureaucrats, visible minorities, and immigrants. Nevertheless, the "agin-the-government" creed rises up from two solid foundations. Whatever may once have worked does not, pretty obviously, work well any longer. Much contemporary anger is directed at those, from governments to special-interest groups, who held power, or appeared to, during the times when everything began to go wrong. As important, at the same time that people have realized they can no longer depend upon government and established institutions, they have developed – by street-smarts, survivalism, education – a new capacity for depending upon themselves. Often what is said and done isn't attractive: Our politics, though, has become more honest and more democratic, also more polarized and visceral, than it's been in a long time.

A related contemporary political development has been a shift in the nature of violent protest. Once it happened in the inner cities, in Harlem and Watts, and Brixton and Toxteth. Today, it's more likely to occur in the suburbs and the hinterland. Its most extreme form involves the formation of militias and acts of terror, like the bombing of the federal building in Oklahoma City. Marginally milder variations include the British soccer riots and the attacks by German skinheads on foreigners, especially Turks.

A repeat of the riots and demonstrations of the Depression years is probable. It will become certain when, after a few more years of "jobless recovery" and widening income gaps, the middle and working classes realize the extent to which they have been disenfranchised permanently. Tellingly, University of Nebraska economist Wallace Peterson describes what's happening to these foundation citizens of nation-states as "a Silent Depression."

Part of the Canadian national myth of egalitarianism is just that, a myth. The degree of corporate concentration in Canada, or of market dominance by a small number of firms, is closer to the condition of Third World countries than to that of typical industrial nations. A study by the Conference Board of Canada found that thirty-two families and five conglomerates control one-third of the nation's non-financial assets. Indeed, Canada has more billionaires proportionately than the United States does. Until the crash of the Canary Wharf project in London, Canadians could count two fellow citizens among the World's Richest Ten – the Reichmanns and Ken Thomson.

A significant part of our inegalitarianism comes in a form that Canadians don't notice. Everyone is fixated on incomes, and therefore secondarily upon the income tax system. What really matters though is wealth, that's to say accumulated capital like stocks and bonds, savings accounts, houses, consumer durables, and private pension plans. In terms of wealth, we are one of the most unequal of Western societies. The reason is straightforward: Wealth is taxed less in Canada than in any other industrial country except Australia. As a proportion of the total tax take, combined wealth taxes (on wealth itself, estate or death duties, gift taxes, and capital gains) account for just 0.03 per cent in Canada, according to the study *Top-Heavy* done by U.S. economist Edward Wolff and funded by the 20th Century Foundation. This is one-twentieth the share of total taxes accounted for by wealth taxes in Britain, even after a dozen years of Thatcher, and one-fortieth of that in Japan. To cite the only comparison that counts with Canadians, our wealth taxes as a proportion of total taxes are one-twenty-fifth their share south of the border. (And one-hundredth the share in Switzerland, a nation scarcely hostile to capital accumulation.)

Thus the income egalitarianism Canadians cherish so much is in some ways a con. Complaints by neo-conservatives and corporate leaders about excess taxes at the top in contrast to our industrial rivals thus are a self-serving con. In almost no other Western country are the wealthy so cosseted, not to mention the fact that our corporate tax level is well below the Western average. Indeed it's high time to tag neo-conservatives, as champions of the well-off and of corporations, as a "special-interest group," the same label they apply so scornfully to representatives of women, racial minorities, and the poor.

Even in the familiar terms of income distribution, we don't rank close to the most egalitarian. On the basis of a complicated formula known as the Gini Co-efficient, Wolff measures Canadian incomes as more egalitarian than those in the United States, Britain, Italy, but less so than Japan, Germany, France, and the Scandinavian countries. As always internationally, we're in the middle. The same UN survey that ranks Canada as number one in living standard ranks us sixteenth in terms of income equality.

Among predominantly Anglo-Saxon countries, though, we are unusual: Only Australian incomes are more egalitarian than Canadian (New Zealand's incomes are less so).

It's as a North American nation that we are unique. Wolff's study shows that the United States is now the world's most unequal society, displacing Britain from the top spot. For almost two decades, income inequalities in the United States have risen steadily and steeply. Just the wealthiest 1 per cent of American households own nearly 40 per cent of the national wealth; the top 20 per cent, or one-fifth, own 80 per cent of the total. All these proportions are increasing each year. In 1978, the average total compensation of the heads of large American corporations was twenty-nine times that of salaried workers; by 1988, it was ninety-three times as large. At the other end of the scale, the after-tax income of the bottom one-fifth of Americans accounts for just 5.7 per cent of the total now, and is shrinking steadily each year.

While the United States is turning itself into an economic jungle, with an increasing number of eight-hundred-pound gorillas and an even more rapidly increasing number of starveling monkeys, we haven't followed its example – so far.

We are in no way a North American Sweden, which anyway is having to cut back sharply its once-famed cradle-to-grave welfare system. The National Council on Welfare has calculated that 4.8 million Canadians were below the official poverty line in 1994, up by 500,000 from the preceding year; among children, the council estimated the incidence of poverty at an appalling 21 per cent, the second highest among developed nations. In Montreal, one in four families earns less than $10,000 a year; in Finance Minister Paul Martin's own east end riding, unemployment is above 20 per cent. In Metro Toronto, once the country's glitz capital, one in five families now depend upon income supplements; users of food banks in the city soared to 110,000 in 1995 from 30,000 a decade ago. Across the country, the more than 2,000 food banks now exceed the number of any fast-food chain, including McDonald's.

Nevertheless we've gone through the "sound barrier" of the near-depression of the early 1990s with our egalitarian ideal, and a fair amount of its substance, still intact. The most encouraging evidence is contained in the study *Are We Becoming Two Societies?* by economists Charles Beach of Queen's University and George Slotsve of Vanderbilt University and published by the C. D. Howe Institute in 1995. They conclude: "The answer suggested by the evidence is 'No.' . . . The eighties were not a new era of polarization in

Canada so much as an era of slower economic growth, higher taxes and two severe recessions that had marked distributional effects." (The data in the Beach–Slotsve study in fact extend into the early 1990s). Beach and Slotsve did find important shifts within this surprisingly static picture: Women's incomes are polarizing faster than men's; younger workers have lost a great deal of ground; the growth in real incomes has stalled, with no increase at all during the half-decade of 1986 to 1992; there has been a marked increase in "insecurity," especially among middle-class males whose post-tax incomes in 1992 were below their peak in 1976.

While the Beach–Slotsve study is impressive and authoritative, its drawback – an unavoidable one – is that it looks at the immediate past rather than at what may lie ahead.

The outlook is exceedingly worrisome. Once, it was popular to suggest that governments ought to become "employers of last resort." Now they're jostling to get towards the head of the restructuring queue. Some forty-five thousand federal jobs are due to be eliminated, while the Harris government will eliminate up to twenty thousand Ontario provincial positions. Public enterprises like Canadian National Railways are being privatized; in preparation, CNR is reducing its workforce by ten thousand employees. Overlaid upon this will be the effects of cuts in transfer payments. Benefits to forty thousand Atlantic fishermen will run out in 1996-97 and are not likely to be renewed. At the same time, private industry restructuring is far from complete: Bell Canada has announced layoffs of ten thousand employees. In the winter of 1994-95, the scale of desperation was measured by the Depression-era flashback of twenty-six thousand people lining up for hours in freezing weather to apply for possible – not actual – new jobs at General Motors in Oshawa.

A disturbing disconnection is developing between the condition of the Canadian economy and the condition of employment in Canada. By mid-1995, the economic recovery had lasted – statistically – for three years. But at a fraction below 10 per cent, the level of unemployment had changed little from its mid-recession peak. Even this mark is largely illusory. Canada's current real rate of unemployment is at least 15 per cent, or about one in six. There are the familiar "discouraged workers" who've given up looking for jobs. There are those working part time involuntarily. There are also now the large number of retirees, often still in their fifties, who've been given pension buyouts as an alternative to being laid off. Large numbers of young people – four hundred thousand by some estimates – are staying in high schools, colleges, and universities often as much to delay their plunge into the labour market as to upgrade their qualifications. A second recession, which many forecast for 1996-97, could push the official rate of unemployment back up to at least 12 to 13 per cent, and the real rate to about 20 per cent.

An entire generation may experience a lost decade, longer still unless the market economy performs as its ideologues keep promising it will. If the Bridges–Rifkin pessimism about the labour-displacing effects of new technology proves to be correct, a large part of today's generations of xers and yers may experience the loss of the greater part of their working lives while at the same time having to pay off the unpaid bills run up by earlier generations.

Creating jobs is the first priority. Scarcely less urgent is the nature of the jobs that may be created. "Virtual corporations" need few full-time employees: most of their other activities can be performed more efficiently by part-timers and contingency workers and subcontractors (greater flexibility; avoidance of payroll taxes and fringe benefits). During the span from 1980 to 1993, part-time jobs in Canada increased by 57 per cent; full-time jobs by a mere 8 per cent. During the half-decade to mid-1993, no new full-time jobs were created. The irregularly employed and the self-employed usually take home smaller pay packets; they also have to pay for their own vacations, life insurance, pensions, dental plans, and when sick earn no pay at all.

Polarization is taking place even among those working full time at more or less the same kinds of jobs. "In today's world, it often seems that the choice is between having a job and having a life," comments Toronto economist Arthur Donner in his 1995 report, *Working Time*, for the federal Human Resources Department. Today, 22 per cent of all employed males put in fifty or more hours a week; two decades ago, even though contractual working hours have shrunk since, only 17 per cent put in that kind of Stakhanovite effort. "Polarized hours of work mean polarization of opportunity and income," remarks Donner. A parallel consequence, he adds, is "the lost time, with partners, children, friends and in the community."

The principal victims of our polarization into two nations are young Canadians. Today's xers and yers are the best-educated generation in history, and they ought to be faring comparatively well because there are proportionately fewer of them because of the baby bust. One in six, though, have no job at all, even when not counting those "hiding" in educational institutions. Of those with jobs, fewer than half are employed full time. We are building walls between the generations as well as between different kinds of workers.

There's no certainty this socio-economic regression will continue. A global boom may unfold. But even a prolonged boom and a proliferation of as yet unimaginable new jobs will not be enough by itself to reverse our division into two nations. In all developed countries "routine production workers" and "in-person servers," in Reich's phrases, will increasingly find their wages and working conditions "capped" by competing workers in developing nations, little different from them in their skills and qualifications and even readier than they to put in fifty and more hours each week.

At the same time, the knowledge workers and the symbolic analysts will take flight, in their travels and in their incomes.

The change in social attitudes that's now taken hold isn't likely to be reversed quickly. The new mood is a contradictory blend of triumphalism and paranoia. In the United States, at least three million Americans now live in what are known as Community Interest Developments. The more common name for these is walled estates. One expert forecasts that by the year 2000, almost one in three Americans will live "segmented spatially in private territories that establish their own rules" for everything from garbage collection to landscaping. They, and their counterparts in luxury apartments, or those residing abroad, all withdrawing themselves into private education, private medical care, private transportation, private security (there are now more private security guards than police officers in the United States), are in "revolt" against Middle America.

Canada's first walled estate, Beacon Hall – a "gated suburb" in the preferred phrase of developers – was opened in Aurora just north of Toronto in 1994. A second is planned. More and more Canadians are sending their children to private schools, despite fees that can top $20,000 for boarders, and later to American colleges and universities. They are paying for specialized medical treatments themselves, here or in the United States, maintaining bank accounts and capital assets abroad, keeping winter and summer houses in the south or in Europe.

These are all individual, private decisions. They also reflect a profound change in the general political climate. Tax loopholes that disproportionately benefit the well-off are old hat, even if these once needed to be justified as necessary to achieve worthy public purposes like promoting Canadian films or oil and gas exploration. Quite new are the now unapologetic arguments for, and actual political commitments (as by Mike Harris in Ontario) to tax cuts designed specifically to benefit the well-off disproportionately on the Reagan-style assumption that a share of this "supply-side" cash will trickle down to everyone else. All of this doctrinaire advocacy of deliberate inequality is justified by appeals to freedom and self-reliance.

The alternative to this neo-conservative dogma is to try to recreate community so that we can continue, to some degree, to be dependent upon one another. Canadian-style egalitarianism and concern about fairness are out of style these days. Yet they may have enough staying power to help us get through even a jungle rampant with eight-hundred-pound gorillas bellowing neoconservative slogans.

6

Feuding with Feudalism

"What is a borderless world? It is a world emptied of every value and principle – except one, accumulation."

— Former Liberal cabinet minister Eric Kierans,
Policy Options, September 1989

Technology cannot be stopped. We can't get off the global economy, most certainly not by ourselves. Many solutions lie beyond the reach of any national government.

But we are not just chaff to be blown around by the gales of the global marketplace. Understanding what's going on has to be the first step towards finding our place in this unbrave new world.

As described earlier, neo-conservatism has immense appeal today – exactly as communism once did. It too is a great simplifier. It too propounds its themes with immense self-confidence. Its basic creed – "Government bad; market good" – has about it the same ring of being a self-evident truth as communism's creed that workers needed only to shake off their chains to become free and equal.

Similarly, just as communists never got round to explaining the implications of "the dictatorship of the proletariat," neo-conservatives have yet to explain the consequences of what can be described best as "the dictatorship of capitalism."

The central point about the revolution – or counter-revolution – now being attempted by neo-conservatives is that the kind of global capitalism they espouse is fundamentally different from all earlier versions. It bears no resemblance to the familiar postwar "mixed economy" in which capitalism was regulated, more or less, by the governments of nation-states. It's different even from the unregulated, union-bashing version that preceded the New Deal of the 1930s. The key difference is that because today's capitalism is global, it eludes almost all the countervailing forces – nation-state governments, unions, public interest groups, let alone public concern about equity. The only check that remains is the marketplace itself; there, no one is a citizen any longer but only a consumer (also a producer, but since there's a surplus of these everywhere such workers are only of marginal interest to global capitalists).

The character of contemporary global capitalism thus has much of the free-booting quality of the capitalism of the early years of the Industrial Revolution. Just as 19th-century industrialists were unhindered by safety and health regulations, environmental regulations, urban zoning codes, unions, bureaucratic oversight, even public opinion, and so could send ten-year-olds into coal mines, so transnational corporations can make their products in a "hands-off" plant in some underdeveloped country where the local authorities ignore environmental and other regulations for the sake of attracting these industries. In its 1995 report, *Workers in an Integrating World*, the World Bank spells out this equation candidly: "Increasing labour market flexibility – despite the bad name it has acquired as a euphemism for pushing wages down and workers out – is essential in all the regions of the world undergoing reform." Nor does the equation end there: The threat by transnational corporations to move production to plants in underdeveloped nations "tames" the governments, and workers, of developed nation-states.

The magic ingredient of contemporary capitalism resides in its discovery of how to evade most regulations and taxes. The more that transnational corporations operate transnationally rather than nationally, the more they can minimize their tax liabilities by intracorporate accounting. In parallel, the more they operate transnationally, the more easily they can play nation-states against one another, especially now that these have bargained away in free-trade deals their one high card – access to their domestic markets in exchange for job-creating plants.

In competing amid today's global economy for the favours of transnationals, nation-states are in roughly the same circumstances as were the 19th-century city councils of Bradford and Manchester, say, when they tried to cajole another "dark, satanic mill" to locate within their boundaries.

The compensation for all of this, according to neo-conservatives, will be the reward of "trickle-down economics." Even if income gaps widen and transnational corporations are less and less regulated, surplus cash will cascade down from the top, like secular manna.

This theory is based upon a breathtaking naïvety, in George Bush's phrase on "voodoo economics." It flies in the face of human nature: Only someone like Ronald Reagan, the first to enunciate the doctrine publicly, could actually believe that those who have it don't always keep it and strive ceaselessly to make more of it. Indeed, belief in trickle-down economics is unnervingly similar to the belief of early communists that workers would actually work forever for the greater good of the collectivity.

In fact, the economic system that trickle-down economics resembles most closely is that of feudalism. Just as barons, earls, and knights once created jobs for their peasants and villeins by their jousts, boar hunts, and crusades, so, in trickle-down theory, will global capitalists and knowledge workers create jobs for others by a serendipitous combination of their entrepreneurship and their conspicuous consumption. The difference over the centuries is that while today's global élite is rootless and transient, back then most feudal barons were rooted in a geographic spot, and so into some form of community.

The real difference over time is that in the Middle Ages, religion framed people's lives. The value system that's replaced it is, in Eric Kierans's phrase, "accumulation."

Despite the power of global capitalism, nation-states are by no means without assets. At the level of the prosaic and practical, transnational *apparatchiks* and knowledge workers have to live somewhere. Canada is a lot more agreeable to live in than the Cayman Islands or Liechtenstein. Developed nation-states offer not only a cosmopolitan lifestyle and a first-rate infrastructure but political security: These add up to a pretty attractive trade-off for actually having to pay a few taxes. Nation-state governments can muster up considerable intellectual capability; some of them can also muster up, unlike the Pope, quite a few divisions and tanks and planes.

The commanding asset of nation-states is that they remain the only source of democratic legitimacy. Their decisions carry an authority that no supranational agency, no transnational company, and no international advocacy organization can match. What they have come to lack is the nerve to act collectively, their reluctance to do so heightened by their mutual competitiveness.

A key test occurred at the G-7 meeting in Halifax in June 1995. In advance, James Tobin, the Nobel Prize-winning economist, deliberately made public his proposal that nation-states should impose a tax on all international financial transactions. This wouldn't be at all easy to do: Any twenty-two-year-old currency trader could do billions of "off-the-book" dollars worth of deals using a laptop computer in a hotel room in the Cayman Islands or Liechtenstein. Even so, the banks and insurance companies and pension funds and so on that are the ultimate sources of these funds all have to have a home base. Their accounts could be laundered only to a certain limit: Spot-checks by central banks and by a reconfigured International Monetary Fund could identify hidden deals that would be, at the very least, highly embarrassing, at the worst, criminal. Despite the considerable technical difficulties, developed nation-states with sufficient political will could regulate international finance in the same way they've learned how to regulate international trade, and, a far more profound challenge, how not to go to war with each other. As host, Jean Chrétien did manage to get the topic added to the meeting's agenda; but he could muster up no support for a serious study of how to implement the scheme. In effect, the seven most powerful nations-states in the world were admitting their irrelevance as global players.

Canada's representatives can prompt and hector other nation-states only so far. On our own behalf, though, we can construct some barricades behind which we can nurture those "values and principles" we care about.

In fact, we're doing a bit better than we allow ourselves to believe. These days, the acid test of governmental competence – at times it would seem the only one – is its ability to get its finances into order by balancing its budget.

The great neo-conservative hero is Ralph Klein of Alberta, with Ontario's Mike Harris about to be elevated into the pantheon. Klein deserves, and no doubt Harris will deserve, some of this applause. Just as much progress towards the Holy Grail of a zero deficit has been achieved, although without the same social polarization and in the absence of windfall oil and gas revenues, by New Brunswick Premier Frank McKenna and by Saskatchewan Premier Roy Romanow. (In fact, per capita provincial spending in Alberta is still higher than in Ontario even after five years of "socialism.") In its last two years, Bob Rae's government attempted, with some success, to develop a "partnership" variant of this approach in Ontario, between government, business, and labour. The federal Liberals have attempted the same inclusive approach: Paul Martin's budget hit, or was seen to have hit, everyone more or less equally hard.

By contrast, south of the border it's still an open question whether the slash and burn policies of the new Republicans – equally, their deliberate widening of income gaps – won't stir up sufficient public resistance to put roadblocks in their path towards fiscal probity. If so, the Canadian way will have been proven not merely the fairer but also the more effective way.

Nor has the Canadian way ever been as extravagant as neo-conservative propaganda suggests: According to the Paris-based Organization for Economic Cooperation and Development (OECD), the size of Canada's federal deficit proportionate to GNP ranked, in 1995, just above the middle among all Western developed nations.

A major study, *Re-Inventing Government*, published early in 1995 by Ekos Research of Ottawa, and based on opinion surveys and focus groups, makes an important discovery about the nature of public opinion about the deficit. "An enormous chasm separates the elite and the general public's perception of government," it declares. The study found that the defining values of the élite group of corporate and bureaucratic managers were those of deficit reduction, small government, and market economics. All other Canadians, or 80 per cent of the total, have similarly accepted the necessity of reducing the deficit and debt. Yet, Ekos reports, "[Most] Canadians are clearly not seeking a minimalist model of government, or even a massive withdrawal of government." Their objective instead is "a leaner, smarter government which works more closely in partnership with other stakeholders."

The report continues, "The secure classes are increasingly loathe to see further expenditures in this direction [of redistribution and social justice] as a function of tax fatigue and deficit concerns." By contrast, "The economically distressed feel increasingly abandoned and see themselves losing touch with the economic

standards of average Canadians." From out of this "growing economic bifurcation of Canada," concludes Ekos, may come "social
class conflict."

The questions then become how to head off social conflict and
how to preserve the Canadian community.

No certain answers exist. One initiative, already attempted in
France, could be a serious study of the usefulness of programs of
work-sharing, or of limiting the maximum hours some individuals can work so that others could upgrade their jobs from part to
full time, or find one at all. The drawback is that it's usually the
most productive workers who put in the longest hours; also, that
payroll taxes add 25 per cent to the cost of each extra full-time
employee. Arthur Donner, who advocates this remedy in *Working
Time*, admits that work-sharing would be "only a partial answer
to the unemployment crisis."

An approach advocated by both Peter Drucker and Jeremy
Rifkin is for a major expansion of the so-called "third sector" of
volunteer and charity work. Rifkin proposes that voluntary work
be encouraged by tax write-offs for unpaid hours contributed;
also that corporations be taxed by a "sliding charitable index
geared to increases in productivity." Rifkin makes the important
point that in comparison to the public and private sectors, the
voluntary and charitable sector "is the most socially responsible
of the three." Drucker argues that organizations and institutions
in this sector serve a vital secondary purpose besides that of doing
for free work that governments can no longer underwrite. "They
create citizenship," an opportunity for participation and for personal and group interconnection. Drucker adds, astutely, that
even the knowledge workers of the élite "need a sphere in which
they can act as citizens and create a community. The workplace
does not give it to them."

Volunteerism is part of the Canadian tradition, yet it is comparatively underdeveloped in contrast to the United States. Like

Europeans, although to a much less degree, we've tended to rely upon our "caring and sharing" state. But the state really is out of money. The "third sector," or "social sector" in Drucker's phrase, represents an opportunity for liberals and social democrats to translate their old collectivist ideals into a contemporary ethic based upon partnership between all the social groups, labour, business, government, interest groups, and individuals themselves. Specifically, it provides older Canadians – the most favoured generation in the country's history – an opportunity to repay their society for some of the advantages they've extracted from it at a cost, however unintended, to future generations. The real issue here is the revival of *civitas*, of a sense of responsibility to the larger society in opposition to the pure price mechanics of consumerism.

From Robert Reich to Peter Drucker, all experts agree that the single certain counterattack nation-states can make upon the income polarization now being inflicted upon them by the global economy and technology is education and training. A specific problem for Canada is that we are the only nation-state in the world in which the national government has no say or role in education at any level, a jurisdictional distinction made in the middle of the 19th century, in the era of one-room schools. Significantly, the Ekos survey found that, in defiance of the Constitution, the highest priority Canadians give to any federal activity is that of assistance to education.

Distinctive to Canada, within North America, are of course our social programs. Certainly, these have to be reformed, revised, and restructured. A comprehensive two-tier health-care system, as proposed by Alberta, would be revolutionary though. It would fracture the vital cross-border difference of universality. Like all revolutions, once done it could never be undone. The point here is that the motive for this revolution is ideological, not fiscal. No evidence has ever been advanced that the existing health-care system, above all one in as affluent a society as Alberta, cannot be reformed, revised, and restructured to make it fit financially universalist demands and needs.

Ultimately, the single most important thing that Canada can do is not to do too much. Travelling too far down the neoconservative road is bound to be disastrous. At that road's end there is quicksand. Early unregulated capitalism brought about repeated depressions through the 19th century. In this century, only the pump-priming provided as a by-product by two world wars prevented capitalism from inflicting more economic carnage than the horror of the Depression. Global capitalism's record is as yet unwritten: It's unlikely to be able to rewrite economic history.

Capitalism is a magnificent instrument for measuring the price of everything. It is supremely unequipped to identify the value of anything. Values derive from people, institutions, elected legislatures, churches, social organizations, and not from entities possessed of no vision but their own bottom line.

Left to itself, global capitalism is bound to need government to save it from itself, as it once was by the New Deal. Its "inner contradiction," to use Marx's phrase, leads inexorably to ever-greater accumulation of capital and to ever-widening gaps in incomes. Unregulated capitalism's inescapable flaw is that the unconstrained acquisitiveness it unleashes dries up all of capitalism's own motor fuel. Endless accumulation by the wealthy eventually leaves ordinary consumers with too little money to buy the products of corporations. It was precisely this imbalance between supply and demand that caused the Great Depression.

Long before this inevitable economic crash, a political backlash will burst out. This revulsion against global corporations and neoconservative ideologues will be far more vociferous and violent than today's – often justified – anger at the excesses of state bureaucracies. Indeed, it will be a backlash of the same order as happened when the people of Eastern Europe and the Soviet Union were allowed at last to say out loud what they thought about that earlier version of politico-economic zealotry – communism.

There is another crucial reason why Canada should not do too much, even while doing enough about the deficit to placate the "stateless legislators," and also, as is overdue to be done for its own sake, reinventing government and public institutions to make them efficient, responsive, and democratic. One organizing principle of the neo-conservative agenda is to dismantle as many public institutions as possible so that these can be replaced by the "invisible hand" of the marketplace.

Institutions, though, are not just bureaucrats, buildings, and budgets. They are memory and spirit, a sense of public duty, and a sense of responsibility to colleagues, present and past. The best of our institutions, the RCMP, the Canada Council, CBC Radio, the foreign service, and the better universities, inspire individuals to reach beyond themselves for the sake of institutional memory and spirit. Once dismantled, institutions cannot be reassembled. Once they go, they are gone forever. Their replacements may be better priced but they will have infinitely less value to the community.

If Canada becomes two economic nations, we will cease, sooner or later, to be a nation-state at all. As individuals living within a polarized community, most of us would be better off becoming Americans, who do thrive amid pure individualism. This is to say that either we decide collectively to resist the forces now polarizing us or we accept becoming nothing more than inhabitants of a region of the United States – one still bearing, for the time being, the title and appurtenances of an independent nation-state.

PART II

The Politics of the Matter

7

The Nation That Dares Not Speak Its Name

"[English-Canadians] have acquired an anticipatory nationalism, getting ready for a future [they] may reluctantly inherit."

— Essay by political scientist Alan C. Cairns
in the 1993 collection *Belonging*

In 1965, English-Canadians, as they still were known then, received two warnings about their future. One was official and formal. The Royal Commission on Bilingualism and Biculturalism, co-chaired by journalist André Laurendeau and former CBC president Davidson Dunton, declared in its interim report that "Canada is in the most critical period of its history since Confederation." To surmount this crisis, Canadians – effectively English-Canadians – had to recognize, and to act upon the recognition, that their country was composed of two founding and equal peoples.

The second warning was personal and informal. Back in 1959, a small book, *Les Insolences de Frère Untel*, had severely criticized Quebec's educational system as backward and regressive. The book was published privately and pseudonymously because the quasi-dictator Maurice Duplessis was then in full authoritarian power. By 1965, with the Quiet Revolution unfolding like thunder, Jean-Paul Desbiens could afford to reveal that he was Frère Untel. In an introduction to a second edition published that year,

Desbiens aimed his thoughts at a wider audience. "We French-Canadians are taking our first breath as a nation conscious of its identity," he wrote. "You too ought to be pondering that question, you people of English-Canada. The danger is you will forget to really give it any thought, while we will have made our choice on our own."

Both warnings were prescient. Prime Minister Lester Pearson responded to the first by "co-operative federalism," yielding to Quebec's demands for an expansion of its jurisdiction by an *ad hoc* "opting out" formula that, the Canada/Quebec Pension plans as an example, allowed the province to run its own affairs within a loose framework of national programs. Soon, Pierre Elliott Trudeau would impose order, and a backbone, upon this system, on the one hand limiting further concessions of jurisdiction and on the other hand expanding the space that French-Canadians could claim within the country as a whole by official bilingualism and by so-called "French Power," or the promotion of franco-phones to prominent positions within the cabinet and the federal bureaucracy. A decade later, Joe Clark, then Opposition Leader, summarized brilliantly the magnitude of Trudeau's achievement: "The country that Mr. [René] Lévesque wants to separate from no longer exists," said Clark at the start of the 1980 referendum.

As for Desbiens's warning, English-Canadians paid no more attention to it than the Greeks did to Cassandra. Three decades later, University of British Columbia political scientist Philip Resnick describes his "half" of the country, in his book *Thinking English Canada*, as, "The nation that dares not speak its name."

In literal terms, Resnick was overdoing it. English-Canadians argued ferociously amongst themselves over the National Energy Policy in the early 1980s, and over free trade at the end of the decade. The debates about economic and cultural nationalism were entirely English-Canadian ones. They were active in lobbying for improvements (inclusion of the disabled; a full gender-equality clause) to the original version of the Charter of Rights and Freedoms. While they said little in public during the Meech Lake affair, they got into the act loudly during the Charlottetown referendum. Once the 1990s began, they became exceptionally fractious politically – the Reform Party; Mike Harris's Common Sense victory in Ontario.

The self-imposed coventry of English-Canadians didn't encompass everything, therefore. What was considered unseemly was talking about themselves, let alone daring to celebrate themselves.

Few historical parallels exist for such loss of ethnic nerve. The unchanging miracle of ethnic identity is its durability. Even small peoples, like Estonians, Latvians, and Lithuanians, have emerged from a half-century of Russification with their identity scarcely diminished; Catalans have survived four decades during which the use of their language was proscribed, even on gravestones. When threatened, the response of all tribes – within Canada, the Québécois and native people – is to hunker down and wait out their time.

There were occasional yelps of outrage from English-Canadians about the national extension of bilingualism, about affirmative action for francophones: All were condemned instantly by the élites. In parallel, there was the cry of despair captured by the Department of Inmigration's poll in 1992 that found that one in two respondents "feared they were becoming strangers in their own land," and also occasional outbursts about the implications of multiculturalism and of mass immigration. Mostly, there was silence.

It hadn't always been like this. The Vimy Memorial, built in mid-Depression to commemorate the great Canadian victory of the First World War, is bold, almost triumphalist. It says, "We were here, and we won." The same sense that the 20th century might really belong to Canada surged up after the Second World War through the golden era of Pearsonian diplomacy, through the breakneck postwar economic expansion (the fastest in the world, as is hard to believe now), and on up to the international triumph of Expo 67.

Canada has continued to progress socially and culturally since those years, and, until the last few years, has also progressed economically. But the "English-Canadian" nation itself has regressed. It has lost a great deal of its sense of self and self-esteem. Quite a few of its members have indeed acquired the lost look of members of a tribe who feel they are becoming strangers in their own land.

Few topics are more difficult to raise in public. The predictable catcalls of "backlash" and "privilege" (meaning the attempt to preserve it) are neither here nor there. The real difficulty is that English-Canadians are almost incapable of talking about themselves – a fundamental cross-border difference at a time when so many Americans so eagerly confess their personal traumas to television personalities Oprah Winfrey, Geraldo Rivera, or Jenny Jones. Uttering personal grievances publicly is the single serious sin an anglophone can commit (all others are exonerated by the liberal doctrine of tolerance). Even feminists among them have felt constrained to advance their cause through surrogates – single mothers, people of colour, natives.

The puzzle about this is it's hard to identify reasons why English-Canadians should feel self-apologetic. They are, certainly, capable of being smug and sanctimonious, and were once singularly stupid about having French "thrust" down their throats.

But to utter a truism that "dares not speak its name," the fact is that the country the UN keeps citing as the most agreeable place to live in in the world is largely the creation of English-Canadians. The contributions of francophones, of native people, of immigrants, have all been significant of course. But what we are now is mostly what English-Canadians, Anglo-Celts to use the more accurate term, once were. They "set down the tramlines" of the Canada of today in the marvellous phrase coined by historian Donald Akenson in an essay in the September 1995 edition of *The Canadian Historical Review.*

It was English-Canadians who explored the greater part of the country, cleared it, and settled it. It was they who contributed the overwhelming majority of men who died fighting in wars for democracy and freedom. It was they who created almost all of the country's political and legal infrastructure (borrowed from Britain of course, but substantively amended here) and who established the social security systems that make this country distinctive in North America. It was they who developed the prevailing mores of civility and tolerance towards pluralism and diversity that make this country unlike any other in the world.

To utter the ultimate un-Canadianism, Canada deserves its UN ranking. People come here eagerly from all over the world. Their principal motivation is of course to better themselves economically. But a powerful incentive among many is the chance to live in a society that is democratic, that observes the rule of law, where the police and the judiciary are impartial, that permits, almost encourages, infinite diversity, and that protects human and civil rights as extensively as does any other society in the world.

Over time, the term English-Canadian has become largely meaningless. Much better described now as English-speaking Canadian, this category has grown to include large numbers of people with z's and w's or multiple vowels in their last names, and in all shades of colour, who have assimilated into what Akenson calls "[the] nation-building, to use an old term, that created a central set of political social, legal and cultural conventions within which all the allegedly separate multicultural groups operate." Indeed, Québécois have become more anglicized than is generally recognized (Lévesque always understood this): Polls now find comparatively few political and cultural value differences between them and other Canadians. The same is true of native people: Native women have relied on the Charter, that surrogate citizenship of all English-speaking Canadians, to press their case for equality within the new self-governing territories.

Perhaps the highest praise ever paid to the Canadian value system – and so to the inheritance created for contemporary Canadians by the old English-Canadians – comes from a conversation with an Italian-Canadian whom I met when he was back "home" for several months to settle some real estate matters. He recounted how he'd described the character of his new country to old friends. That Canada was civil, orderly, and tolerant, everyone had found both delightful and credible. A further description, though, was met with bafflement: "In Canada, there's no point in trying to bribe the judges."

It's no easier to explain diffidence in a people than extreme shyness in an individual. Like all northerners, we tend to be reticent and introverted. A colonial tic is an obvious cause. At some level of their consciousness, Canadians don't take Canada seriously, only the United States and Europe. A certain self-protective pragmatism applies: Those who hang back remain clear of the firing-line, and escape the challenge of daring to be excellent. The flipside of Canadians' egalitarianism is a fear and envy of those who are first rate: These threaten the self-esteem of the less gifted, except when they display their qualities outside the country and so bring honour to everyone in it.

Beyond this, all that can be attempted are some wing-shots at the phenomenon.

English Canada's most obvious handicap is that it doesn't exist. It has no capital and no centre; Toronto, the single credible candidate, inspires fear and envy among all others. English Canada is fractured into regions and provinces – "identity is local" Northrop Frye has commented – and more recently into ethnicities, races, and even genders. Officially, it doesn't exist at all. The phrase English Canada has become politically incorrect. The proper terms are either TROC (The Rest of Canada), which makes its inhabitants sound vaguely gnome-like, or ROC, which sounds inert, if solid. The point about these acronyms is that within them, English-Canadians, the country's principal architects, vanish.

Relevant also is that English Canada has never had a "real" history in the European sense of decapitated kings and revolutions. Nowadays it is fast losing much of its own local history. Mention of English-Canadian achievements in the two world wars (except in revisionist CBC programs) has slipped away – quite unlike in Australia – no doubt so as to not remind Quebeckers they once were largely absent from them, perhaps also to not remind today's young how militaristic their fathers once were. More recently, Canadian history has often been positively scorned as a chronicle of sexism, racism, homophobia, anti-Semitism, environmental degradation, and militarism. The entire doctrine of "historical disadvantage" that underpins employment equity schemes presumes that, unlike their sensitive descendants, all earlier Canadians were uncaring, discriminatory brutes.

English Canada hasn't, for a long time, had any political heroes. Pearson and Diefenbaker were the last. Since then, not only have all the prime ministers been Quebeckers, "blips" excepted, but, from René Lévesque through to Lucien Bouchard, so have all of the country's larger-than-life politicians, with perhaps the single exception of Alberta's Peter Lougheed. Indirectly, English-Canadians have been told for three decades they are second-rate politically; as indeed they have been.

A major factor has been the steady diminishing and outright elimination of the tribe's symbols. "Dominion," once a distinctively Canadian term meaning dominion by all Canadians over the territory rather than of any imperial outreach, went long ago. The monarchy has been marginalized. The military, during

Trudeau's long term, was regarded with amused contempt. Power has been shifted from the Commons, where so much English-Canadian history resides, to the provinces and to the courts. The RCMP has had to fight off an attempt to replace its distinctive name with the impeccably bilingual "Police," and to accept turbans as the head-dress for its Sikh members. Metrification, a pointless exercise anyway since Americans haven't budged from their inches and pounds, has eliminated all the familiar weights and measures.

No conspiracy was involved in any of this, or certainly not much of one. Instead, there has been a carelessness, almost a frivolousness, in the treatment given to the second of the *deux nations*, quite unlike the intense focusing of political and academic attention upon Quebec over nearly four decades now. Books about what Quebeckers want and need overflow the library shelves; there are perhaps half a dozen titles devoted specifically to English-Canadian topics. A revealing moment occurred during the free-trade debate. Aware of the angst the impending pact was causing amongst many English-Canadians, two of Mulroney's key aides, Allan Gotlieb, then ambassador to the United States, and Derek Burney, then Mulroney's chief of staff, urged him to offset the psychic sense of loss that the vanishing of protective walls would produce by implementing new policies to enhance pan-Canadian cultural expression. Mulroney took no action because he simply didn't understand the point.

The assumption, never stated but also never examined, has been that English-Canadians, as the majority, as the holders still of so many economic, financial, and cultural resources, needed no nurturing and would just sort of always be there and be in charge.

Even today, to suggest the opposite provokes incredulity. Yet this has already happened. Four decades ago, Anglo-Montrealers *were* the city, financially, economically, culturally; today, they are a dwindling, ageing rump. Across the country, English-Canadians are scarcely likely to vanish as fast. But in their cities, they *are* becoming strangers: Shortly after the year 2000, the majority in Toronto will be non-white, and in Vancouver soon afterwards. Increasingly, English-Canadian culture will be a culture of the hinterland, of the farms, of small towns, and of the suburbs.

Another reason why English-Canadians are so quick to be apologetic, even while almost certainly having less to be apologetic about than any other people in the world, can be suggested. Guilt itself is integral to their character. Indeed, whenever English-Canadians aren't feeling guilty about something or other, they quickly feel guilty about not feeling guilty. Perhaps this addiction is a kind of penance for the luck of having been born in what has to be the most fortunate country in the world – no enemies; natural wealth; easy access to the super-abundant opportunities south of the border. Perhaps its roots lie deeper, in Scottish Calvinism and in Jansenist-tinged Irish Catholicism. Whatever its cause, the "guilty" certainly do not go in for talking about themselves.

English-Canadians' collective silence may be prompted also by a more visceral motive. They may be preparing themselves for their inevitable collective downgoing. One of the great political dramas of the next century is going to be the transfer of power away from European peoples to leaner, harder, hungrier others. This doesn't mean a "clash of civilizations," as suggested by American scholar Stanley Huntingdon. What's happening may be more a case of one of those transfers of energy between people that, in the thesis of historian Arnold Toynbee, causes a rising civilization to displace a played-out one. The hallmark of an exhausted civilization is that it no longer possesses the self-confidence to reproduce itself: It cannot be a coincidence that the birthrate of English-speaking Canadians is well below the replacement rate now. (Nor a coincidence that "old stock" Quebeckers have entered the same "demographic winter.")

Such an instinctual motive is quite in character for a pragmatic, ex-colonial people. Above all in this age of tele-politics, it is personalities, not ideas, that inspire or deflate us. That part of the change in consciousness amongst English-speaking Canadians of the past three decades that wasn't written in the wind anyway was written out for them by a particular individual. He was, of course, Pierre Elliott Trudeau.

Trudeau was – is still – just too damn good, too cerebral, too elegant, too sophisticated, too graceful, too sexy, too intimidating, and too ruthless (that least English-Canadian of all character traits). He made everyone else look like klutzes, whether anglophone opponents like Robert Stanfield and Joe Clark, or his own ministers, Robert Winters, Mitchell Sharp, and John Turner.

The most insightful comment ever made about Trudeau came from an old, close friend: "He sucks up all the oxygen from the room." For a decade and a half, Trudeau mesmerized us, seduced us, hypnotized us, until almost nobody else was breathing normally. While everyone else was off-balance, Trudeau made his personal agenda the national agenda. On many matters he was a pretty indifferent prime minister: His economic legacy to Canadians is today's national debt; as was wilful and naïve, he spent much of his time pretending the United States didn't exist. But on what really mattered to him, national unity and the Constitution, he was sublime. In retirement, as he showed during Meech Lake and Charlottetown, he has lost none of his allure, nor his ruthlessness.

Today's Canada is Trudeau's Canada. Multiculturalism is his creation, reinjecting back into Canada the hyphens Diefenbaker had tried to scour out by his policy of "un-hyphenated Canadianism." It was during Trudeau's term that the phrase "English-Canadian" began to vanish from official discourse: this was a quid pro quo for the new rule that French-Canadians were to be described officially as French-speaking Canadians (and so, similarly, English-speaking Canadians). In a splendid assertion of identity, though, French-Canadians renamed themselves Québécois. During the greater part of his term, Trudeau rejected economic and cultural nationalism – effectively, English-Canadian nationalism – because he was concerned it would catalyse a counterpoint French-Canadian nationalism. It was only during his last term, from 1980 to 1984, that Trudeau embraced economic nationalism, in the form of the National Energy Policy and the Foreign Investment Review Agency. His concern then was strictly tactical: to gather up allies for his monumental project of patriating the Constitution.

All of this was for the sake of fulfilling Trudeau's vision of "One Canada." In fact, it isn't easy to know just how differently things would have turned out had the national vision he pursued so relentlessly been displaced by the alternative *deux nations* concept called for by Quebec nationalists and supported by both Robert Stanfield's Conservatives and the New Democrats. Despite national bilingualism, French Power, and the rest of it, Quebec is about as much a distinct nation today as it would have been had the *deux nations* formula been applied. Contemporary Quebeckers have plenty of problems. Conspicuously absent from the list, though, is their original existential doubt about being *maîtres chez nous*. A side consequence of this achievement by Quebeckers, also of the reinforcing of their sense of self-esteem because their interests have so continuously dominated the national agenda, is that it's now the second nation, the one so long taken for granted, that has lost its cohesion, and that has developed doubts about whether it is master of its own house.

Other Canadians were very slow to realize this. Few had the nerve, or wit, to complain about how their ethnic distinctiveness was being surreptitiously strip-mined out of them, and out of their country. To say any of this publicly would have been embarrassing, possibly treasonable; most certainly it would have inspired some withering retort from Trudeau. It was only after he was gone that English-Canadians began to notice their own silence.

In March 1991, *Saturday Night* fulfilled its duty to be provocative by printing an article by journalist Rick Salutin that quite clearly was treasonable. "Perhaps the time has come for Canada to get out of Quebec," he wrote. Having tossed his cap over the wind-mill, Salutin followed with an entire suit of clothes. The rest of the country had become "in many ways a far more interesting place than Quebec," he wrote.

The unsayable had been said at last: Not so much Salutin's notion about Canada getting out of Quebec, which was an atten-tion-getting provocation, as in his daring proposition that the rest of Canada might be the "more interesting place." This was indeed a headlong assault on the conventional wisdom. For decades, Quebeckers – Trudeau as their single-combat champion – had seemed so superior (he was), so elegant, so intellectual, so *formi-dable*, and everyone else so provincial and bland.

By the early 1990s, though, Canada (outside of Quebec) was well on its way to becoming postmodern. That condition may be scary and unsettling. But it is creative and energetic. Major cities, Toronto, Vancouver, to a lesser extent Calgary, Edmonton, and even Ottawa, were now multicultured and multiracial in a way that, within Quebec, only central Montreal was. Having taken the great historical dare of negotiating continental free trade, and having survived it (sort of anyway), other Canadians had gained a confidence in their capabilities as survivalists. There was a growing appreciation that no matter its supposed parochialism, TROC or ROC or whatever was capable of producing an excep-tional number of international artists of the first order – notably writers like Margaret Atwood, Robertson Davies, Mordecai Richler, Michael Ondaatje, Alice Munro, and Carol Shields. Raw energy was suddenly bubbling up all over the place: From out of depressed Newfoundland came Fisheries Minister Brian Tobin to perform as "Captain Canada," and the iconoclastic satire of "This Hour Has 22 Minutes." In the entire country, the most interesting city potentially has become Vancouver, as it transforms itself from the terminus at the end of a transcontinental railway into a bridge between this continent and the Pacific Rim. Except perhaps for Los Angeles, Toronto is now the most polyglot city in the world. California political scientist Joel Kotkin identifies Toronto and Vancouver as among only a dozen "global cities" that he calculates have the population mix to thrive in the global economy.

Collective creativity always expresses itself politically. In the mid-1990s, Quebeckers were arguing about the same themes – distinct society, sovereignty, sovereignty-association – they had been arguing about since the mid-1960s. By then, other Canadians had opened an entirely new book. From out of the western bedrock of old English Canada emerged the Reform Party to perform as a "conveyor-belt of ideas to the political system," in the phrase historian Desmond Morton once applied to the CCF and NDP, on everything from direct democracy to devolution to fiscal frugality to personal political integrity. Harris's Common Sense agenda is the most radical agenda – or revolution – in postwar Canadian political history, certainly in the context of centrist, bland Ontario. All of the "sacred trusts" about the role of government, the desirability of public institutions and redistributive programs, and the universality of social programs are being questioned now with an attack and energy Canadians haven't possessed politically in decades. To return to a point made in the Introduction, Canadians (outside of Quebec) are demonstrating a readiness to debate ideas that completely contradicts our image of being parochial pragmatists.

One consequence of discovering that they actually are interesting is that English-speaking Canadians no longer find what's going on in Quebec particularly interesting. To say the truly unsayable, many are bored to death with the entire national unity issue.

This change in attitude has been building up for the better part of a decade. Robert Bourassa's unilingual sign legislation of 1987 caused a click of consciousness: If Quebeckers weren't interested in bilingualism, they couldn't be much interested in Canada. Thereafter, many people stopped feeling guilty about Quebec. (Even earlier, the cold-bloodedness of Bourassa's policy of *fédéralisme rentable*, profitable federalism, dried up the reserves of sympathy.) The free-trade debate produced a louder click. Many English-Canadian nationalists came out of it deeply disappointed and resentful that their counterparts in Quebec had paid no attention to, had taken no interest in, the same kind of contest between head and heart going on in the rest of the country that had happened in Quebec during its referendum of 1980. The same 1988 election left many New Democrats similarly resentful. Despite a major effort in Quebec in terms of campaign funds and the allocation of the time of the leader, then Ed Broadbent, Quebeckers as always voted overwhelmingly for one of their own – Mulroney. During the later Meech Lake and Charlottetown affairs, many anglophone artists and intellectuals, the very ones once-active in Parents for French and lifelong supporters of Trudeau, sat on their hands.

From these years on, many in the rest of the country have been disengaging themselves emotionally from Quebec. All kinds of subtle factors are in play: multicultural Canadians, and especially multicoloured ones, now provide the cultural excitement and edge that English-Canadians once searched for in Quebec in order to liberate themselves from their own WASPishness. The global economy has turned everyone's eyes outwards: Young people are now having to make the decision whether to immerse themselves in French for the sake of qualifying for jobs in a shrinking federal civil service, or to cram up on Spanish, Mandarin, or Japanese to qualify for a job with a transnational. Arguments about the difference between sovereignty-association and sovereignty *and* association aren't merely stale but are irrelevant to the kind of arguments going on in the rest of the country about the role and purpose of government itself.

No one – or a number too trivial to be worth calculating – wants Quebec to go. Often, though, the motive for wanting the "two halves" of the country to stay together is now self-interest – that a breakup would be exceedingly expensive, at worst that it might be catastrophic, with the other nine provinces finding it impossible to stitch together a workable federal community because one, Ontario, would encompass half the new country's total population. The obvious alternative scheme of governance for what might be called Canada Two, a radical decentralization of power to all provinces, would leave the community without any centre, and so without any collective sense of itself.

Other Canadians have thus acquired what political scientist Alan Cairns described in his essay in the 1993 collection *Belonging* as "an anticipatory nationalism, a getting ready for a future [they] may reluctantly inherit . . . a nationalism by default, created on the re-bound."

One change catalysed by this "anticipatory nationalism" is that other Canadians have stopped fighting one another. For the past four decades, off and on ever since Confederation, the axis around which all of Canadian politics have revolved has been that of feds versus provs. Unlike in Europe and the United States, the major part of Canada's social security system has been created by equalizing opportunities and income protection across the provinces rather than of doing this among individuals – a technique that got the job done in a properly federal way while avoiding class politics. The federal government initiated most programs, levering the provinces into taking part by funding them in large part; the actual delivery of services, though, has been exclusively a provincial responsibility, hence the wide variations in supposedly pan-national programs like health care and welfare (let alone in exclusively provincial programs like workers' compensation and higher education).

The effect of all of this – compounded by Quebec's insistence on *de facto* autonomy, which all the other provinces copied from the mid-1970s on – has been to make Canada either the world's most decentralized country or, after Switzerland, the second most decentralized. (Ottawa accounts for only 40 per cent of total government spending, as opposed to 48 per cent by Berne; Switzerland, though, is really run by its banks, not by its governments, national or cantonal.) Canadians have been very slow to recognize this cardinal characteristic of their country. Trudeau, for example, was attacked constantly as an "arch-centralist"; in fact, in 1977, in a precursor to today's "block grants," Trudeau handed over to the provinces $6 billion worth of shared-cost programs for health, welfare, and postsecondary education in a devolutionary move that economist Thomas Courchene described at the time as a "substantial devolution of power . . . a reworking, *de facto*, of the Constitution."

In this sense, a great deal of the endless federal–provincial war has always been largely a phoney one, prompted much less by Ottawa's attempt to impose common or hegemonic standards than by the fact that fighting with, at the very least complaining about, other Canadians is one of Canadians' favourite indoor sports. As well, ambitious provincial politicians and bureaucrats have always been more than willing to lead the cheering. (Similarly, carping at the CBC for being centralist ignores the reality that it is, and has been for decades, the most regionalized national network in the world.) Regional wars have been our substitute for the customary class wars.

Reality has at last caught up with perception. Ottawa's weakness is now visible to all. Even some Quebec sovereigntists understand that the old order they so often have struggled against has been turned upside down: Jacques Parizeau has repeatedly argued that the reason why Quebec must leave is to save itself from the unworkable, Yugoslav-type confederation to which Canada has been reduced by its attempts to accommodate Quebec's incessant jurisdictional demands.

One consequence of the shift in the public's perception has been the vanishing of that staple of English-Canadian regional identity, the East–West struggle. Suddenly, it has lost most of its substance, even its point. Western hotline radio hosts can still stir up listeners by making cracks at Toronto and Ottawa, and business types there complain about the "$2,000 cup of coffee," meaning the day lost flying east to do bureaucratic or bank deals. But yesterday's sense of deep grievance about all this has been replaced by a laidback jokiness.

Jean Chrétien's "My Rockies" popularity in the West is clearly a factor. The severity of the recession in "privileged" central Canada (Greater Toronto accounted for more than one in two of all jobs lost), in contrast to its minimal impact in at least the far west of British Columbia and Alberta, matters too. Lastly, there's the fact that on the cardinal issue of free trade, the West won – big – over central Canada. British Columbia and Alberta in particular are now arranging their own affairs with their neighbouring states or the Pacific Rim. Albertans, naturally more pugnacious than British Columbians, know they'll never again be afflicted with the National Energy Policy. In a poll, Ekos Research found that only 10 per cent of British Columbians (even fewer elsewhere in the West) now say they want their province to leave Confederation.

. True, in some important respects the provinces are more at odds with each other than ever. New Brunswick's Frank McKenna has "stolen" industries destined for other provinces, like Purolator and United Parcel Services; Saskatchewan persuaded Crown Life Insurance to shift there from Ontario; Nova Scotia made a pitch (sweetened with a $2.3-million loan offer) for Ottawa's high-tech Systemhouse. Looming ahead, with Alberta in the lead, will be interprovincial competition to persuade industries to shift head offices and plants by the lure either of low general corporate taxes or of special tax deals. At the very least, the more they contend with each other, the less all the provinces will be able to contend with the national centre.

An important new pan-Canadian factor is that all provinces will be gaining autonomy out of Ottawa's commitment to "flexible federalism." This involves making a virtue out of the necessary. The new block grants system announced by Paul Martin in his February 1995 budget will give provinces unchallenged jurisdiction, limited only by some very general national standards, over health, welfare, and postsecondary education. Although with less money ($7 billion less in 1996-97), each province will be able to do things its own way.

This devolutionary deal has still to be negotiated. Some provinces are far from happy at the trade of more jurisdiction for less money. Nevertheless, after decades of attacking Ottawa's "imperialism," it's difficult for them to work up a full-throated righteous-indignation roar about being offered more power.

A province-run Canada would be radically different from a Canada-run as a nation-state, or a state-nation. As B.C. commentator Gordon Gibson remarks tartly, even though himself a supporter of substantial devolution, the premiers "could not agree on the same time even if in a room with a single watch." Not until mid-1994, and then only partially, did the provinces agree to dismantle internal trade barriers between them that, until then, had been higher than those among the independent nation-states of the European Union. The provinces' failure to establish national standards for those programs they administer exclusively, such as education, is likely to be extended to social programs, thereby widening still further the gaps between Canadians. In the phrase of political scientist Thomas Courchene, "Social Canada is going to have to be re-built from the bottom up." Canadians themselves will have to impose pan-national standards upon their provincial governments once Ottawa's ability to define and enforce these standards – those for health care as the most important – dwindles away at the same time as its financial involvement in them dwindles away.

In a reversal of Canadian history, though, the provinces (Quebec excepted) are no longer "ganging-up" on the feds. Some provincial leaders have even taken to worrying there may be too little left at the centre. Former Ontario premier Bob Rae has warned that Martin's budget could mean "The end of Canada as we have known it." Saskatchewan Premier Roy Romanow has talked about the need for a national debate about "shared common values." In an interview for this book, Rae worried about the future of equalization payments to the poorer provinces: "It isn't yet respectable to say this out loud but you're going to hear it said sooner or later." (Logically, the step beyond neo-conservatives' current attacks on "welfare dependency" is an attack upon equalization dependency.)

How the new, devolved Canadian universe – in the limit perhaps some form of association of ten quasi-sovereign states – will actually unfold will depend a great deal upon whether the federal government can exploit its continuing symbolic authority to mobilize Canadians and the provinces into maintaining national standards and programs. Whether it possesses the will and skill to do this is an open question. The answers Canadians themselves provide are nevertheless intriguing. According to Ekos Research, "Extreme alienation and regionalist aspirations seem to have dropped in recent years." Canadians, it reported, had lost all interest in "territoriality" and in fed–prov squabbles. They wanted their governments to work in partnership, and were unconcerned who did what: indeed, the most commonly cited area for federal action was that most sacrosanct of provincial jurisdictions – education.

Regionalism is as integral to the Canadian mystique as scraping windshields. It's bound to revive: Indeed, early in 1995 several provincial attorneys general told Ottawa bluntly they might not enforce its new gun-control legislation. A major confrontation is inevitable over Alberta's plans for a two-tier health-care system. Once the Quebec referendum is safely over, a number of provincial premiers, especially those in Alberta and British Columbia, are bound to revive demands for more devolution of jurisdiction.

For the time being though, Canadians (outside of Quebec) are less combative towards each other, and trust each other more than they have in decades. This attitude bespeaks one major political consequence: If the apocalypse of Quebec's separation actually happens, other Canadians are in a mood to work with each other to try to keep their community going.

As soon as Rick Salutin said the unsayable, everyone started saying it. In the collection of essays 'English-Canada' Speaks Out, published in the fall of 1991, Reg Whitaker, a political scientist at York University and not coincidentally an anti-free trader and a leftie like Salutin, writes, "If English-Canada is to find a mechanism for articulating its own authentic voice, it must confront what the preachers of National Unity seek to avoid at all costs. We must explore the idea of Canada without Quebec." In Thinking English Canada, Philip Resnick argues, "There will be no resolution to our crisis as a federation as long as English-Canadians refuse to think of themselves as a nation." Resnick had in mind a "sociological [his italics] nation," not a political one. In their book Deconfederation, Calgary professors David Bercuson and Barry Cooper proclaim bluntly, "To restore the economic and political health of Canada, Quebec must leave."

Such calls for Quebeckers to actually go were rare, and were usually the product of frustration rather than of real intent. What was noticeable, though, was the self-confidence with which commentators now breached all the old rules of national unity – the key rule always having been to never say anything that might upset anyone. In Plan B: The Future of the Rest of Canada, Gordon Gibson, despite having once been an aide to Trudeau, argues for a radical decentralization of Confederation whether or not Quebec separated. "If Quebec folds in the crunch, as it may well do," he writes, "in another decade the triggers to political change will be in B.C. and Alberta."

The mood in the rest of Canada during the runup to the 1995 referendum was quite unlike that back in 1980. Then, no one had said anything upsetting or indeed anything at all, but had relied on Trudeau to speak for all Canadians. This time, entire forests were scythed down to produce the scores of books, pamphlets, essays, and speeches on the topic. One debate that shattered all the old rules was about how to deal with Quebec *after* it had voted to separate: Osgoode Hall's Patrick Monahan argued that a fallback offer of some form of special status should be prepared in advance of the referendum because to wait until afterwards would mean that TROC or ROC would be unable to get its negotiating act together, with Queen's University's Robert Young countering, on the basis of the Czech–Slovak experience, that separation negotiations would go quickly and easily. Some, after analysing the entrails of the kind of negotiations that might follow a vote for sovereignty, almost welcomed a division of the spoils. "A Canada without Quebec would be a much more cohesive and governable political entity. The incessant wrangling over Quebec's place in Confederation would be over, once and for all," writes journalist Allan Freeman and economist Patrick Grady in *Dividing Up the House.*

All of this was "anticipatory nationalism." It reflected also a sense of how interesting the rest of Canada had become and, to say the unsayable one last time, of how boring the national unity issue had become. There was even a new attitude of assertiveness among English-speaking Canadians. The support Mike Harris received from Ontarians because of his promise to abolish employment equity revealed a quite new readiness to draw lines in the sand beyond which "old stock" Canadians were no longer prepared to allow themselves to be pushed. The increasingly uninhibited public criticisms of official multiculturalism revealed the same attitude. English-speaking Canadians, it seemed, were laagering themselves down for "a future [they] may reluctantly inherit."

There is a paradox in all of this. These new attitudes mean that Trudeau has emerged the eventual winner in his contest with Clark to define Canada's character. His policies, from bilingualism to multiculturalism to native self-government to the Charter of Rights and Freedoms, have made Canada an incomparably more interesting society – if decidedly a more cantankerous and divided one – than it was when he started reshaping it into his own image almost three decades ago. Indeed, all of this has turned the country into such an interesting place that hardly any English-speaking Canadians want to leave it even if they may have to scramble to reinvent it if Quebeckers vote to separate. The idea of "One Canada" endures; it keeps on enduring, therefore, even if those living in it find themselves, unwillingly, sadly, living in Canada Two.

8

Our Cold War

"I think we've won the Cold War and don't yet know it."

— James "Scotty" Reston, in his last column
for the *New York Times*, August 2, 1987,
two years before the Wall came down

As the Cold War has been to the United States, so the national unity crisis has been to Canada. It's because our all-consuming national challenge isn't yet resolved that the comparison is worth making.

Nations often grapple with prolonged, defining issues of this kind: The long quest by British monarchs to maintain "their" territories in France, that ended with Queen Mary dying with Calais carved upon her heart; the struggle over Alsace–Lorraine that petrified German–French relations for a century, causing them periodically to explode; China's long obsession with the "unfair treaties" of the colonial powers; Mexico's enduring fear of the gringos because they "stole" half of the country above the Rio Grande.

So long as issues like these last, they define everything. Then, abruptly, they shrink down into a few paragraphs in the history books. They all end differently; they usually end without warning; but they do all end.

Insofar as the Cold War and national unity are concerned, the two issues could scarcely be less alike. Yet they have an astonishing symmetry. By the standards of modern tele-politics, both have lasted an extraordinarily long time. The Cold War's beginning can be traced to Winston Churchill's 1946 warning that an "Iron Curtain" was descending across Europe; its end to the fall of the Wall in 1989. National unity has fixated Canadians for roughly one decade less – so far. Its start can be dated to the 1965 warning of the Royal Commission on Bilingualism and Biculturalism that "Canada is in the most critical period of its history," followed by a call for "a true partnership, as between equals." Its end is not yet.

The similarities continue. The United States' unremitting waging of the Cold War not only defined and dominated its politics, but to a considerable degree distorted and deformed them. We, too, have made national unity our political organizing principle. At times it has come to seem to be the primary reason for our existing as a nation-state, not that much differently from the United States in its life or death struggle with "Godless communism." Just as the Cold War enlisted successive generations of the best and brightest, so the cause of national unity has mobilized entire generations of our governing class of politicians, bureaucrats, academics, lawyers, and mainstream journalists. It's been remarked often that almost all of the sovereigntist leaders are baby boomers or older, still pursuing the long ago dreams of their youth. The federalists likewise: Their moments-of-glory memories stretch back to Trudeau as justice minister one-upping Quebec's nationalist Premier Daniel Johnson during the 1967 federal–provincial conference, just as those of the nationalists go back to René Lévesque bravely quitting the Liberal Party in 1965 to found his seemingly forlorn *Mouvement souveraineté-association*.

Both sides have devoted time and energy to their quarrel – in many respects, their civil war – that they would have applied to other political, economic, and social concerns. The United States, while winning the Cold War easily, crossed the finishing line badly winded; in the same way, Canadians have entered the 1990s incomparably weaker economically than we were when we began this journey, and far more fragmented politically and socially.

The comparison can be pushed nearer to the bone. Our national unity equivalent of the "military-industrial complex" was small-scale stuff, within bureaucracies and on campuses. Conspicuously, though, most of the members of our political class who were on the "right" side during the various national unity crises have benefited with appointments, contracts, honours, and patronage (Norman Spector, the bureaucratic architect of the Charlottetown Accord, became ambassador to Israel). Conversely, the Economic Council of Canada was disbanded soon after issuing a report calculating that an independent Quebec could be viable economically.

Pressing right against the bone, the Cold War, at least in hindsight, can be seen to have been wildly exaggerated as a struggle for national existence. No evidence has ever been found that Stalin or his successors ever intended "lunging" across Western Europe, as the alarmist phrase went. Despite some self-serving calculations by the CIA – one of these, in 1990, estimated the Soviet economy as the same size as Japan's – the actual industrial output of the Soviet Union was a pitiful one-tenth of the United States and its allies. Perhaps the real fraud of the Cold War was that some Soviet leaders were sufficiently impressed by the alarmism in Washington to imagine that with large numbers of heavy missiles, all in fact clumsy and inaccurate, their country might actually be a co-equal superpower, and so proceeded to bankrupt it.

It's far too early to cast the cool light of hindsight upon the national unity crisis. Yet time and again there was a quality to its management that was almost hysterical. In mid-1992, Joe Clark, then minister of intergovernmental affairs, actually warned that failure to pass the Charlottetown Accord could put Canada at risk of becoming "another Beirut." Earlier, when Meech Lake was failing, many members of the political class proclaimed that the consequences would be Quebec's separation and the collapse of the dollar. The truth is that while Quebeckers' opinions about sovereignty have oscillated wildly, the peaks of support for it have always occurred during those "safe" periods, such as immediately following the collapse of the Meech Lake deal, when no actual referendum was in prospect.

None of this is to say that the national unity crisis was just fantasy. On November 15, 1976, on the night of René Lévesque's election triumph, even strong Quebec federalists were deeply moved as they watched him tell fifteen thousand singing, cheering supporters in Montreal's Paul Sauvé Arena, "I have never been so proud to be a Quebecker." But for the policy of Cold War-style containment that Trudeau then adopted, Quebeckers might well have skipped and danced their way right out of Confederation. With nerveless brilliance, Trudeau sidestepped every confrontation with Lévesque, never criticizing Quebeckers for their choice, maintaining his stance all the way through Lévesque's unilingual legislation, Bill 101, and deliberately avoiding challenging it in the courts despite considerable pressures to do so within his cabinet and across the country. When eventually implemented, this legislation exorcised the primal anxieties of Quebeckers by creating a linguistic safety zone within which they can forever feel *maîtres chez nous*.

Trudeau saved Canada then, as only he could have done. He did it again during the referendum of 1980, not so much by his brilliant performance during the campaign as by what he'd done much earlier. Clark's comment, this time an astute one, that "The Canada Mr. Lévesque wants to separate from no longer exists," captured Lévesque's frustration at finding himself, right after any declaration that there was no place for a Quebecker in Canada, arguing with francophones in power at Ottawa like Marc Lalonde, Gérard Pelletier, Jean-Luc Pepin, not to mention Trudeau himself, or with anglophone politicians and officials who were at least functionally bilingual.

Much of what has happened since that decisive – 60 per cent – vote by Quebeckers for federalism has been determined by sheer accident more than by policy or shifts in public attitude. Quebec nationalists now proclaim that Trudeau's enactment of the 1982 Constitution over Quebec's objections was a great "humiliation." Whatever did or did not happen during the "Night of the Long Knives" at the 1981 First Ministers conference where Lévesque was outmanoeuvred by Trudeau mattered less than what didn't happen afterwards. In 1982, when the new Constitution was signed into law by the Queen on Parliament Hill, there were no public demonstrations or protest marches in Montreal or elsewhere. Quebeckers by this time were preoccupied with their "Quebec Inc." version of the long casino boom.

What started everything up again was Mulroney's decision to try to one-up Trudeau by negotiating a deal with Premier Robert Bourassa, trading his signature to the Constitution in exchange for "distinct society" status. To sell the deal to the rest of the country, Mulroney went into rhetorical overdrive. The Constitution "imposed" upon Quebec had been "one of the greatest disappointments in the history of the province," he declared. This stirred up the Quebec nationalists. It also stirred up Trudeau.

Mulroney lost Meech Lake in-between the rock of Newfoundland Premier Clyde Wells's adamantine opposition and the hard place of Bourassa's enactment of unilingual sign legislation. Raining down on the scene were Trudeau's thunderbolts. Mulroney then lost the Charlottetown Accord, an expanded version of Meech, to cross-Canada public opinion in the 1992 referendum, as hostile to the accord in the rest of Canada as within Quebec, if for quite contradictory reasons.

Accident now became self-fulfilling. The failure of Meech, escalated to flash point by the burning of a *fleur-de-lis* flag by a half-dozen louts in Brockville (a sequence replayed constantly on Quebec's TV stations), sent support for sovereignty shooting above 60 per cent. Parti Québécois Leader Jacques Parizeau, a true believer in outright independence in contrast to Lévesque's ambivalence about making a clean break (shared by Bloc Québécois Leader Lucien Bouchard), capitalized on the moment to reinsert a promise to hold a referendum on sovereignty back into the PQ platform.

In September 1994, Quebeckers punished the tired and stale Liberal government for the preceding four years of recession, just as Ontarians would do nine months later to their New Democratic government. The only alternative available to Quebeckers, though, happened to be the pro-sovereigntist PQ. Ever since, our "cold war" has resumed.

As this is being written, our internal cold war has dimmed into a phoney war. Despite the considerable propaganda powers available to it, the PQ government has failed to lift support for outright sovereignty above the 40 per cent mark – the same losing level as in 1980. It's not even clear how many of the separatists really want to separate. A February 1995 poll by SONDAGEM of Montreal found that two in five of those who intended to vote for sovereignty believed that a sovereign Quebec would still be part of Canada.

Quebeckers' attitudes, and their understanding of the rest of the country, thus have changed astonishingly little in the twenty years since comedian Yvon Deschamps pronounced that what Quebeckers really want is "*Un Québec indépendant dans un Canada uni.*" Parizeau was exploiting this ambivalence when he promised Quebeckers in his sovereignty bill they would be able to retain their Canadian passports and currency. Later, under pressure from Bouchard, Parizeau magnified the ambivalence to bursting point by proposing that the question, in a referendum by then delayed until the fall, should now be sovereignty *and* association. That combination did shift the separatist vote towards the 50 per cent mark. Yet the new numbers were based on an illusion. In Jean Chrétien's neat phrase, sovereignty and association amounts to "a divorce followed by remarriage." In fact, for lack of any interest in the rest of the country in any association except one that reduced a sovereign Quebec to political impotence within the reconfigured pan-Canadian association, Parizeau's new formula was meaningless, other than as a tactic to convince "soft nationalists" to edge over to the sovereignty side in order to avoid the humiliation of a severe referendum defeat.

At the time of writing, it's impossible to know whether the referendum will be postponed again, this time indefinitely, or be held and lost, or be held and won on a "soft," Deschamps-type question. In one possible scenario, Parizeau would eke out a narrow win on the sovereignty-and-association question, wait for the rest of the country to say no – which it most certainly will – then proclaim humiliation and rejection and proceed directly to his lifelong objective by way of UDI, a unilateral declaration of independence.

How Quebeckers would react to such an outright political fraud is as unknowable as the outcome of the referendum itself. The most that can be attempted with reasonable safety is to make a couple of comments about the context within which this latest national unity crisis is unfolding, and, much more riskily, to suggest where a resolution might be found.

Whatever the result of the referendum, including even a decisive victory for federalism, it's been a long time since Quebec and the rest of the country have been so far apart. In a certain sense, the long battle between Trudeau's dream of "One Canada" and the opposed *deux nations* vision of Quebec nationalists has ended in a victory for the nationalists. This is because Quebec has already largely separated from the rest of Canada – emotionally and psychically, as well as administratively in most practical respects. It is also because many other Canadians have, substantively, withdrawn from Quebec.

The decisive difference between this referendum and that of 1980 is the absence of emotion – on either side. The economic stresses and strains have of course frayed people's reserves of sentiment and idealism. But underlying attitudes have changed also, on both sides.

Some years back – anyone can pick their date – Quebeckers in effect gave up on Canada. They simply lost interest in it, and stopped being worried about it. That they were secure linguistically made a critical difference: Noticeably absent this referendum around has been angry rhetoric about "Westmount Rhodesians" or pained recollections of having once had to speak English to buy socks in Eaton's. While Bouchard is adept at pressing the nerve of past "humiliations," the official attitude in Quebec is that the issue is no longer ethnic survival but rather the survival of the pluri-cultural people living in the territory of Quebec by the device of separating from a sinking Canada.

That Quebec is now almost entirely self-contained administratively – even while receiving a net benefit of federal spending over taxes of some $3.5 billion a year – matters a good deal to this relaxed mood. Moreover, Quebec's self-containment is about to be increased significantly by the devolution of power to all provinces – so-called "flexible federalism" – made necessary by Ottawa's financial constraints. Indeed, it isn't easy to identify many practical ways in which a fully sovereign Quebec (already possessed of its own immigration program, as an example) would be significantly more independent from the rest of Canada than it is now, especially given the contemporary porousness of all nation-states and the commitments Quebec would have to abide by under NAFTA.

Always it's the emotional distance that matters the most. A prominent Quebec federalist, Alain Dubuc, editor of the province's largest newspaper, *La Presse*, sums up this sense of detachment: "I don't really care about Canada. I don't have much energy to put into that country. All my energies go towards Quebec."

Much the same is true on the far side of the Ottawa River. It isn't that other Canadians want Quebec to go; it's that many no longer care about keeping it in the way they once did. The Canadian Labour Congress, for example, has accepted the withdrawal of the Quebec Federation of Labour into a new arrangement that CLC President Bob White has described as "sovereignty-association."

One of Parizeau's deftest political sallies since gaining office was to warn in a speech to the Canadian Club in Toronto that, no matter the outcome of the referendum, Quebeckers' demands on other Canadians would persist "like endless trips to the dentist." Overwhelmingly, other Canadians are exhausted by the latest national unity crisis, and so, largely, are indifferent to it. No mood of rejectionism exists. But nor is there much generosity. Other Canadians are impatient for Quebeckers to decide, and are prepared to wait for the television anchors to pronounce the referendum result as *oui* or *non*. Scarcely a scrap of patience exists in the rest of the country for any new initiatives – some constitutional offer or special administrative deals – to convince Quebeckers to decide to stay. Exacerbating the exhaustion and boredom is a disbelief that any new deal that might be done would long remain a done deal. On both sides, the contemporary mood is bleak. Which may be to say that it's realistic.

So it may be time to make a suggestion that, initially, may seem quixotic.

Even if the sovereigntists lose the referendum decisively, a large number of Quebeckers, probably a majority of francophones, and an overwhelming majority of its influential intellectual élite, will remain profoundly dissatisfied with Confederation in its current form. One of the most eloquent expressions of this attitude is contained in Laval University political scientist Guy Laforest's book, *Trudeau and the End of the Canadian Dream* (English version, 1995). "We Quebecers are being asked to accept the principle of limited and shared national sovereignty in this era when integration in all its forms is being reinforced. So be it," writes Laforest. "But Canada should do no less. Let Canada renounce the sovereignty and monopoly on the Canadian national identity by creating a space for Quebec by its side in the definition of our political system."

Although he would never admit it, and no doubt doesn't realize it, Laforest is virtually pleading with the rest of Canada to offer Quebec *something* – for face, for pride, for reassurance.

Assume that the sovereigntists do lose. Even federalist Quebeckers would fear afterwards that their province will lose its bargaining leverage within Confederation. Inexorably, that leverage is eroding already. Quebec's share of the national population has slipped below the symbolic mark of 25 per cent, or one-quarter. Its share of national economic output – overtaken in 1993 by British Columbia and Alberta combined for the first time – is dipping down towards the 20 per cent level. Montreal's economic future is questionable: It's missing out on trade with the Pacific Rim and Latin America; its infrastructure is crumbling visibly. Before long, Vancouver will displace Montreal as Canada's second-largest city. The province's entire economy is weak. Its net debt level, at 68 per cent of its total output, is the highest in the country (even after almost five years of "socialism," Ontario's is 42 per cent); Quebec's rate of poverty – one in five – is also the highest. Its "hole" card, a major new hydro project in James Bay, has been blocked by the opposition of native people while some of Hydro-Quebec's existing export contracts have been cancelled.

Already wounded economically, Quebeckers are at risk of being wounded psychically by a humiliating loss in the referendum. Afterwards, the PQ government, despite its considerable ministerial competence, may lose its will, certainly its credibility, to manage the province's affairs effectively by imposing the long-delayed spending cuts that will be needed to shrink the budget deficits to bearable size.

In the specific terms Laforest uses – "Let Canada renounce the sovereignty and monopoly on the Canadian identity" – he, and others like him, are asking for the impossible. Other Canadians will never agree to some form of special status or of *deux nations*, will not even stir themselves to discuss it. Further, as Quebec nationalists have always lacked the honesty to admit, as soon as Quebec became "special" it would become more disadvantaged within Confederation than it is now. Any provincial gains would be offset by federal losses. Never again, virtually certainly, would a Quebecker be prime minister, in contrast to their hold on that office for almost thirty years now but for three "blips" – Clark, John Turner, and Kim Campbell. Quebec's federal ministers and MPs would lose influence over national policies. Increasingly, discretionary federal spending would be directed elsewhere. As for the ultimate of sovereignty-association, even if such a pact could be negotiated, Quebec would be reduced under any imaginable terms to a junior, largely powerless, partner.

While equality, in the form of *deux nations* or of special status, let alone of sovereignty-association, is unattainable, the unalterable fact remains that Quebec is and will be forever distinct among the provinces.

Brian Mulroney's solution was "distinct society." (A variation of the old B&B commission's term "autonomous society.") Its lethal defect was that while Mulroney kept saying this would give Quebec no new powers, Bourassa kept saying it would enable Quebec "to gain new ground." (Equally lethal, by then few believed anything Mulroney said.)

Quite different would be what could be called "symbolic distinct society" status. The technique for achieving this would be to identify Quebec as a distinct society in the preamble to the Constitution as opposed to proclaiming this status in the body of the document. Indeed, this was Bourassa's initial demand; Mulroney later rolled the dice towards Bourassa by agreeing to enact distinct society status as a separate clause in the Constitution itself, where it would have had the same over-arching legal implications as the existing clauses about gender equality, multiculturalism, and native people. As a perambulatory declaration, though, distinct society status would be only a state-ment of good intent, without legal or political implications.

Such an offer, made after the referendum and only after a victory for federalism, would of course be rejected contemptu-ously by Parizeau – although not absolutely necessarily by the more ambivalent Bouchard. Quebeckers themselves, though, might respond differently.

The truth is that Quebeckers have been badly misled by their recent leadership. Bourassa's unilingual sign legislation in 1987 dried up almost all the reserves of sympathy, and guilt, in the rest of the country. The subsequent "knife at the throat" policy of threatening to separate pursued by the nationalists took no account of the fact – self-absorbed narcissism as a major cause of the misunderstanding – that other Canadians could no longer be intimidated. Lastly, Parizeau, by misreading temporary support for sovereignty in the polls of a half-decade ago, committed Quebeckers to a referendum that, most probably, will end in yet another "humiliation." After so many "defeats," the securing of symbolic distinct society status would at least give Quebeckers a moral victory.

Extracting such a compromise from other Canadians will not be easy. For the time being at least, Chrétien has immense politi-cal credit in the bank. Certain premiers, Roy Romanow of Saskatchewan, Frank McKenna of New Brunswick, and, because of his role in Meech Lake history, Clyde Wells of Newfoundland, could exercise influence beyond their own borders. Leaders like these might be able to lead the rest of the country because what they would be calling for would be an act of generosity from Canadians that, if the referendum indeed is already lost, there's no "need" for them to make.

Even if the offer of symbolic distinct society status is rejected officially, the offer itself will signal to Quebeckers that other Canadians have not rejected them. A gesture towards reconciliation would have been made.

Such a gesture, let alone some implausible constitutional offer, would not solve the national unity crisis. The truth is that Quebeckers' wholly legitimate anxieties and grievances as a minority are no more soluble definitively than the anxieties and grievances of the Scots, of the Catalans, of the Walloons and Flemings, and of every minority nation-people around the world. A gesture might – just possibly – reduce the national unity crisis to a national unity concern, at the very least for a few years.

Our private cold war is finished, although it is not yet over. It is possible, although not probable, that Quebeckers will allow themselves to be trapped like "lobsters" – in the phrase Parizeau apparently used in a private briefing with European ambassadors – and vote for sovereignty as a kind of downpayment to win for themselves the association that they really want. Such a tactical vote would enable Parizeau, once the association has been rejected, to hustle them out of Canada by an UDI. Much more probably, Quebeckers will recognize Parizeau's manipulation in asking them to vote for what he cannot deliver, and will vote *non* to a sovereignty that only a minority really want.

What will remain, in either case, is the angst of Quebeckers about their status as a minority. Their angst is real. It's time, though, for Quebeckers to recognize that the "other" of the two nations, their old opponents the English-Canadians, are similarly becoming a minority within the country, numerically and emotionally. Separated, we will both vanish, they to become an insignificant nation-state that no one in the continent will care about or even notice, we, after a defiant battle against the odds, almost certainly to become Americans.

In one form or another, the national unity crisis will continue as long as Canada continues. Once reduced to a national unity concern, though, Canadians will be released to apply their time and energy to talking about all the other economic, cultural, and political changes taking place within our society, and about how to cope with, and capitalize upon, them. These are our principal concerns now: They apply equally to both of the *deux nations*, and to all others in the Canadian community.

PART III

The Culture of the Matter

9

More Equal Than Thou

"The desire for equality becomes more insatiable in proportion as equality is more complete."

— Alexis de Tocqueville, *Democracy in America*, 1835

The defining differences between the Canada of the early 1990s that I returned to and the Canada I had left the better part of a decade earlier were those of economic angst and identity anger. More people, in incomparably more kinds and circumstances, were more clamorous about their separate identities and were more urgently insistent that these identity rights be recognized and realized than ever before in Canadian history, or in any of the transatlantic societies I'd just been exploring.

Much of this reflected the new kind of Canada that was emerging. Much of it derived from the recently enacted Charter of Rights and Freedoms. This new Constitution handed around more rights to more different people than any equivalent national document (except, possibly, the old Yugoslav constitution). All individuals were equal, before and under the law. But all kinds of groups were also more equal than other individuals: Women, in Section 28, aboriginals in Sections 25 and 35, multicultural Canadians in Section 27, also French-speaking Canadians and underdeveloped provinces (by way of equalization), and, by way of Section 15(2), all kinds of unnamed "disadvantaged" groups. All of this was exceptionally ambitious. It was also exceptionally popular. With astonishing speed (reminiscent of the way we quickly embraced the once controversial maple leaf flag), Canadians made the Charter into an emblem of citizenship, as revered as was their two-hundred-year-old constitution by Americans. Combined, the emerging new Canada and the implanted new Charter would unleash what Madam Justice Rosalie Abella, now a member of the Ontario Court of Appeal, would describe as a "rights frenzy."

As a direct consequence of our new national emphasis on relying upon the law to extend rights to all people deserving of them or claiming them rather than, as in the past, of addressing political problems by log-rolling out solutions among competing interest groups, we became victims of "Constitutionitis." From early 1987 to the end of 1992, a period that coincided roughly with my time abroad, a major part of our national energy was expended in trying to revise our brand-new Constitution in order to define a whole new range of group rights, most importantly those of Quebeckers as members of a "distinct society" and those of native people as possessing an "inherent right to self-government."

While all of this was going on, the nature of some of the problems Canadians were now attempting to cure had changed markedly. Discrimination in its classic sense of actual injury to an individual or group ceased to be the only criterion for remedial action: Hurt feelings, meaning those allegedly created by a "hostile environment" or a "chilly climate" produced by sexism and racism, had become major subjects of concern. Whenever our energy flagged in our attempt to create a no-fault society as defined by intangibles like these as well as by old-style, tangible wrongs, guilt spurred us on. The most remarkable aspect of former UN ambassador Stephen Lewis's description of Canada as a "systemically racist" society in a 1992 report to the Ontario government was that this unsubstantiated proclamation was widely accepted as a statement of self-evident truth.

Much that was happening here was also the product of the *zeitgeist*, or spirit of the times, particularly the public temper south of the border, where affirmative action was being enforced rigorously and comprehensively and where Bill Clinton's new cabinet would turn out to be the most "diverse" ever (even while containing more lawyers than ever before). The baby boomers, who'd come of age in the 1960s, were now coming into positions of power. Back then, they hadn't been able to change the world, but they could now make it a fairer, more equitable, and most certainly a more sensitive place.

In both countries, the feminism of the 1970s had blazed a trail – beginning with equality of opportunity, equal pay for work of equal value, through employment equity, and on to long hidden issues like spousal violence, sexual harassment, and date rape – that other identity groups now followed. Gays and lesbians, for example, began calling for same-sex benefits and a redefinition of the concept of the family. We – ourselves and the Americans – were evolving into what were beginning to be called "postmodern" societies, radically different from the societies of our past or of any others anywhere.

Alexis de Tocqueville had foreseen all of this (and a good deal else) a century and a half earlier. The more nearly that equality is achieved, the more insistently it is demanded, in particular because of the "vague dread" (of missing out on something) that de Tocqueville observed seemed to envelop the outwardly ebullient and self-reliant ex-colonists.

Canadian philosopher Charles Taylor adds a contemporary gloss to de Tocqueville's insight. "The core problem of identity politics," Taylor remarks in his 1992 book, *The Politics of Recognition*, "is that it fails if equality is achieved because the differences, and therefore the identity, would vanish."

What was new, as Taylor observes, "is that the demand for recognition is now explicit." Identity politics wasn't really about equality; it was about recognition. Mere equality of opportunity no longer attracted people to the barricades. Their rallying cry now was "Equality of results," sometimes known also as "real equality." Rather than being potential, or an opportunity to be seized, equality had to be actual, in the now; rather than being specific, as in non-discriminatory hiring practices and before the law, it had to be comprehensive, encompassing not only employment but language (hence political correctness), attitudes, feelings, and thoughts (hence the popularity of "sensitivity training" sessions, compared by critics to the re-education sessions of Mao's Red Guards).

Even "real equality" or "equality of results" was insufficient. The achievement of these would threaten the identity of the group by making its members like everyone else. Hence the incessant search for new targets. For example, actions to prevent explicit sexual harassment were succeeded by a demand for "zero tolerance" of sexual harassment in its broadest definition, and this in turn by demands for elimination of a "chilly climate" – meaning in effect a perception of patronizing attitudes, no matter the absence of any alleged, let alone proven, instances of explicit sexism or racism. Indeed, "real equality" has been redefined to legitimize inequalities. In a 1993 report to the Canadian Bar Association, former Supreme Court judge Bertha Wilson called for women lawyers to be paid the same as male ones while working fewer hours in order to care for their children. Since recognition rather than equality is the real objective, there is, at least theoretically, no limit to such proposals.

Canadians (and Americans) would have saved themselves a good deal of guilt-ridden angst, most certainly a considerable amount of self-flagellation, had they paid attention to the insights of de Tocqueville and Taylor.

In Canada, the battles over identity politics were waged on four specific fronts, to be discussed in succeeding chapters. These were: The interpretation of the Charter of Rights and Freedoms; employment equity; official multiculturalism; and immigration. This last is a quite different program from the others. Its objectives are economic (and political) rather than cultural. But the new policy of continuous mass immigration initiated in 1989, if only by the happenstance that most of these newcomers came from entirely different cultures from that of "old Canada," significantly affected what could be called the "in-house" identity programs. It was around this time that the long-established program of official multiculturalism became, *de facto*, a policy concerned principally with the narrower, and much more demanding, phenomenon of multicolouredism or, in that curious bureaucratic term, multi-racialism. As well, because of mass immigration, the numbers eligible to benefit from the new employment equity programs (also the numbers likely to be made losers by them) increased towards some critical political mass. Chapter Thirteen describes the impact of all these developments upon the ultimate commonality of every national community – our citizenship.

While we, and the Americans, are well ahead of everyone else, we nevertheless have been travelling a path mapped out by the Western liberal tradition.

During the 20th century, all developed societies have behaved in a manner without precedent in human history. A few earlier touchstones exist: The French and American revolutions; welfare legislation in Bismarckian Germany; and its comparatively timid equivalents in Victorian Britain. It's only quite recently, though, that developed nation-states have accepted establishing equality among all their citizens as a national obligation and necessity. With, again, occasional exceptions – the Soviet Union, where "real socialism" turned quickly into "command socialism"; Scandinavia, where the Middle Way dates from the 1930s – developed countries only really launched themselves upon this extraordinarily ambitious project once the guns had stopped firing at the end of the Second World War.

By equality these governments, and all the experts who concocted the specific policy proposals for them, meant two things. The first was equality of opportunity. Everyone should start life's race on the same line, with equal access to resources, educational and otherwise, and an impartial system of justice (including various forms of legal aid). Later, the meaning of equality of opportunity was extended to encompass protecting individuals against catastrophes, like serious illness and endemic poverty.

The second meaning of equality was economic. This meant full employment, with social security substituting for its temporary absence, and a progressive income tax to at least narrow the gaps in the widths of everyone's wallets. All states, most particularly the United States, accepted that income inequalities remained a necessity in order to actually create wealth that could then be redistributed. The function of the rich, their wallets reinflated by tax loopholes, was to *encourager les autres*, even perhaps to benefit the less fortunate a bit by trickling down upon them a share of their surplus cash. (To their eventual great cost, communist societies ignored this truth of human nature.)

Canada largely achieved these objectives sometime during the mid-1970s: Trudeau's "Just Society" was as much a statement of fact as a promise. Three decades of resource boom had generated ample amounts of wealth to be redistributed. We had redistributed that wealth pretty evenly. The 1995 Rowntree Commission in Britain rated Canada near the top among those industrial democracies that had achieved major gains in income equality over the preceding half-century. Especially generous were the new income supports for the elderly and, by way of equalization and unemployment insurance, to those living in underdeveloped regions. (Through the 1970s and 1980s, in contradiction to their objective economic circumstances, the Atlantic provinces experienced actual population increases.)

We were by no means the most equal society in the world, certainly not compared to the Scandinavians, Germans, or Japanese. In practice, as noted in Chapter Five, our egalitarianism is riddled with holes, and with loopholes. An ever-increasing number of Canadians escape the tax system, and the egalitarian ethic, by moving their funds abroad – the Irvings of New Brunswick are the most notorious escapees. At the other end of the scale, the living conditions of most native people remain a national disgrace. Comparative poverty continued of course, as it always must when measured comparatively. Most disturbing by far is that, at one in five, the rate of child poverty in Canada is the second highest among developed countries. Almost as disturbing, evidence has begun to accumulate of "welfare dependency," or of state-induced, and subsidized, poverty.

As North Americans, though, we are almost defiantly egalitarian. Even after about five years of dominance of the neo-conservative, free-market ideology as a result of the Canada–U.S. free trade deal, egalitarian attitudes remain remarkably strong in Canada. The media (its one saving grace is that it gives readers and viewers more or less what they want) persists in seeking out exorbitant executive pay packages, many of which indeed reflect not much more than competitive corporate machismo, and very few of which reflect the market rules of supply and demand (there being no shortage of candidates for CEO jobs).

Within the broad limits of the possible, Canada achieved well over a good decade ago its transcendent postwar task of extending equality of opportunity and a respectable degree of economic equality to the great majority of its citizens. As the result of this achievement, the issue of equality has moved to the top of our national agenda for most of the time since.

The de Tocqueville thesis, as updated by Taylor, has proved to be dead on. The more equal society became, the more anxious people became to be equal. To rephrase an even earlier philosopher, the defining creed of many Canadians became "I am unequal, therefore I am." This has been transmuted into the doctrines of real equality and of equality of results.

In fact, the concept of equality of results wasn't entirely new. Successful empires, like the Roman and British, practised a version of it, distributing honours, appointments, status, and wealth among leaders of their subject peoples, and then conscripting these leaders' subjects into their armies. Indeed, the most fully realized equality of results system was practised more than a century ago in a part of Canada then not part of Canada. In the wake of late 19th-century Catholic–Protestant riots, the Newfoundland government awarded all public offices, civil service positions, and school grants, on a strict proportional basis, to Catholics, Anglicans, and Methodists. It's a nice irony that today's identity politicians are advocating a policy first implemented by long-dead white males in an imperial colony.

Debating-points like these aside, today's version of equality of results has no precedent in history. The shift from equality of opportunity to equality of results means that any inequalities that persist are immoral, even evil, rather than the consequences of the rough justice of the marketplace or of innate human tendencies such as favouring one's own family and friends. At best these continued inequalities are the product of a deliberate attempt to maintain "privilege"; at worst they are the product of ingrained racism and sexism. Equality of results thus is demanded as a right, on par with rights to freedom of speech and freedom of association.

This is why reverse discrimination, although inevitable since an "A" cannot be moved to the head of a job queue unless a "B" is shuffled to its rear, doesn't trouble identity groups, except in public arguments. All minority groups *are* equal, morally and philosophically. The majority – always described as the "dominant" or "privileged" majority – thus *must*, morally, yield space for these groups. In the 1990 book, *The Law of the Charter: Equality Rights*, Dale Gibson writes that "while the *means* typically employed by affirmative action schemes are discriminatory in the short run, the *goal* of equality to which they are directed is the antithesis of discrimination." In her 1993 report on gender equality, *Touchstones for Change*, to the Canadian Bar Association, Melina Buckley, the CBA's executive director, dismisses counter-arguments about reverse discrimination on the grounds that "Affirmative action programs do not result in special treatment, they result in *appropriate* [her italics] treatment."

Whether appropriate or discriminatory, all the techniques used to achieve equality of results, from affirmative action to multiculturalism to equal "representation" on everything from government and corporate boards to TV panel discussions, are, although important, only means to an end. That end is recognition. The objective isn't just a no-fault society with zero tolerance for any residual inequalities and discrimination: It is a society filled up with the faultlines of all those who possess an inherent right to define their identities and to secure societal recognition of these distinctive characteristics.

Such recognition derives from the groups themselves. It isn't a gift to be distributed around by the "dominant" majority. The identity of all minority groups pre-exists that of the majority and is merely being suppressed temporarily. Hence the manner in which groups take charge of their own identity by redefining it themselves. In Canada, the most expressive examples are of French-Canadians in Quebec renaming themselves Québécois, and of native people renaming themselves First Nations. Blacks have renamed themselves Afro-Americans (and Afro-Canadians). Homosexuals, who once condemned the term "queer," now celebrate it in Queer Nation.

The result has been the development of a new concept of

community. Canada no longer consists of a continuous, organic community forged out of the traditional regional and provincial communities arising out of our history, from out of our very rocks and forests. In theory, more accurately in dogma, Canada consists now of an agglomeration of all the identity communities, each of which must be recognized as distinct from the "dominant" majority and so entitled to equality on its own terms. Logically, the doctrine of "self-governing territories" as applied now to native people could be extended to all identity groups. While there are severe practical limits to the extent to which identity communities could ever become distinct political entities, there are few theoretical limits to the dogma: One American feminist has identified "gender nations." A shade less extravagantly, dub poet Clifton Joseph writes in left-centred *This Magazine* that the objective of ethnic groups is "to really and equitably redefine the country, taking all its cultures into *full* [his italics] consideration," thereby displacing Canada's "Eurocentric and ultimately soft-sell white supremacist framework of a French and English battle royale." That's to say that your house, into which you once invited me, is now my house.

That geography and history have already made Canada a community of communities makes it easier for us to become a community of an infinite number of identity communities. Inherent divisions – Québécois; native people; the provinces – create the precondition for potentially limitless division.

There is another reason why identity politics has had so much impact upon contemporary Canada. The core claim of identity groups is that they are victims. To Canadians, most especially English-Canadians already burdened by a legacy of guilt, victimhood is the most persuasive appeal anyone can make.

There are unquestionably more victims in Canada than there are in any other country. All francophones are victims of all anglophones, all natives of all non-natives, all ethnic groups of all WASPs.

Also, as a consequence of today's identity perceptions, all women of all men, all people of colour of all whites, all disabled of all abled, all gays and lesbians of all straights. Distinctive to Canada, and quite aside from the endless "humiliations" the Québécois have suffered, has been the victimization of the West by the East and of the Atlantic provinces by central Canada. Indeed, the depredations of the "pale, patriarchal, penis people," as they've been memorably called, have been inflicted upon an extraordinary number of victims by extraordinarily few victimizers. Excluded from the "dominant majority" must be all those WASPS who are homosexual or disabled, poor or unemployed, all those underdeveloped regions, and within the wealthy provinces, all those in small towns and on farms, and all those in the metropolitan suburbs who are patronized by the clever sophisticates of the inner cities. This equation leaves thirty million Canadians being victimized by roughly three thousand well-off metropolitan WASP males.

Only the boldest of Canadians have been brave enough to question the validity of victim culture. Environics pollster Michael Adams once dared to lob out the notion of "psychological affluence," meaning that those who've gained acceptance as victims have the moral edge over supposedly advantaged types – mostly white males – who must struggle along under their burden of guilt.

Certainly, the victim culture fits perfectly our far from fully exorcised self-image as ex-colonials who liberated ourselves from exploitation by the imperialist and snobbish British just in time to fall prey to the aggressive, and equally imperialist, Yankees.

It's an open question whether we harbour proportionately more victims and therefore more identity groups than Americans do. Quite certainly, the two North American nations are in an international political correctness division all of their own.

Objectively, the United States ought to be in a class by itself. No Canadian equivalent exists, except to a degree in our treatment of native people, to the "historical disadvantage" inflicted upon American blacks by slavery, segregation, and legalized discrimination. Economic inequalities, which magnify identity inequalities, are far more marked south of the border. The unique litigiousness of Americans makes that society a natural one in which to conduct legal battles over identity rights.

Yet the cross-border differences are slight. Affirmative action programs were initiated a good decade and a half earlier there. But the Ontario program that began to go into effect in the winter of 1994-95 before being drastically rewritten by the new Harris government was the most comprehensive of its kind in the world. The nuttier versions of American political correctness, like the successful demand by a University of Michigan professor that a reproduction of Goya's *Naked Maja* be taken down because it "objectified" her, are matched by the world's first example of "look-ism" that happened here when a University of Toronto professor was disciplined for allegedly staring at a student in the college swimming pool. No Canadian equivalent exists to the famous Antioch College regulation requiring each partner to give explicit verbal approval at each stage of a seduction. Statistics Canada, though, yielded to feminist pressure to include in a survey on violence questions, such as "Has a man ever leaned over you unnecessarily?" "Have you ever been the subject of unwanted male attentions (i.e. whistling)?" Lastly, while the California legislature once debated (without approving) legislation that would have required state universities to develop equity graduation marks as well as an equity enrolment program, no American campus has matched the "chilly climate" policies of the universities of British Columbia and Victoria, which allow students to make complaints against "any combination of attitudes, practices and structures [that create a chilly sexist or racist climate] . . . rather than . . . discrete incidents of harassment."

The most obvious explanation why Canadian identity politics should be so much like those in the United States is that, by way of TV, films, and the rest, we take so many of our cultural cues from it. Identity politics started there: Most of the gurus of identity politics are American, from Charles Reich to John Bradshaw (who discovered both the inner child and the fact that 91 per cent of American families are dysfunctional) to theorists and propagandists like Gloria Steinem, Andrea Dworkin, and Shulamith Firestone (who argues the need to change "not just all of Western civilization but the very organization of nature"). So also are their principal critics, Allan Bloom, Robert Hughes, Camille Paglia, Katie Roiphe. By contrast, the first book-length Canadian critique of identity politics didn't appear until 1995; this was Trent University professor John Fekete's *Moral Panic*, a scrupulously researched denunciation of the exaggerations of the extent of male violence. (One study cited by Fekete calculated that 98 per cent of Canadian women had suffered sexual assault.) To a considerable degree, we are deep into identity politics for the same reason we are deep into multichannel, multimedia communications – because it rolls right over us from next door.

There is one especially disturbing aspect to this cross-border similarity. With its demonizing of the "privileged majority" and its indifference to legalities, identity politics has in many ways become the McCarthyism of the 1990s. As was true for those accused of being communist sympathizers in the 1950s, those accused today of sexism and racism are for most practical purposes guilty the instant the allegation is made. Four decades ago, though, Canada largely resisted McCarthyism. That identity politics should now be as dominant here as there reveals the extent to which Canadian value systems have become Americanized.

There are some distinctively Canadian aspects to the equation. Accepting the supremacy of group rights over individual rights is part of the warp and woof of our history. Our original BNA Act accorded equality as provinces to Prince Edward Island and Ontario, and conferred distinct society status upon numerically unequal Quebeckers by recognizing their common law, their education system, and their language. The 1982 Charter thus came directly out of Canada's bedrock.

We are especially susceptible to identity politics because we have no over-arching national creed. Most nation-states are defined by their ethnicity. Americans know, or think they do, what it is to be American. Canada's equivalent is a vague reformist liberalism, or a widespread acceptance of the ideals of tolerance and pluralism that can easily shade into non-judgementalism about anything.

More subtly, identity politics suits the traditional Canadian political culture of deference to authority. While identity groups want to be liberated from the pale, patriarchal, penis people, they depend on the state to do this, even though according to their definition the state is run by their "oppressors." Multicultural groups depend upon government for grants. Far more important, they depend upon government for recognition, in a sense for their very existence. The Ukrainian-Canadian community, say, exists principally because the government says it does.

But for this legitimizing by the state, Ukrainian-Canadians would have no more distinctive validity than would individuals who get together to perform Highland dances or, for that matter, to play chess. Feminists are equally dependent upon the (male-dominated) state. The saying of Pierre Trudeau's that everyone remembers is "The state has no place in the bedrooms of the nation." Today, a major objective of feminists is to get the state into the bedrooms to prevent spousal abuse, child abuse, sexual harassment, date rape, and "chilly climate."

Lastly, colonies never escape their past. One of colonialism's legacies is a conviction that all the decisions that matter are made by others – the global economy, the *zeitgeist*, the imperial capital. With her unfailing prescience, Margaret Atwood titled her seminal study of the grand themes of Canadian literature *Survival.* "Survivor" is the politically correct way of saying "victim."

By definition, victims are not responsible for their inequality. By logical extension, victims are blameless for actions they may take, more accurately are forced to take, to end their condition of oppression.

Hence the phrase "blaming the victim" hurled back at any members of the dominant majority who dare to criticize the conduct of specific members of minority groups. The phrase comes from sociologist Willam Ryan's 1971 book, *Blaming the Victim,* in which he attacks U.S. Senator Daniel Moynihan for his famous 1965 analysis that a major share of social problems in ghettos derived from the collapse of black families.

Blaming the victim is central to contemporary analysis of the proper treatment of claims of sexual harassment, date rape, and violence against women – essentially, that these be accepted as justified unless the defendant can prove otherwise. That victims must not be blamed for their behaviour was the reason why wild accusations of "racism" against June Callwood, a lifelong fighter against discrimination in any form, were given sufficient preliminary credibility to force Callwood to resign from the board of directors of a shelter for battered women that she had created.

"Victim theory" challenges liberal democracy at its very core. One liberal verity now under attack is due process. The Ontario government's internal guidelines on sexual harassment identified as an offence the making of "unwelcome or unwanted gestures or comments." The mere fact that a complaint has been made confirms that the act was "unwelcome," leaving the onus of proving innocence upon the accused. In a paper to the Ontario Human Rights Commission, researcher Donna Young urges that in instances of alleged racism the presumption should be that "the complainant has a legitimate complaint and oblige the respondent [accused] to demonstrate otherwise."

By contrast, members of minority groups, as victims, are always inherently innocent. Young argues that visible minorities "who engage in anti-white verbal behaviour" were not guilty of racism because whites belonged to the "dominant group." The most radical version of "victim" theory has been applied in the areas of sexual harassment and date rape. That any "no," no matter preceded by what encouraging acts or words, means "no" stretches common sense but not logic. Fantastical is that the reverse may not be true. Susan Estrich, a leading American feminist theoretician, argues that "So long as women are powerless relative to men, viewing 'Yes' as a sign of true consent may be misguided."

Among more advanced identity politicians, the old concepts of guilt itself, let alone of innocence until proven guilty, are irrelevant, or worse, patriarchal. "Findings of discrimination are not predicated upon a finding of culpability or 'guilt,'" writes sexual harassment "expert" Jean McEwen in her report on allegations of sexual discrimination in the University of British Columbia's political science department. "Such laws are premised upon the effects that certain behaviours have on the recipient." In other words, discrimination exists, and must be punished, whenever it is claimed, or felt, to exist.

The other fundamental challenge is to freedom of speech. Draft regulations circulated to universities in 1994 by the Ontario Ministry of Education proposing procedures to ensure "zero tolerance" of sexual harassment made no mention of the countervailing value of academic freedom nor of the convention, and rule, of the independence of universities. (After a public protest, these regulations were withdrawn.) Conspicuously few fellow academics argued the case for freedom of speech in defence of Jeanne Cannizzo, curator of the controversial 1990 *Into the Heart of Africa* show at the Royal Ontario Museum, or of eccentric University of New Brunswick professor Martin Yaqzan after he'd written a paper arguing that victims of date rape might sometimes be responsible themselves. At a seminar held at UNB in the spring of 1994 to try to put a cap on the "Yaqzan affair," Svend Robinson, an NDP MP and leadership candidate, declared, "Who says that freedom of speech is more important than equality?"

The answer came from Alan Borovoy, president of the Canadian Civil Liberties Association. After describing Yaqzan's paper as "a silly bit of work," Borovoy criticized the professors and students for "inadequately developed loyalty to liberal democratic values."

With some exceptions – Cannizzo, an unworldly academic, was so traumatized by being attacked as a racist that she quit her job, and the country – most of these incidents have been marginal to national affairs. Moreover, the majority was only might-have-beens. The Ontario Human Rights Commission quickly disowned its researcher's "reverse onus" paper once it had been leaked to the press, and the Ontario Department of Education withdrew its "zero tolerance" ukase to universities.

There were, though, an awful lot of might-have-beens. The original version of then Justice Minister Kim Campbell's "rape-shield" bill provided for what amounted to a reversal of proof of innocence. As will be described in more detail in the next chapter, the concept of reverse discrimination has been sanctified by the highest court in the land: "Equality does not connote identical treatment" declared Supreme Court Justice Gerald LaForest.

The excesses of the ideology of the identity politicians were bound to bring the entire doctrine imploding upon itself sooner or later. The first warning that too much had become far too much occurred in the winter of 1994-95. Suddenly, special-interest groups lost credibility with the media, which until then had provided them with a megaphone in return for quotable sound-bites. A sign of a shift in the intellectual climate was the publication, early in 1995, of John Fekete's *Moral Panic*. Few publishing houses would have dared print so revisionist a text much earlier.

The decisive event was of course Mike Harris's massive victory

in the June 1995 Ontario election. Only Harris's promise to reform welfare evoked more favourable responses to Conservative
canvassers at the doorsteps than his pledge to abolish the New
Democrats brand-new employment equity scheme.

The supposed backlash was so inevitable that it raised the suspicion that many identity politicians prefer defeat to working out
sustainable solutions to existing inequalities. That's to say they'd
much rather work outside the community while hugging onto their
grievances from the moral high ground, than inside the very community they demand must include them. If this is so, it's because so
long as they remain on the outside, they remain distinct.

The predictability of the backlash also raises fundamental
questions about the contemporary validity of liberalism and
social democracy (in the latter case because the NDP since the late
1970s has increasingly focused its attention on cultural issues as
opposed to those of class and economic disadvantage). If the only
ethic these creeds now subscribe to is that of non-judgemental
tolerance – "different strokes for different folks" – they themselves
no longer have any centre.

The apparent backlash, though, doesn't mean that those now
cheering the end of employment equity in Ontario want the
various subcommunities to be repressed or discriminated against.
It means, rather, that they want an end to the building of walls
within their community.

10

A Frenzy of Rights

"Why can't I be proud of being white and male?"

— high-school student to Naomi Klein,
former editor of *This Magazine*

In November 1984, when the Royal Commission on Equality in Employment, appointed sixteen months earlier by the Trudeau government, turned in its report, the phrase "affirmative action" was used universally. The great contribution to the cause of equality of the commission's chair and sole member, Rosalie Abella, then a provincial court judge, now a member of the Ontario Court of Appeal, was to mint the much less threatening and quintessentially Canadian term "employment equity." In another demonstration of her political smarts, Abella, even though her research focused almost exclusively on gender differences, multiplied her political allies by recommending that employment equity be extended to racial minorities, native people, the disabled. As cannily, she urged that no specific quotas be set for members of the disadvantaged groups.

Abella's recommendations covered a broad span, from publicly funded day care to changes in labour practices and the education system. The Mulroney government's need for showy action prompted it to implement only her headline-making proposal.

Parliament enacted the Employment Equity Act in 1986. It applied to all federally regulated companies and Crown corporations with payrolls of more than one hundred, or to some six hundred thousand workers – although, curiously, not to the public service itself. The legislation passed after little debate, and amid widespread public applause.

The same attitudes applied in the summer of 1994 when the New Democrat government of Ontario enacted its own Employment Equity Act. This legislation, which applied to the entire public sector and to all private companies with payrolls of fifty or more, thereby covering 75 per cent of the provincial labour force, was the most comprehensive of its kind in the world.

It was the world's most comprehensive for the briefest possible time. Not long after the scheme had begun to go into effect in the winter of 1994-95, the newly elected Conservative premier of Ontario, Mike Harris, fulfilled one of the most popular of his election pledges by making radical reductions to the scope of the program.

Employment equity is thus, largely, yesterday's politico-cultural scenario. The federal program (extended, in December 1994, to the entire public service) remains in place. It is unlikely to be enforced rigorously, though, because of the public scepticism expressed by Ontario voters and also because it will be predominantly members of the supposedly "advantaged" group – white males – who will be most affected by the layoffs of forty-five thousand federal civil servants.

For a decade, though, Canada was a world leader in achieving the identity politicians' goal of "equality of results." A royal commission suggestion had been turned into a rule of working life intended to compel employers to hire employees according to a strict proportional representation of all the various segments of the population by means of the technique of annually scrutinized "numerical targets" (a softer term for quotas). During this period, any criticism of this essay into social engineering was met by a barrage of accusations of "privilege" (as in clinging to it) and "denial" (as in denying the existence of "systemic" discrimination), followed by the neutron bombs of "racism" and of "sexism."

Very few dared raise their heads above the parapets to get a clearer view of what was going on. One of them, however, was Abella herself.

Abella expressed her doubts about what she had helped bring about in a brilliant essay, "The New Isms," in the 1991 collection 'English-Canada' Speaks Out. She didn't question employment equity itself; indeed she defended it staunchly. "The reason in human rights we do not treat all individuals equally is that not all individuals have suffered generic exclusion because of group membership," she wrote. "Otherwise we could never correct disadvantage, chained as we would be to the civil libertarian principle of equal treatment for every individual."

But Abella recounted her concerns about what relying upon the rigid prism of the law was doing to the originally idealistic concept of equality of results. One was that the Charter of Rights, Canada's new carving of constitutional law upon stone, was "ideologically schizophrenic on the key issue of group versus individual rights." Another was that "Everyone now claims a monopoly not only on truth but on justice itself." The third was that the entire country was in the grip of "a rights frenzy."

By this time, Trudeau himself, Sphinx-like about everything but the national unity issue, must have been wondering just what it was he had brought about. The Charter fulfilled to the letter his concept of the defining sovereignty of each individual, and therefore of their absolute equality. As had been his lifelong ambition, the Charter's key Section 15(1) proclaimed unequivocally that "Every individual is equal before and under the law and has the right to equal protection of the law without discrimination."

The clause immediately following this Trudeauesque one, though, proclaimed the exact opposite. The Charter's Section 15(2) declared that the general guarantee of the equality of all individuals "does not preclude any law, program or activity that has as its object the amelioration of conditions of disadvantaged individuals and groups."

Back in 1982, this had been almost a throwaway clause. Over the objections of those like Saskatchewan Premier Allan Blakeney, who worried that it would justify federal intrusions into their jurisdiction, the subsection had been added to meet the concerns of feminists that 15(1), unless qualified, could be used to strike down any future affirmative action programs.

Intended originally as only a minor modifier, Section 15(2) evolved, quite quickly, into the essence of the Charter. Those who achieved this evolution were neither the elected politicians nor even the identity advocates, much less the public at large. The rewriting, *de facto*, of the Charter was done by those in whom Canadians place their highest trust according to all the polls – their judges, above all those in supreme juridical authority as members of the Supreme Court. Deference to judges has become the last manifestation of Canadians' famed deference to authority.

One unanticipated consequence of the Charter has been to Americanize our political system – an outcome anticipated at the time only by Manitoba Premier Sterling Lyon, his views having been discounted because he was assumed to be hostile to Quebec. A major share of power over social and cultural issues has shifted from Parliament to the courts. Parliament's legislative powers remain unaltered. But the courts can now interpret legislation, that is they can say what it was the parliamentarians meant to say, or should have said. In July 1992, in a decision written by Chief Justice Antonio Lamer, the Supreme Court ruled that judges could "read into" legislation meanings not specifically spelled out in them. Implementing this updating of the "living tree" legal doctrine, the Ontario Court of Appeal one month later "read" sexual orientation into the prohibited grounds for discrimination enumerated in the Canadian Human Rights Code.

This was an act of judicial creativity. One of the great defects of all human rights laws is that they reflect only the conventional wisdom at the time of their enactment. Thus, the disabled were added to the list of disadvantaged groups enumerated in the Charter only at the last minute, as a result of the eloquence of their representatives in their appearances before the Senate–Commons committee.

In the process, though, the Charter became more the property of judges than of the people's democratically elected representatives.

This process has been called the "judicialization of politics." In a 1994 essay for the C. D. Howe Institute, University of Toronto political scientist Richard Simeon observes, "The judicialization of politics represents a fundamental shift from the bureaucratic politics of the postwar model. If bureaucratic decision-making is characterized by consultation, expertise, trade-offs and compromise, the judicial process is adversarial, rules-driven and black and white." Astutely, Simeon focuses his analysis upon the particular politico-legal implications of identity politics. Because the real issue in identity politics was always recognition rather than the resolution of specific grievances, these issues were "inherently less amenable to the kind of splitting the difference solutions central to the interest politics of the post-war period." In other words, as soon as the battleground was shifted from Parliament and the legislatures to the courts, identity politics was about all or nothing, either a crushing defeat at the hands of members of the privileged majority or a long-overdue triumph in which no prisoners were taken.

It's certain that ordinary Canadians didn't understand this transformation in the nature of social and cultural decision-making. It's questionable whether the judges involved fully understood it.

Comments made by Chief Justice Lamer, though, strongly

imply a sense of proprietorship about the resolution of these kinds of issues. "A democracy pure and simple is not necessarily the best nor the most tolerant society in which to live," Lamer said at the University of Toronto's law graduation in July 1992. "Democracy only ensures majority rule which, by itself, is insufficient to ensure human flourishing."

It's most unlikely that Canadians really want their judges to perform as benevolent monarchs: Even the most benevolent of monarchs, deeply concerned in the manner of Prince Charles to "ensure human flourishing," are unaccountable. The court's rulings on the Charter – following the three-year delay until it came into full effect in 1985 – have been predominantly liberal. Most of these decisions have been applauded by identity groups. Future courts may well be more conservative (as is happening now in the United States); identity groups would then find these judges equally unaccountable while at the same time conservative-minded observers would be applauding.

The disturbing fact is that the Supreme Court, whether acting benevolently or merely trendily, has used Section 15(2) to advance group rights over individual rights further in Canada than in any other jurisdiction, and, certainly, considerably further than most Canadians realize. In a sense the court has made the "equality of results" concept, of which employment equity was the fullest practical realization, into the foundation of a new legal structure.

In a key statement in 1991, Chief Justice Lamer declared that the "overall purpose" of Section 15 was "to remedy or prevent dis-crimination against groups subject to stereotyping." Lamer thus reversed the order of priorities of Section 15's two clauses. The first, which guarantees equality of all individuals, was henceforth to be subordinate to the second. As actually written, though, the second clause merely states that 15(1)'s commitment of the equal-ity of all individuals "does not preclude" programs to remedy existing inequalities. This reinterpretation of a "does not preclude" into "overall purpose" really does move judges towards monarchical status.

While the Supreme Court as a whole did not in any way become an advocate for identity politics, some judges appeared to, most particularly Madam Justice Bertha Wilson. An individual of exceptional ability and persuasiveness – nothing is more persuasive than deep convictions expressed in a soft Scottish burr – she came to perform as a kind of conscience to the court during a period when its members, some of them pretty unworldly types for all their intellect and career accomplishments, were trying to grapple with social and cultural issues of a kind no previous court had ever encountered, and were having to do this under the felt pressure of identity groups that themselves were deeply convinced of the morality, and necessity, of their causes.

Certainly, some court rulings seemed to be grounded as much in the doctrines of identity politics as of legal precedent. The 1985 Singh decision, for example, as a result of which Canada, uniquely in the world, extends the full protection of the Charter to non-Canadians, specifically to applicants for refugee asylum. The unparalleled rate of approval of refugee applications probably owes as much to the "rights-centred" adjudication process implemented to fulfil the Singh decision (full right of appeal up to the Supreme Court, representation by taxpayer-paid legal-aid lawyers) as to the humanitarian instincts of the members of the Immigration and Refugee Board.

The Conway decision of 1993 was perhaps the most extreme example. A male prisoner at a federal penitentiary had challenged the legality of frisk searching of male prisoners by female guards. "Given the historical, biological and sociological differences between men and women, equality does not demand that practices which are forbidden where male officers guard female inmates must also be banned where female offices guard male inmates,"

ruled Mr. Justice Gerald LaForest. He argued that for lack of a
sufficient number of female inmates, female guards would be disadvantaged in their opportunities for promotion unless they engaged in "cross-gender frisk searches."

Other comparable rulings include the 1989 Andrews decision
that Canadian citizenship is not required in professional practice.
Indeed, according to Justice Wilson's commentary on this case, all
non-citizens belong to "a disadvantaged group in our society."
Similarly the 1993 ruling by Mr. Justice J. A. Linden of the Federal
Court of Appeal that discrimination in the Income Tax Act against
married couples does not constitute grounds for a claim under the
Charter's prohibition against discrimination because, "It cannot
be said that married persons have been socially, politically or historically disadvantaged" and indeed, "may well have experienced
some privilege and advantage as a result of their status."

The most important decision of this kind was the Supreme
Court's 1992 Butler ruling in which Canadian judges became the
first in the world to accept the "hostile environment" thesis of
American feminist Catharine MacKinnon. Henceforth, pornography should no longer be determined by the traditional "community standards" test (whether the material is offensive to local
mores), but whether it created a negative or hostile environment,
in this specific instance for women. Following this decision, a
claim was made to the Ontario Human Rights Commission that
magazines like *Penthouse* and *Playboy* should be banned from
corner stores as offensive to women. More consequentially,
Canada Customs has repeatedly cited the "hostile environment"
ruling as justification for seizing gay and lesbian literature – in
direct contravention of the original intention of the organization,
LEAF, the Women's Legal Education and Action Fund, that had
argued the hostile environment thesis before the Supreme Court.

All these decisions derive from the "ideological schizophre-
nia," in Abella's phrase, in the Charter itself. They have been

magnified by a judicial tilt towards identity politics, made explicit by Justice Wilson's 1990 claim that male judges were "inherently biased" and so could not be impartial in cases where the accused was a woman. The tilt is implicit also in Justice Linden citing the "historical disadvantage" rule as reason for disallowing claims of tax discrimination against married couples. This phrase, which identity politicians so often rely on, appears nowhere in the Charter. The government itself has rejected the concept's validity: "History cannot be re-written," Multiculturalism Minister Sheila Finestone declared in December 1994 in explaining her rejection of claims by Chinese-, Italian- and Ukrainian-Canadian groups for compensation for wrongs done to them during the Second World War.

Because everything goes in cycles, it is probable that the court will soon draw back from identity politics' interpretations of the law. Indeed, some recent court judgments have expressed a new concern about the costs to the public treasury of implementing rights-based rulings. Keeping up with shifts in Canadian public opinion, though, is another form of trendiness. The court risks losing some of the aura of detached objectivity that causes it to be so widely respected. Above all in this era of populism, the question is bound to be raised whether Supreme Court and other judges should not be subject to congressional-style confirmation hearings to determine their political and personal biases. The logical consequence of a "judicialization of politics" is the politicization of the judiciary.

Even though this wasn't at all its intention, the court helped legitimize the doctrine of "equality of results" and also to magnify its implications. Judicial sanction for the "hostile environment" doctrine legitimized the demands on university campuses for enactment of "chilly climate" regulations, in which proof of actual personal injury has become secondary to vague claims of an atmosphere of sexism or racism. As important, when such distinguished

and impartial adjudicators were saying "right on," it became far
more difficult for others to say, "Wait a minute."

Although of secondary political importance now, employment
equity merits a backwards glance. But for the circumstance of
Harris's victory, it would be defining the working lives of most
Canadians. Almost more important, it's a classic example of a
good social idea turned into a political disaster by a mixture of
moralism and arrogance, and of passivity and timidity.

The root problem is easy to identify. "Historical disadvantage,"
which so often is used to justify everything else, particularly
"reverse discrimination" against the inheritors of historical privilege (i.e., white males), is a concept imported here from the
United States. There, it is totally valid. That American blacks have
been disadvantaged historically and continue to be despite the
Civil Rights Act is clear, unarguable, and shameful.

The same simply isn't true for the "designated" groups
identified in Canadian legislation. Certainly, all blacks here have
to contend with mindless stereotyping. But only a relatively small
number of native-born blacks have had to endure historical discrimination; while none of it is excusable, none was in any way
comparable to the slavery and legalized segregation suffered by
their counterparts in the United States.

To this rule of comparative Canadian benignity, there is one
glaring exception: native people. As will be described in Chapter
Thirteen, they are "Canada's blacks."

It is true beyond any argument that women in Canada have
had to struggle far harder than men to climb the corporate ladder,
or to be paid the same for work of equal value, and they have been
patronized, harassed, bumped against the glass ceiling. The salaries
of those employed full time are only 72 per cent those of equivalent males. But to compare their past and present condition to
that of blacks is to trivialize real oppression.

In fact, because "muscle" jobs, as in mining, forestry, agricultural and fishing, heavy construction, and industrial metal-bashing, are in decline while service employment, especially personal service employment, is expanding, the unemployment rate among all women today is *lower* than for men. Among young women, those most likely to benefit from employment equity as they compete for starter jobs, the rate of unemployment is close to one-quarter lower. As well, now that women account for 55 per cent of the enrolment at universities, they are doing far better than young men at preparing themselves to compete for, and win, tomorrow's jobs. Studies by the Demos think-tank in Britain suggest that the "loss of self-esteem" once observed among young women is now found far more commonly among young men. Indeed, a whole new literature is appearing about the rootless condition of many men now that they've lost their role as family breadwinners and who, once a separation occurs, very often lose their families as well.

Apart from blacks, more particularly black males, most particularly young male Jamaicans, evidence of explicit discrimination against most racial minorities is difficult to find. Most have higher incomes and lower unemployment rates than the national average after account is taken of the standard ten-year time lag before newcomers enter fully into the mainstream. Indeed, the single most successful group of postwar immigrants are not Jews, as is widely assumed, but the Asian refugees from East Africa: Because so many were businessmen and professionals, they achieved salaries higher than the national average within just one year of arriving. Today, only the stupidest of human resource directors would not be delighted if an East Asian walked through the door to apply for a job.

Instead, for most of the groups labelled "disadvantaged" in the Canadian legislation, the problem has been what's been called "soft discrimination" – misunderstanding, awkwardness, social avoidance – rather than explicit oppression in the American black model. In pursuit of their goal of "recognition," identity groups have reinterpreted Canada's past (in fact, most explicit historical discrimination in Canada concerned religion rather than race or gender) and then applied it here as if Canada was the United States. This intellectual deception created a hollow at the centre of employment equity programs that was bound to cause trouble. Expecting white males to feel guilty forever about what their ancestors may or may not have done was expecting far too much. Neither, for long, were their partners, mothers, and sisters likely to accept that those they loved should be punished forever for yesterday's "sins."

There were all kinds of other problems. No one had the faintest idea (or the right to challenge) whether an individual one-quarter, one-eighth, one-sixteenth a native person or other racial minority really qualified to be "designated." Conspicuously absent from both the federal and Ontario legislation was any definition of "merit." Most conspicuous by its absence – an unbelievable omission in the instance of the legislation drafted by New Democrats – was any mention of by far the greatest disadvantage any individual can suffer: to be poor, unemployed, poorly educated. Semi-skilled young men moving south from Northern Ontario in search of jobs in Toronto (or Newfoundlanders, the poorest of all Canadians, moving westwards to Ontario now that there were no fish in their bays) were nevertheless assumed to be deserving of "reverse discrimination" as a function of the colour of their skin and the shape of their genitals.

Just one factor sustained all these nonsenses and inequities: guilt. When guilt began to ebb, the motive for continued silence became fear – the fear that to criticize, even to express any public doubts, was to earn condemnation as a racist and sexist. Besides Abella's indirect intervention, two individuals found the courage to speak out.

One of those who kept his nerve was Robert Martin, a professor of law at the University of Western Ontario. His most extended critique of employment equity came in the form of a long essay, "Challenging Orthodoxy," published in the spring 1993 edition of the *Canadian Law Journal*. Martin revisited Abella's original report to point out that it contained no statistical or other evidence of discrimination suffered by the then newly designated group of racial minorities but had simply declared, on the basis of unsubstantiated statements made at public hearings, "People of colour undeniably face discrimination, both overt and indirect." Martin notes that two recent reports by the Economic Council of Canada, in 1990 and 1991, had concluded, "no evidence exists of systemic pay discrimination on the basis of colour." Martin suggests that the rule of "historic disadvantage" was irrelevant to Canadians of colour since there were so few of them in historical Canada. Martin (himself a former anti-apartheid activist) concludes by warning, "Quotas are racist, they are immoral, they are anti-democratic, and they are unabashed class warfare."

Alan Borovoy, president of the Canadian Civil Liberties Association, was a good deal more judicious. In a 1993 brief to the Ontario legislature committee studying the employment equity legislation, Borovoy reveals that of fifteen private employment agencies tested by his organization, twelve had agreed to refer job applicants on a "whites-only" basis to a mythical company. He cites organizations that resorted to the trick of requiring "Canadian experience" where none was needed for the jobs being advertised.

Closet discrimination was undeniably real, therefore. Yet Borovoy remains deeply troubled: "It is unacceptable to punish innocent people for the sins of others." He then makes his central point: "The legitimate purpose of employment equity is not to compensate for yesterday's sins nor to quickly mirror the community mix. It is to *avoid discrimination from now on* [his italics]."

Had Martin's warning been heard and had Borovoy's intelligent suggestion for concentrating upon avoiding discrimination "from now on" been acted upon, the inevitable backlash against the illogicalities and inequities of employment equity could have been avoided.

The first warning sign came in the spring of 1993 when the autoworkers union local in Oshawa disaffiliated from the NDP. There were many reasons for this. One, as explained by a dissident to a reporter, was: "I've realized my son will never be able to join me on the assembly line." Then came the vote by 20 per cent of Canadians for the Reform Party, again for mixed reasons, but with Reform's criticisms of multiculturalism and immigration serving as hot-button issues. Afterwards, there came an ever-increasing number of complaints, and of bitter jokes, on hotline radio programs.

The most expressive sign of change was spotted by Naomi Klein, the twenty-five-year-old former editor of *This Magazine*. As a role model, she's often invited to give what she calls "My Feminism 101 speech" at Toronto high schools. On one of these occasions in the winter of 1994-95, Klein remarked as usual how important it was for women, and students of colour, to be proud of who they were. This time, a male student raised his hand and asked, "If it's right for women to be proud of being women and for blacks to be proud of what they are, why can't I be proud of being white and male?"

Klein recounts that she could think of no answer. This was because no answer exists. Dividing a community on the basis of colour and gender creates an absolute certainty that those left out will, sooner or later, stop feeling guilty and fight back.

As so often happens, real change didn't happen in Canada until it had happened in the United States. The 1994 congressional elections became known as the Angry White Males election after 62 per cent of them (along with quite a few of their wives and partners) voted Republican. Right afterwards, two California professors initiated a campaign for a referendum ballot to prohibit "discrimination on the basis of gender, race, ethnicity" – an ironic, and astute, repetition of the wording of the 1964 Civil Rights Act. Polls have shown overwhelming support for the ballot, including among women, Hispanics, Asians. In anticipation, the University of California has voted to abolish its affirmative action programs. The issue now looms as a potentially decisive one for the 1996 presidential election. All the Republican candidates are committed to abolishing affirmative action. By contrast, Clinton, after initially wavering, now stoutly defends the concept with the slogan, "Mend it, don't end it."

Canada's equivalent backlash happened during the June 1995 Ontario election. Immediately afterwards, mainstream commentators started declaring – for the first time – that the New Democrats' legislation had been "poorly thought out."

It's impossible to know how much change even long-running employment equity schemes like the federal one have actually achieved. The high probability is that most of what has happened would have happened anyway. Chartered banks are by far the best performers. But the proportion of racial minorities among bank employees was already double what was required officially the year *before* the federal scheme went into effect. Conversely, the increase in the numbers of native people employed by the federal government has been shamefully slow.

The tragedy is that the ideals of employment equity couldn't have been more valid. Equity *is* equitable. The need for education and information is real. Role models do make a difference to other members of "designated groups." Systemic discrimination, of the kind reported by Borovoy to the Ontario committee, deserves to be cracked down on hard.

At the practical level, even a small technical change limiting the power of equity commissions to making spot-checks of selected companies and institutions, and with the results being well-publicized instead of the bureaucratic and expensive nightmare of detailed annual reports, would have significantly increased public support for the programs. The omission of references to "merit" as a criterion for hiring was needlessly provocative. The omission of any reference to the disadvantage of poverty and unemployment as a mitigating factor in qualifying for "reverse discrimination" was a scandal, above all for the New Democrats.

These defects aside, employment equity programs – more exactly, the publicity about them – did play a part in sensitizing employers to the new demographic and cultural realities. They helped companies learn how to turn their newly diverse staffs into genuine teams and how to reach out for new talents. Beyond any question, the personnel of most large corporations and institutions have acquired a rainbow hue over the past decade and their managers have become far more sensitive to gender differences.

Complacency by liberal-minded politicians and the moralistic arrogance of identity politicians, compounded by the timidity of opinion leaders, though, have damaged employment equity programs, probably fatally. Whether by legislative revision or by benign neglect, they will die little mourned.

Aside from being an American import, the "equality of results" doctrine that underpins employment equity programs and a succession of Supreme Court judgments, has always run counter to the Canadian grain. The reason is simple. The defining Canadian ethic *is* equality, or egalitarianism. Often this isn't fulfilled, or is ignored, or is blatantly transgressed. But the ethic itself endures. In the United States, most public debates are won by whomever demonstrates that their argument is based on efficiency and effectiveness. The winners in Canada are most often those who can show that their proposals are fair and equitable.

Few societies in the world are less in need of social engineering to achieve equality for all than Canada. A society with the world's most politically correct Constitution, with the world's largest immigration program and most generous refugee program, and with, uniquely, official multiculturalism simply isn't an especially racist and sexist society.

This isn't to say that the sadly universal defects of racism and sexism do not exist here. The number of violent incidents involving black males and police officers is inexplicable except by perverse stereotyping. But by exaggerating the extent of the discrimination that actually exists, and by then escalating cultural differences into a right to claim different forms of citizenship, we have put our community at risk of becoming a society in which everyone is different and no one, therefore, has anything in common – except that we're all victims.

11

Dividing the Culture

"We are strongly attached to our weak attachments to each other."

— Michael Adams, Environics Research,
comment to author

During a panel discussion on CTV's W-5 on January 31, 1995, the secretary of state for multiculturalism, Sheila Finestone, got herself into terrible trouble for saying, "In my view, there isn't any one Canadian identity. Canada has no national culture." The host, Susan Ormiston, replied sharply, "No national culture? I think a lot of people will feel uncomfortable with that." Media commentators denounced Finestone for reducing Canadian identity to a thousand unfocused points of light.

The commentators ignored, or chose discreetly to overlook, that another panellist had said exactly the same thing. "What is a Canadian value?" Cham-Wah Yuen, head of the Chinese Parents Association of Richmond, British Columbia, had asked. "Can someone define to me what's a Canadian value? Then we can talk about it."

As probably few commentators were aware, Pierre Trudeau had said almost the same thing a quarter-century earlier. "There is no such thing as an official culture. . . . Nor does any ethnic group take precedence over any other," he had remarked on

October 8, 1971, while introducing into the Commons An Act for the Preservation and Enhancement of Multiculturalism in Canada. It's unlikely that Trudeau really meant what he was saying since the dominance of francophone and anglophone cultures was then a self-evident fact of Canadian life, or indeed that he cared greatly about the matter except in terms of political advantage. Between Trudeau's statement and Canada's contemporary multicultural condition, though, the line is unbroken, widened a bit by Mulroney's revision and expansion of the original multiculturalism act in 1987.

It all started out as so little, and was so little understood. After generalities about "willingness to share ideas, attitudes and assumptions" and about being "sensitive and responsive," about the only piety omitted in the original 1971 act was "be kind to your four-footed friends." The program only became real two years later when, looking for votes after his near-defeat in the 1972 election, Trudeau abruptly tripled multiculturalism's budget to $10 million. At the same time, his government started advertising heavily in ethnic newspapers.

The only strong criticism came from francophones. René Lévesque denounced it as a "red herring" to distract attention from Quebec's demands for special status. Guy Rocher, vice-chairman of the Canada Council, warned sadly, "Outside Quebec, I am nothing more than a member of an ethnic minority. The Canada I belonged to no-longer exists."

This, precisely, was Trudeau's intention. By making Canada multicultural, he was forestalling its evolution into the biculturalism − as opposed to the bilingualism − of *deux nations*. French-Canadians escaped easily from the thicket of hyphens Trudeau was trying to plant amongst them by renaming themselves Québécois − ironically, the only unhyphenated Canadians remaining today. Nominally a national program, multiculturalism has always taken an entirely different route in Quebec. There, the rule, and more important the practice, has always been "cultural convergence": As in Europe, and to a considerable degree in the United States, all newcomers must either assimilate to Quebec's "national culture" or remain forever on the society's margins, like expatriates living in London, Paris, Hong Kong, or Singapore. The crowds who chant "Québec aux Québécois" at the annual *Fête Nationale* on June 24 know perfectly well who they mean by Québécois. That the official justification for sovereignty is now "territorial nationalism" rather than the old, now faintly embarrassing "ethnic nationalism" has changed nothing in the place that matters to Quebeckers – their hearts.

While multiculturalism has had no effect in achieving Trudeau's objective of making Québécois any the less distinct in feeling or in fact, neither, for quite a long time, did it have much of an effect anywhere.

There was genuine idealism amid the original political opportunism. Multiculturalism's transcendent purpose, in the phrase of one of the key bureaucrats of the time, was "to get the people with the 'funny' last names on an equal footing with the Macdonalds and the Cartiers." Instead of Diefenbaker's dream of One Canada in which everyone would be equal because no one had hyphens, celebrating hyphens would make all Canadians equal. It worked. Each year, Canada became more pluralist and more tolerant. A decade or so later, there was no longer anything unusual in people with "funny" last names climbing to the top of the ladder, a Don Mazankowski as deputy prime minister, a Ramon Hnatyshyn as Governor General.

It's extremely unlikely that much of this, if any of it, had anything to do with official multiculturalism. Mostly, the program dished out grants, including to ethnic organizations specifically created for the purpose of receiving them. Worthy projects were undertaken to produce local histories of Ukrainian-Canadians, Italian-Canadians, Finnish-Canadians, and, since it was essential to be "fair," of Celtic-Canadians as well. There were lots of festivals and dances but also, occasionally, some well-chosen recipients: M. G. Vassanji, winner of the first Giller Prize for Canadian literature for his 1994 novel, *The Book of Secrets*, was encouraged with several small grants, including one to publish a magazine of South Asian writing.

Mostly, if not entirely, the reason why Canada became an increasingly tolerant society was that Canadians had become an increasingly tolerant people.

Those "tramlines" of Canadian culture, in Donald Akenson's lovely phrase, started out pretty bumpily. Historian Michael Bliss makes the neat point that today's black-white tensions are "probably no worse" than those between Irish Catholics and Anglo Protestants a century ago. Indeed, until comparatively recently – the 1950s – the most explicit discrimination in Ontario was the almost-total exclusion of Catholics from positions of financial, economic, and political power in the province – theoretically entitling them to a claim of having been "historically disadvantaged."

Mostly, that old Canada was parochial and colonialist. Think of the whole country then as a bit like the Royal Canadian Legion today: Old guys afraid of change.

That old Canada imposed a head tax on Chinese brought over to work on the railways and turned away a boatload of starving Sikhs. During the First World War, it interned Austrians, Germans, Ukrainians, and stripped naturalized Canadians of their vote. During the Second World War, it once again interned citizens originally from those countries and also from Italy and Japan. Its attitude towards Jews in their years of horror was "None is Too Many." In Halifax, Africville was as desperate a ghetto as Davis Inlet is today. The enduring mark of shame – cut especially deeply into the national memory because its inspiration was pure racism – was the treatment of Japanese-Canadians. Wartime hysteria explains some of the treatment but not the fact that, in the confiscation of property, the ban on military service, and the postwar prohibition against Japanese-Canadians returning to their old communities (some four thousand were sent all the way back to their "homeland"), it was so much more racist than the equivalent measures against *nisei* south of the border.

Some vestiges of those attitudes linger on. That no Jew has yet been appointed to head any of Canada's chartered banks is explicable only by residual, social anti-Semitism. Had the issue been one of baseball caps rather than turbans, the Legions would not have banned all headgear. During the Gulf War, many Arab-Canadians were made to feel that they personally were enemies of the state. Young black men driving cars are stopped by the police far more frequently than are white men.

So it isn't enough to say that that was then and this is now. Whatever we once were, we remain, to some degree, still. But we've stopped being that way for quite some time: Within the lifetime of almost every Canadian adult, our attitudes have undergone a sea change.

Canada's Citizenship Act of 1947 *was* the first in the world to make no distinction between native-born and newcomers. The postwar opening of the country to mass immigration from all over Europe was unprecedented in our history, even if catching up belatedly with the demographic ambitions of the United States during the preceding century. Prime Minister John Diefenbaker's 1958 declaration of his determination to "bring about a Canadian citizenship that knows no hyphenated considerations" was exceptionally daring and imaginative for those times, even if grievously inadequate in its understanding of the anxiety of French-Canadians to hold onto their hyphens. Canada's immigration policy of 1962, formalized by the Immigration Act of 1967, *was* the first in the world to abolish all quotas or preferences on the basis of race, national origin, religion, or culture. The later definition of "family class" immigrants was the most generous in the world.

From Hungary, Czechoslovakia, Uganda, Vietnam, more refugees were accepted here than by any other country in the world, earning Canada's the UN Nansen Medal for work with refugees. No other nation has a policy of official multiculturalism.

Affluence was a major factor. Generosity comes readily to the well-off. Urbanization mattered too: As we became less parochial, we became less defensive. Equally important, multiculturalism and immigration were so clearly a net national benefit: The country simply became livelier, more interesting.

During this period, wop and uke and polack jokes dropped from the national vocabulary to be replaced, alas, by Newfie jokes (bafflingly, these were especially popular in Quebec), thus confirming that people always need to feel superior to some other people.

For most Canadians through the 1970s and 1980s, multiculturalism became a synonym for tolerance. Since this by now had become central to their self-image, they supported the program enthusiastically. Canadian nationalists often cited official multiculturalism as one of the characteristics, along with bilingualism, that made Canada distinct from the United States.

Criticisms were rare. Intriguingly, and no doubt because they couldn't be counterattacked as racists, these carpings were most often expressed by those who were themselves beneficiaries of multicultural programs. In 1978, feminist and author Laura Sabia told the Empire Club of Canada in Toronto, "A dastardly deed has been perpetrated upon Canadians by politicians whose motto is 'divide and rule.' I, for one, refuse to be hyphenated. I am a Canadian, first and foremost." In her book *The Middleman and Other Stories*, Bharati Mukherjee, an immigrant to Canada who has since moved to the United States, warned that multiculturalism "by preserving differences, preserves biases." While the casino economy roared on and real estate values soared, few others wanted to be bothered by this kind of cultural quibble.

The differences, though, kept on multiplying. From the mid-1970s on, the majority of immigrants came from Third World countries, and so from societies where many of the basic Canadian values, such as democracy and the rule of law, and Western-style education or either of the official languages were non-existent. Simultaneously, as a function of sheer numbers, reinforced powerfully by the official "hyphenated" legitimacy now accorded to them by the Charter as well as by the multiculturalism legislation, multicultural groups became ever more insistent in their demands for distinctive treatment, in everything from turbans in the RCMP to state-supported segregated schools. Relevant to this new sense of entitlement was that while the Charter and the act defined as rights those of "preserv(ing)" and "enhanc(ing)" the distinctive cultures of newcomers, neither made any reference to any responsibilities these individuals might embrace to enhance the broader Canadian culture by making themselves a part of it.

The crucial difference, as political scientist Richard Simeon writes, "is not so much in diversity as in a *politicized* [his italics] diversity."

The political class never explained to Canadians what was happening. During the 1970s, no politician or official told the people of Toronto and Vancouver that within a quarter of a century their cities would be predominately non-white, or the northern echoes of Los Angeles. Except in pieties, the topic of multiculturalism has never been debated in Parliament.

A presumption of its own innate high-mindedness in contrast to the presumed closet bigotry of ordinary Canadians explains much of this silence by the élite. So does the fact that its members, while keen to implement multiculturalism, themselves had little idea what multiculturalism was. Neither the act nor the relevant clause in the Charter contained any explanation of the defining word "culture." In fact, back in 1971, the term was generally taken to mean either folklore or high art. It was only later, among experts and the public at large, that "culture" was expanded into its anthropological meaning and came to encompass the entirety of a people's life. Between folk songs and all of life there's quite a difference.

To put the problem at its starkest, if female genital mutilation is a genuinely distinctive cultural practice, as it is among Somalis and others, then since official multiculturalism's purpose is to "preserve" and "enhance" the values and habits of all multicultural groups, why should this practice be disallowed in Canada any more than singing "O Sole Mio" or Highland dancing?

The élite had never thought about – never had dared to allow itself even to begin thinking about – such questions. When ordinary Canadians began to ask them about multiculturalism and also about immigration, it had no answers other than guilt-tripping – much the same policy adopted to try to silence critics of Meech Lake.

The economic downturn that began in 1990 quickened the pace of the backlash, even while giving the élite an opportunity to dismiss it as caused only by temporary "employment anxiety." The real anxiety was cultural.

Almost frantically, Canadians began searching for ways to express their frustration and unease. The 1991 Spicer Commission – set up in the wake of Meech Lake's failure in the hope of mustering up support for the impending Charlottetown Accord by giving the public a chance to vent its frustrations – reported that what Canadians were most angry about (other than Mulroney personally) was multiculturalism. Nothing was done. In a 1992 poll, the Immigration Department found that one in two Canadians "expressed the fear they were becoming strangers in their own land." The immigration quota, then at an all-time high of 250,000 each and every year, continued unchanged. In the 1993 election, the Reform Party broke all Canadian political precedent by calling for the abolition of official multiculturalism and for cutbacks in immigration: almost unanimously, mainstream media commentators dismissed Reformers as bigots.

The political élite's refusal to recognize the extent of ordinary Canadians' cultural anxiety was almost identical to its prolonged failure to come to terms with the seriousness of the debt and deficit problems. There were no bond traders, or "stateless legislators," though, to force the élite to recognize cultural reality. Until the June 1995 Ontario election, the élite ignored the accumulating evidence of cultural unease, and continued in a state of denial.

The reality, though, was easy to discern. As early as 1989, a survey by Decima Research made the unnerving discovery that fewer Canadians (34 per cent) favoured allowing immigrants "to maintain their distinctive cultures" than did Americans (47 per cent). Tellingly, opposition to multiculturalism ran strongest among the very groups of European-Canadians for whom the program had been created in the first place. Indeed, majority support existed among just one group – college-educated English-Canadians. These élite attitudes were motivated by idealism. Self-interest was equally a factor since mass immigration and multiculturalism both served them with lots of ethnic restaurants as well as nannies to provide quantity time for their children, and also gave them little trouble by way of competition for jobs.

In 1993, a survey by the Canadian Council of Christians and Jews found that 72 per cent believed that ethnic groups should adopt Canadian values. A repeat survey in 1995 found that support for this proposition had increased to 77 per cent.

In that year, Mike Harris challenged directly the first of the three cultural verities of the past decade – employment equity. By then, immigration policy had been subjected to a major review, but, as will be described in the next chapter, this was only tentative and constrained by a great deal of political calculation.

To date, official multiculturalism remains in an ongoing broken state of élite denial. What follows is an attempt to explore the subject itself.

During the winter of 1994-95, Canada's media became fascinated by the *hijab*. Newspapers, magazines, and TV networks ran long articles and documentaries about young Muslim girls in Montreal and Toronto who turned up in high-school classrooms wearing the same formless gown and hair-concealing shawl as their religious kin in Tehran, Riyadh, Damascus, and Algiers. The commentaries steered a self-consciously careful course between exploring the legitimacy of people's concerns about the implications of the phenomenon and of respect towards those who choose to separate themselves from the rest of society behind a veil. The question the articles and documentaries tried to address was whether the *hijab* represented a legitimate form of multicultural pluralism or was the latest example of national fragmentation.

This was the wrong question. To be a teenager is to be an idealist; whether the outlet chosen to express these romantic and generous impulses is a cult, or a mainstream creed like Islam, or secular equivalents like environmentalism, feminism, anti-racism, is secondary. Anyway, grunge clothes, little differently from the *hijab*, provide young girls with a protection from the alarming implications of their newfound sexuality.

A quite different question ought to have been put – and ought to be put now – to all the multicultural experts and to the young girls proudly wearing their *hijabs*. This question was why scarcely any members of the Muslim-Canadian community have protested against the *fatwa* death sentence pronounced against writer Salman Rushdie by Ayatollah Khomeini in February 1989. The community's silence hasn't been absolute. Soon after the decree, *Ottawa Citizen* editorial writer Mohammed Azhar Ali Khan criticized the *fatwa* in a long article, concluding, "The fulminations of a million Rushdies cannot much damage Islam. The words and deeds of the followers of Islam can. That is the real tragedy."

The great majority said nothing. Understandably, many practising Muslims in Canada regarded Rushdie's book *The Satanic Verses* as disgusting and blasphemous. Yet all these individuals would have known full well that the pronouncement of a death sentence against an individual without a trial, as was done by Khomeini, violates all the canons of the Koran.

The *fatwa* was also a crime against international law. By his personal dictat, an Iranian politician was condemning a non-Iranian citizen to death. In December 1992, when Rushdie came to Canada to make a surprise appearance at the annual fund-raising benefit staged by the Canadian branch of PEN International, the *fatwa*, which applied to all practising Muslims no matter where they lived, similarly violated Canadian law. Those Canadians most knowledgeable about the matter, though, thus said – essentially – nothing about it. Initially, public comment would have been difficult, and may well have been dangerous. But, six years later, the silence of the Muslim-Canadian community about the *fatwa* remains as absolute.

To return to the *hijab*, the real question that ought to have been asked wasn't about that particular article of clothing; it should have been about the definition of Canadianness. Is this a quality that each person is free to determine for themselves? Or does Canadianness constitute an over-arching set of values and cultural assumptions that apply to everyone, no matter that pluralism and tolerance of differences are among the most important of those values? Is being welcomed into a country any different from being welcomed into a house where if the domestic rules happen to be, say, no smoking, no liquor, vegetarian food, every guest observes them?

Questions of this kind apply every bit as much to all multicultural groups. During the massacre in Tiananmen Square in 1989, a young Chinese-Canadian businessman in Vancouver, Raymond Chan, organized public protests against the repressive regime in Beijing. His protests mirrored those of the Canadian government and ordinary Canadians. Few members of his own community joined him, though, and its leaders criticized him for speaking out; later, once Chan became minister of state for Asia-Pacific affairs, their attitudes towards him changed considerably.

By far the best-organized multicultural community in the country is the Jewish-Canadian one. Yet during the long decades of tension in the Middle East, this community made virtually no attempts to engage in dialogue with members of the Arab-Canadian community – the conferences about the economic consequences of peace in the region organized by the Bronfman Foundation of Montreal being a rare exception to the rule.

This kind of self-centred self-absorption is by no means unique to the Jewish-Canadian community (which has made repeated efforts to reach out to the black community with which it has had so many hurtful misunderstandings). Precious little dialogue, if any at all, about historic rivalries and cultural tensions has taken place between Serbian-Canadians and Croatian-Canadians, between Ukrainian-Canadians and Russian-Canadians, between Chinese-Canadians and Vietnamese-Canadians, between Hindu-Canadians and Sikh-Canadians, between Japanese-Canadians and Korean-Canadians, between Turkish-Canadians and Armenian-Canadians, and on and across almost every last particle of the Canadian mosaic. (To all rules there are exceptions: Unlike their American kin, Irish-Canadians have kept a conspicuous distance from the quarrels of Northern Ireland.)

Nor has common misery created much kinship. A great disappointment of the Somali refugees has been the failure of any of the other black communities, whether native-born or from the Caribbean or Africa, to provide help. In some "high diversity" schools, like Toronto's Bloor Collegiate, the worst schoolyard rumbles aren't between white skinheads and students of colour but between ethnic gangs, such as the Lethal Punjabis and the L.A.s (Latinos).

Many multicultural groups don't practise multiculturalism. They practise what can best be described as mono-culturalism within the multicultural context that Canada provides for everyone. Thus, on his appointment as president of the Canadian Jewish Congress in May 1992, University of Toronto professor Irving Abella declared that his top priority was to fight "assimilation." Too many Jews were intermarrying, he said, and bringing up their children outside the faith. Preserving the collectivity identity of Jews in Canada, he said, "is the agenda."

The determination by many multicultural groups to remain quasi-Canadians on their own terms is striking. Many of the Croatian- and Serbian-Canadians who enlisted in either side of the civil wars in former Yugoslavia were second- and third-generation descendants of immigrants. A variant on this apartheid concept occurs in the demand for "self-government" by native people, and as a consequence of that, at least among the Mohawks of Kanesatake, a new "blood quantum" system to determine whether, by being at least 50 per cent native, individuals are entitled to live on the reserve and to enjoy its benefits (such as paying no income tax).

Forgotten amid all the pieties involving the necessity of respecting cultural diversity is that most ethnic cultures the world over are defined in significant part by their dislike of, or fear or hatred of, a neighbouring culture. Preserving cultural differences means importing and preserving those biases. Official awareness of this reality is limited. Overwhelmingly, the anti-racist programs of the Department of Multiculturalism are directed at white or European-Canadians, as if racism were a function of colour and not of race itself.

Differences *are* difficult – for everyone. Those between franco-phone and anglophone Canadians, for example, aren't much closer to being healed than a quarter-century ago, or for that matter two centuries ago. Nor are those between natives and non-natives.

These unresolved tensions, though, are the consequences of historic pacts, or accommodations, or misunderstandings entered into long ago during the building of this country. These quarrels are *ours*. However inadequately, the attempts to resolve them have most often been marked by goodwill, have often been exceedingly expensive, and most certainly have never lacked for any measure of that Canadian habit of dialogue.

That the intercommunity quarrels of so many multicultural groups have been imported here from distant places isn't the point. We accept the songs, food, and dress of all newcomers. We most certainly cannot therefore deny them their feelings. The point instead has to do with Canada's nature. Here, a new per-spective is beginning to take hold. This is that multiculturalism now *is* Canada. A good example is Clifton Joseph's declaration in *This Magazine* that the objective of ethnic groups was "to really and equitably redefine the country" thereby displacing, in Joseph's listing, the classic Canadian concerns of " 'Quebec's sep-aration,' 'Western dissatisfaction' and 'national unity.' " Between Joseph's provocative exaggerations and the declaration by Multicultural Minister Sheila Finestone that "Canada has no national culture," there is remarkably little difference.

If an ever-increasing number of newcomers have come to wonder whether Canada has any "house rules" at all, their bewilderment at finding themselves in a community with so many of the char-acteristics of a chameleon is entirely understandable. They keep being told that Canadian *is* a chameleon – ever-changeable; infinitely mutable – by many more than Finestone.

It's the fact that these changes have so often been imposed, or proposed, from the top down rather than demanded from the bottom up that makes Canada so different from other societies. The original multiculturalism act of 1971, for example, was demanded by very few Canadians – indeed almost exclusively by Ukrainian-Canadians on the prairies. As the preceding chapter described, the doctrine of "historical disadvantage" that is the foundation of all employment equity programs was bootlegged in from the United States.

One of the most vivid of recent examples of this kind of top-down social engineering involves a "consultation paper" about possible improvements to the Criminal Code, made public by Justice Minister Allan Rock in the fall of 1994. His policy suggestions ranged from the possible need to redefine the appropriate use of force to protect private property to the newly troubling question of the use of the defence of intoxication in cases involving sexual assault.

One section of Rock's paper broke entirely new legal ground. In the more than one hundred years since the code's original enactment, "Canada has been transformed into a more diverse society in terms of race, ethnic origin, religion and culture," the document notes. This raised the question whether "the criminal law should be amended to accommodate such cultural and religious practices." Specifically, whether there should be "a general cultural defence" to enable persons "not [to be] found guilty for conduct that would otherwise be criminal, when the person acted in accordance with his or her customs or beliefs." Examples cited included Canadians whose religious beliefs required them to carry ceremonial knives, or to take prohibited drugs, or to marry more than one spouse.

Confronted by a public furore, Rock declared that "cultural defence" was only a theoretical idea, one that, on reflection, he himself opposed. The fact remains that none of the officials and aides who'd edited the paper, nor Rock himself, had noticed anything unusual in the notion of a "cultural defence" based on self-proclaimed beliefs. Far more disquieting, the "cultural defence" concept was not in any way novel.

A variation of the cultural defence concept is the justification for the revision of the RCMP's dress code to allow its Sikh members to wear turbans, this decision residing on an acceptance of the claim that the turban is a religious symbol, although it is the uncut hair, *kes*, one of the five sacred k's, that is the religious symbol. In Ontario, pilot projects have been planned for so-called "demonstration schools" for black students, with a "black-focused" curriculum. Again in Ontario, a "court diversion" program has been initiated for special treatment of visible minorities, primarily blacks. Specialized judicial and legal systems exist for native people, including, in the instance of "sentencing circles," totally autonomous systems.

Nor is "cultural defence" new to Canadian courts. In January 1994, Quebec County Court Judge Raymonde Verrault sentenced a man to twenty-three months in jail rather than the four years requested by the Crown on the grounds that while he had assaulted his eleven-year-old stepdaughter over a two-year period, he had "only" sodomized her, thereby, in the words of the judge, "preserv[ing] her virginity, which seems to be a very important value in their [Islamic] religion."

An important variation of the cultural defence concept resides in the attempt by an ever-growing number of groups, initially Orthodox Jews and evangelical Christians, later supported by Muslims, Sikhs, and Hindus, to secure state funding for independent religious schools. Their legal case is based on the Charter of Rights' guarantee to all of equal benefit of the law, in this specific instance the Constitution of 1867, which provides for state funding to Catholic schools. In March 1995, the Supreme Court granted these groups the right to appeal. Most observers expect the Supreme Court to confirm an earlier negative decision by the Ontario Court of Appeal. This will require some legal adroitness though. In his decision of July 1994, Ontario Chief Justice Charles Dubin writes that the Charter "does not provide, in my opinion, state support for the exercise of one's religion." Indeed, it does

not. Left unresolved, though, is the political and legal justification
for treating Catholic schools differently (also those for small
groups like the Amish and Mennonites) from those to which an
ever-growing number of Canadians now are sending their children in order to preserve their "distinct cultural heritages" as
guaranteed to them under both the Charter and the multiculturalism act.

Many of the new programs, especially those directed at native
people and at black youths, can easily be defended as imaginative
attempts to deal with specific social problems no differently from,
say, hostels operated specifically for battered women.

The problem is that, because of sheer numbers and diversity,
practical and sensible solutions to specific problems now set
precedents that, especially because these are legitimized by the
official rubric of "preserving" and "enhancing" distinctive cultures, can be extended to ever-growing segments of the population. The standard liberal democrat solution of "let's be tolerant
while looking the other way," now encounters the real-life
problem that the entire population is watching, either for precedents that can be applied to themselves or in fear that the community is going be fractured beyond recovery by some metastatic
combination of segregated schools, separate justice systems, and
an RCMP parading in yarmulkas, chadors, saris, and kilts.

The most extended critique of the divisiveness of official multiculturalism in the form in which it has developed has been Neil
Bissoondath's best-selling 1994 book, *Selling Illusions*. Immune as
an Indian immigrant from Trinidad to the standard attack of
"racism," he's instead been damned as a "coconut" – brown on the
outside, white on the inside.

The most striking aspect of Bissoondath's critique of multiculturalism, though, isn't what he says about multiculturalism itself.
His comments about it are comparatively conventional, if ele-
gantly expressed. It had acquired "aspects of a holy cow for many,

a cash cow for some," he writes. Much of the program is folkloric. "Our approach to multiculturalism encourages the devaluation of what it claims to protect and promote. Culture becomes an object for display rather than the heart and soul of the individuals formed by it." He compares Toronto's annual Caravan to, "a folksy, Canadian-mosaic version of the Jungle Cruise at Walt Disney World." Even the best of multiculturalism, he argues, is "vicarious" and sentimental.

Bissoondath explores insufficiently the extent to which multiculturalism limits cultural identity. Hyphens don't simply describe people; they entrap them, as if in aspic. To describe someone as Italian-Canadian, say, is to categorize them as being half-Italian, when that part of that individual's identity may be no more consequential than the Irishness of Brian Mulroney while singing "When Irish Eyes Are Smiling." People become the stereotypes they're supposed to be.

What's so absurd about this encouraged separateness is that it's being done at the very same time as Canadians are getting together as never before. In 1986, census takers found that one in three marriages in Canada was "mixed," with the highest proportion – 50 per cent – found among Japanese-Canadians. This exaggerates the degree of the phenomenon: In its literal way, Statistics Canada classifies the marriage of an Irish-Canadian to a Scots-Canadian as cross-cultural. Nevertheless, the number of cross-cultural marriages in the common-sense meaning of the term is rising sharply. Most important, Canadians now welcome them. Between 1965 and 1988, opposition to mixed marriages declined from 52 per cent to just 16 per cent, according to the Gallup Poll. On the ultimate "Guess who's coming to dinner?" question, 73 per cent of Canadians now say they favour white-black marriages. Indeed, the strongest opposition to the true multiculturalism of cross-cultural marriages comes most often now from newcomers who fear losing control over their own children. (Some try to hold on to their children culturally by arranging marriages for them with spouses in their country of origin.) Through its obsessive categorizing by ethnicity and race, multiculturalism becomes an absurdity in instances of mixed marriages: Bissoondath's daughter is the child of a Québécoise mother and an Indian-Trinidadian father who insists upon calling himself a Canadian.

Moreover, the official phrases, Italian-Canadian, Sikh-Canadian, Ukrainian-Canadian, imply that the core identity of these individuals is Italianness or Sikhness or whatever, with Canadianness as a kind of add-on. Often, the reverse is true. South-Asian writers, like Bissoondath, Rohinton Mistry, Michael Ondaatje, Shyam Selvadurai, and M. G. Vassanji, have flowered here rather than in their "homelands." It's a case of the East being liberated by the West. In the same way, almost all black music, from spirituals, blues, and jazz to hip hop and gangsta rap, has been created in the West rather than in Africa.

Bissoondath's use of the word "vicarious" is nevertheless exceptionally apt. Outside of its native soil, ethnicity is ethnicity lite; "safe nationality" in the phrase of Ukrainian-Canadian writer Myrna Kostash. Italian-Canadians, say, may be wholly Italian inside their homes and within their neighbourhoods, but they are untouched by the Italianness of their homeland, which encompasses not just its landscape and its uninhibited delight in life but also endemic political corruption, systemic bureaucratic inefficiency, the Mafia, and the need to pay *tangenti*, bribes, for any service from garbage collection to actually getting treated in hospital. Similarly, during the decades that their homeland was ruled by the Soviets, Ukrainian-Canadians preserved like icons its traditions and customs. Many of those who've since visited there have undergone a severe culture shock at discovering that the land of their dreams is repressive, authoritarian, chauvinist, and fiercely intolerant of any cultures except its own.

The true originality of *Selling Illusions* resides in what Bissoondath has to say about Canada. His tone is regretful, tender, elegiac. "If Canada, as an historical, social, legal and cultural concept, does not demand respect for itself and its ideals, why should any respect be expected?" he writes. He keeps wondering why Canadians have apparently lost the nerve to demand respect for the kind of society they have created. He writes of "[the] basic flaw in the Canadian character, our traditional modesty as a country, metastasizing into an inability to see the positive." Lamenting the collective inability to see the magnitude of what has been achieved, Bissoondath remarks that "Canadians, because they are of so many colours, are essentially colourless in the best sense of the word." He notes the collective inability to recognize just how challenging it has been for us to come as far as we already have. Discussing the fracas over the Legions' ban on turbans, Bissoondath's tone is both disapproving and empathetic. He writes that the veterans, "though many of them are physically diminished by age, their handshakes tend to be firm, their gazes frank. But they are also people prey to the insecurities of change."

Most perceptive of all, perhaps, are Bissoondath's comments on the country's contemporary social and political context. At the same time as "English-Canada saw its defining Britishness dismantled, Quebec saw its defining Frenchness strengthened." Cut adrift from their familiar moorings, "in a country weak in symbols and homegrown traditions, people grow jealous of what they have. . . . Sometime the fear of loss can prove paralyzing; it can lead to perception of threat and a rigidity of mind, to the appearance, at least, of intolerance."

Bissoondath's great contribution to the debate about multiculturalism ultimately has comparatively little to do with his criticisms of the program itself. His achievement has been to reassure Canadians, as only he, a brown immigrant could get away with doing, that being concerned about the consequences of official multiculturalism is not the same as being bigoted, intolerant, or racist. More importantly, he has told Canadians that a people who do not demand respect for what they are cannot expect to receive respect.

In reply, the minister responsible, Sheila Finestone, declared, "I don't enjoy Bissoondath. I don't enjoy his lack of understanding of choice."

The federal Liberals are so dependent upon the votes of multicultural Canadians – with Quebeckers turned skittish, this is really the last bloc vote left in the country – that they aren't very likely to undertake a serious review of official multiculturalism.

A continuation of this denial by the élite could be disastrous. Something far more damaging to the community than a backlash may happen. English-Canadians, including those other Canadians who've assimilated to that culture, may start to think of themselves as, and increasingly to act as, just another multicultural group. From the vote for Reform in 1993 to the far stronger vote for Mike Harris's Conservatives in Ontario, there are signs that this is happening.

If English-Canadians, and those who think like them, do withdraw from the centre, and grumpily marginalize themselves, the Canadian centre will simply no longer be able to hold. The same thing will happen if English-Canadians are excluded from involvement in the new multicultural Canada on grounds such as that of "cultural appropriation" – effectively, cultural apartheid – or the dogma that the identity of identity groups is exclusively their own concern. The pushing out of middle-class whites, often women who've been engaged in the struggle for years, from positions of influence in multiracial organizations like women's shelters and the National Action Committee on the Status of Women, and in a different form from the Writers Union of Canada, is the mindless behaviour of the kind that courts in exile engage in: Since their members are largely powerless within the larger society, their one source of power is to turn upon each other.

In the end, the identity politicians may still occupy the moral high ground, if only in their own minds. But they will have created around themselves a swamp that others will keep well clear of. If too many of these "others" retreat into their own forms of ethnic ghettos, the Canadian community will lose its cohesion, its very sense of being a community.

Canadians still support overwhelmingly the *idea* of multicultural tolerance. The same Ekos survey that recorded rising opposition to mass immigration found that 75 per cent of Canadians believe that "a mix of cultures makes Canada a far more attractive place to live." The 1995 survey by the Council of Christians and Jews found – despite by then a great deal of public criticism of multiculturalism – that 55 per cent supported multiculturalism as against 31 per cent opposed.

Most Canadians not only support multiculturalism, they are immensely proud of it. Tolerance towards diversity and the acceptance of pluralism have become the defining characteristic of the country and its citizens. International successes are probably more important to Canadians than they are to any other peoples: That others know we exist confirms that we really do exist. There is an almost tangible expression of public pleasure whenever the Canadian mounting the podium to receive some international athletic or arts prize is someone who happens to be black or brown or Asian. Each success of this kind magnifies – and enhances – the contemporary meaning of the word "Canadian." Without needing to utter a word, these individuals are telling the world, "We come in all types and all colours, and yet we are all Canadians." The subtext to that silent boast is, "We are all Canadians in ways you others dare not be."

The single important statement to be made about multiculturalism is that Canada *is* multicultural in the only dimension that matters – in reality. The largest proportion of Canadians are now neither francophone nor anglophone. One in six are first-generation immigrants, the highest proportion for any country except Australia. We are multicultural linguistically. In Vancouver, a majority of students in public schools now speak at home a language other than English. Soon, Chinese will be more widely spoken than French in the three-quarters of the country outside of Quebec. We are multicultural visibly. By the year 2000, estimates Carleton University demographer John Samuel, close to one in five Canadians will be non-white (excluding aboriginals). While the change is most dramatic in Toronto and Vancouver, the non-white proportions will reach up to 25 per cent in Calgary and Edmonton in just half a decade, and to 20 per cent in Montreal and Winnipeg. Outside of the official multicultural program as such, and so often overlooked are the effects of the rapid, natural expansion of Canada's native population. From the year 2000 on, one of two new entrants into the Saskatchewan labour force will be aboriginal or Métis. Louis Riel may win in the end: One day, the populations of Saskatchewan and Manitoba may well be predominately Indian or Métis.

This is the Canada that we *are*. Far from clear, yet, is whether we can reinvent ourselves into a community that is larger than the sum of its parts.

12

A Nation of Immigrants, or For Them?

"It [immigration] is creating a new pattern of human co-existence."

— Joel Kotkin, *Tribes*, 1992

Even though fewer than a dozen countries still maintain immigration programs in the normal meaning of the term, it would be hard to find one that does not accept any newcomers at all. Even Switzerland, officially a "non-immigrant country," accepts a few thousand citizens each year – provided they are wealthy enough. Similarly, it would be hard to find any country that is mono-cultural these days. Iceland may come closest.

Three nations nevertheless stand apart from all the others. They are the United States, Canada, and Australia. Uniquely, all are nations of immigrants.

Even for them, that statement is only half-true. Aboriginals excepted, all Americans, Canadians, and Australians are indeed either immigrants or the descendants of immigrants. But it's stretching reality, and dislocates feeling, to classify someone born in a country as the descendant of earlier immigrants rather than as native-born. People are what they were at birth.

The quality that really defines the United States, Canada, and

Australia as nations of immigrants is that they are the only countries to have realized their national potential by mass immigration. (Not coincidentally, all possess the space and natural wealth to do this.) Many other countries have of course been influenced by and have benefited from immigration. Without mass immigration, though, the United States, Canada, and Australia would be quite different from what they are now: smaller, poorer, less powerful, much more parochial, less optimistic, and less expansive. The United States would be a kind of Anglo-Mexico rather than a superpower. Immigration transforms a nation's future. Mexican-American writer Richard Rodriguez has made the deft point that it is now more often immigrants than the often self-doubting white Anglo-Saxons who believe most fully in the American Dream (just as it was so often Jewish-American producers and directors who most lovingly expressed American values in the movies of the 1940s and 1950s). In Canada, immigrants have made their greatest impact on our cities. But for them, Toronto's most attractive attribute would still be its nearness to Buffalo, and Vancouver's to Seattle.

As a deliberate national policy, Canadian immigration dates only from the late 1940s. (The 19th-century influx of Scots and Irish was really an internal migration from the British Isles to British North America, that of the "men in sheepskin coats" at the turn of the century a temporary expedient to people the prairies.) We first opened our doors wide to all of Europe; in 1962, we opened them to the entire world, formalizing this policy by the revised Immigration Act of 1967.

In its scale, no international equivalent to Canada's postwar policy exists, except perhaps that of 19th-century America when that country's need to fill up its limitless spaces made mass immigration a national imperative. Contemporary Canada thus wasn't so much built by immigrants – almost all the heavy lifting had been done earlier – as enriched by them.

In modern times, the magnitude of immigration to Canada is without equal. Some eight million newcomers have arrived since the Second World War. Among these are more than three-quarters of a million refugees, initially in four major waves, from Hungary, Czechoslovakia, East Africa, Vietnam, and now in an annual stream of 25,000-30,000. About one in six Canadians is now an immigrant (or refugee); the U.S. equivalent is only about one in fifteen, even though that country is considerably wealthier and has a much lower unemployment rate. (Australia's immigrant proportion is actually higher than Canada's but much less diverse and so less ambitious.)

For a nation that once worried about its "absorptive capacity" and that will worry forever about the fragility of its identity, this policy has been marvellously daring and imaginative. It has had more effect upon our national character than any other single social policy enacted since the Second World War. Our large cities are now not simply far larger than they would have been otherwise, creating a cosmopolitan Canada for the first time outside of Montreal, but they are multicultural, multiracial, multilingual. They are consequently now quite different from the old Canada of the hinterland. Hand in hand with cosmopolitanism has come a surge of human energy. By contrast, Europe, from which Canada once imported its political and legal systems and upon which we still retain a certain cultural and intellectual dependency, is today an ageing, conservative, subcontinent entering what has been called its "demographic winter." (So is Japan.)

The future of the Judeo-Christian culture, of the Western tradition going back to the Greeks, thus resides largely now in the United States, Canada, and Australia. All three are still comparatively youthful nations; all possess optimism and expansiveness, as well as naïvety. All owe a major share of these attributes to their immigrants who are energized – in contrast to the native-born who tend to take them for granted – by the qualities of these societies, such as democracy, the rule of law, gender equality, multiculturalism, none of which, at best few of which, exist in their homelands.

At the same time, immigrants are moderating the Judeo-Christian, or European, character of these countries. By the year 2050, the United States' population is projected to be majority non-white. No comparable forecast has been made for Canada but with higher immigration rates offsetting a much smaller native-born black population, we should arrive at about the same point at about the same time. In his book *Tribes*, describing "global tribes" such as the Chinese, Japanese, Indians, Jews, and also Anglo-Saxons, whom he identifies as able to function anywhere in the world while retaining their ethnic identity, California political scientist Joel Kotkin has described what's happening in the United States, Canada, Australia and in a few other places like London and Hong Kong as "a new pattern of human co-existence." Call it the serendipitous synergy of West and East. Call it postmodernism.

Ideas like these have never been debated in Canada. There's been no equivalent here either to the futuristic optimism of a Kotkin or to the angry pessimism of *Alien Nation*, the recently published diatribe against immigration by New York journalist Peter Brimelow (an ex-Brit and ex-Canadian). Indeed, in our quintessentially Canadian way, until very recently there has been no real debate about immigration at all. It's just sort of happened.

There was in the 1970s a nasty outburst of so-called "Paki-bashing." Occasional commentators, like Doug Collins in Vancouver, inveighed against the vanishing of the old Anglo Canada. There have been mutterings about the "monster houses" built by some Chinese newcomers in Vancouver. The scale of discontent was trivial, though, compared to that expressed in roughly similar circumstances in liberal countries like Britain, France, Germany, and in the United States in the "nativist" outbursts of popular commentator and Republican presidential candidate

Patrick Buchanan. The occasional criticisms of immigration policy voiced by politicians were almost always to the effect that the policy was too restrictive. Just about any refugee whose claim was disallowed could count on sympathetic media reports about the "insensitivity" of departmental officials. Academic analysis was invariably supportive.

Some of this was smugness: Racial confrontations of the "rivers of blood" kind in Britain just couldn't happen here, because, well, Canada was Canada. It was taken for granted we had infinite space, and that bigger was always better. A good part derived from the fact that, from the early 1970s, Canadians came to embrace tolerance of diversity as the characteristic, along with our social systems, that defined our national distinctiveness. No doubt, we really were no "better" than anyone else, but our self-image, and therefore the axis around which the occasional discussions about immigration revolved, was that we *were* better, or ought to be.

Tolerance reached its limits soon after 1990. Canada's infinite space, it began to be realized belatedly, was beside the point, which was that all immigrants crowded into a few cities. The economic downturn was a major factor. As significant, after having resisted Meech Lake and Charlottetown, Canadians had acquired the confidence to resist change imposed upon them without explanation or justification from above.

Discontent showed itself first in the criticisms about multiculturalism made to the Spicer Commission of 1991, followed by a steadily growing number of ever-more critical comments on hotline radio shows and letters to the editor. Next came the opinion surveys: Support for the retention of cultural diversity by immigrants and for mass immigration dropped sharply. In Toronto, the city to which by far the largest numbers of newcomers came, a February 1994 Ekos poll recorded discontent at a stunning 67 per cent. In the 1993 election, large numbers of Canadians voted for a party, Reform, that actually dared to criticize multiculturalism and mass immigration. Specifically, Reform proposed a cutback to 150,000 from the current immigration intake of 250,000.

Whenever people want to say the unsayable, they find ways to say it. At this time, a series of incidents made it possible for ordinary Canadians to express their long-repressed fears and grievances out loud. In one well-publicized incident, one "refugee" turned out to be the wife of a Somali warlord. She was sufficiently unconcerned about being "persecuted" back home to have twice revisited there, and to have been able to pay the fare even while living on welfare. Another was the discovery that twelve hundred illegal immigrants had received tax refunds from National Revenue (properly, the source of these incomes was none of the department's business). There was also the report that so many sponsored relatives were being abandoned by their kin that the welfare costs of caring for these indigent newcomers had risen to $700 million a year. To provoke parallel unease about the implications of official multiculturalism, the House of Commons replaced its 120-year-old daily prayer with a properly ecumenical version from which all references to Christianity were exorcized while an official of the Sudbury City Council issued a directive that "Christian iconography" should not be shown in public places during the Christmas season in order to show "sensitivity" to non-Christians.

Frustration and unease were soon replaced by outright fear among sizeable sections of the population. A Toronto police officer, Todd Baylis, was gunned down, allegedly by an immigrant who had been ordered to be deported for earlier crimes. A young woman, Georgina Leimonis, was killed by a random bullet in a popular mid-Toronto cafe, again allegedly by immigrants already liable for deportation. In announcing a special task force to track down these offenders, Immigration Minister Sergio Marchi estimated that perhaps six hundred immigrants and refugees had escaped deportation orders; departmental officials later revised the figure to thirteen hundred. For a time, the *Toronto Sun* was able to run daily exposés of refugee and immigration scams and scandals leaked to it by disaffected departmental officials. And, whether the police were to blame or ethnic communities were for failing to discipline their members, there was a constant series of violent incidents – over drugs, gang wars, "house-knappings" – involving black and, to a lesser extent, Vietnamese and Chinese newcomers.

The decisive force that fragmented consensus on immigration was of course the deep recession. From 1990 on, more Canadians were out of work than in any period since the Depression; at the same time more newcomers than ever before were being brought in to compete with them for the dwindling supply of jobs. Environmentalism played a small part: Concepts like "sustainable development" challenged the presumption that to be bigger was always better. Cost played a significant part, especially once the scale of the debt and deficit problems were recognized: The annual total costs of Canada's refugee program (from administration to welfare to health care and education) were calculated at an incredible $1 billion.

As important as anything else was that immigrants were visible now in a way they had never been before. The country's very face was changing, rapidly and unmistakably. Since the mid-1970s, some 70 per cent of newcomers have come from the Third World. To heighten their visibility, almost all settled in a few cities – principally Toronto and Vancouver, to a lesser extent Calgary, Edmonton, Montreal, and Ottawa. Demographic change thus was far more concentrated here than in the United States. According to the 1991 census, Toronto's non-white population was higher than Los Angeles' at 38 per cent to 33 per cent, and Vancouver's over New York and San Francisco by 30 per cent compared to 26 and 21 per cent respectively. The same was true for Calgary, Edmonton, and Montreal: each was at or close to 20 per cent in comparison to the 12 per cent non-white populations in Chicago and Boston (most of these being native-born blacks). Nor did demographic change manifest itself only in ethnic neighbourhoods dotted with a few local shops; a new phenomenon was that of so-called "Asian malls" in which, from their products and signs to the language of the sales clerks, all the stores catered only for members of a particular ethnic group.

Change always provokes unease. Rapid, concentrated, visible change almost always provokes fear. Change to which those in authority are, or appear to be, indifferent is absolutely certain to do this. The one in two Canadians who told pollsters they feared they were becoming "strangers in their own land" were expressing some of the primal feeling of helplessness of a people defeated in a war.

None of this had any effect upon those in authority. During the 1993 campaign, the Liberals promised in their *Red Book* to increase the immigration intake, then fixed at 250,000 a year, to about 300,000 (or to 1 per cent of the population). Given the Liberals' dependency on ethnic votes, it was certain they would fulfil this promise. Late in 1993, the new immigration minister, Sergio Marchi, launched a cross-country review. Thanks to Marchi's choice of supportive immigration "experts" for all of the public hearings organized as part of the review, it was clear that the purpose of the exercise was to validate a political decision already taken.

The trouble was that by now too many Canadians had lost their fear about saying out loud what they really thought, about immigration, or about anything else. As significantly, the first serious intellectual criticisms of the policy had just been put forward. In September 1992, the *Toronto Star* published a series of articles about immigration by journalist Daniel Stoffman based on research he had done during a year-long Atkinson Fellowship. These articles constituted the first attempt in decades at an informed and objective analysis of Canada's immigration policy and program.

Stoffman asked a series of "Is the Emperor really wearing a suit?" kinds of questions. Were newcomers actually bringing with them the kinds of talents and skills the country needed, and if so, why was the intake comprised largely of "self-selected" immigrants who spoke neither official language nor commanded more than minimal education or skills? Did Canada any longer actually need more people to fill up its empty spaces, as popular sentiment supposed was the policy's purpose? Or was the issue "not whether Canada is under-populated but whether Metro Toronto and other large cities are under-populated?"

Stoffman's articles in the *Star*, later expanded and published in 1993 by the C. D. Howe Institute under the title *Towards a More Realistic Immigration Policy for Canada*, were followed by an ever-growing number of root and branch criticisms. What was immigration actually *for*? Was it really any longer in the control of the authorities when so many immigrants were "self-selected?" And, the most fundamental question of all, had an immigration policy for *Canada* somehow got turned topsy-turvy into an immigration policy for *immigrants*?

Stoffman, and other critics like him, were attacked at the time as, at best, mean-spirited, at worst, racist. But the questions themselves had been released into the political ether. As soon as they'd been asked, it became clear that answers were very difficult to muster up.

The core justification for immigration has always been the common-sense assumption that the more people, the better the economy. By this time, though, studies by the Economic Council of Australia and by the Organization for Economic Cooperation and Development had shown that little or no connection exists between immigration and economic growth. (Non-immigrant

countries like Japan and Switzerland have done fine with almost
no newcomers.) Even these recalculations failed to take account
of the offsetting environmental costs of rapid population growth,
from urban congestion to the loss of prime farmland. The other
common-sense economic presumption justifying mass immigration – that newcomers create new trade links with their "home"
countries – had become similarly suspect. In fact, Canada's greatest postwar trade growth has been entirely with countries, the
United States, Japan, South Korea, from which we attract few
immigrants; conversely, we've experienced declining trade with
the European countries from which so many Canadians once
came. Even the core economic argument, that by expanding the
domestic market, immigrants create economies of scale for local
industries, has been made irrelevant by the reality that industries
like these now survived or failed in the global economy.

The eroding of the quantity argument shifted attention to the
issue of the quality of immigrants. Here, it turned out, the circumstances were even more suspect. In the early 1970s, one-third
of all newcomers to Canada were "independents," or individuals
with specific education and skills (later capital), to contribute to
the economy. By the early 1990s, though, "independents" comprised only one-sixth of the intake. Back then, three times as
many immigrants had gone to university as had native-born
Canadians; by the early 1990s, three times as many were functionally illiterate. In the most dramatic shift, in the early 1970s,
just 5 per cent of immigrants arrived unable to speak either of the
official languages; by the early 1990s, the comparable figure was
41 per cent, or almost one in two.

As soon as looked at closely, most of the justifications for mass
immigration simply crumbled. Back in 1978, without the public
being advised of the implications, and very possibly with those in
authority themselves having little understanding of what they
were doing, the traditional "family class" category of immigrants

had been broadened to its extreme limits. Indeed, the department thereafter identified as its *first* priority: "reunit[ing] Canadian residents with close family members from abroad." Henceforth, all immigrants could bring in by entitlement not just their immediate dependants of spouse and children but parents and grandparents of any age. Once arrived, these parents could in turn sponsor their other dependent children; those among these who were married could sponsor their spouses' parents. This daisy chain could be extended sideways by immigrants sponsoring more distant kin like brothers and sisters, uncles and aunts, nieces and nephews, giving them an advantage in securing the number of points needed to qualify for entry as "independents." Entire new chains could be created by dispatching a family member to marry someone in the "home" country. By making full use of the "family class" and the "assisted relative class," one immigrant claimed to have brought in more than sixty relatives. It was in this sense that immigration had been transformed from being a policy for Canada into a policy for immigrants – more exactly for the relatives of recent immigrants (who gained the sponsorship entitlement as soon as landed rather than only when they had become citizens).

In parallel, and once again without any explanation to the public, immigration policy had been disconnected from Canadian economic policy, or from its original *raison d'être*. From 1989 on, the immigration intake was fixed for the next five years at a level that rose quickly to an annual intake of 250,000 (by far the highest in the world, proportionately). In contrast to the policy decisions taken by every preceding government from Louis St. Laurent to Pierre Trudeau to reduce the level during periods of economic downturn, the annual immigration intake now no longer bore any relationship to the state of the domestic economy. The consequence was that at the same time that Canadians were experiencing their highest rate of unemployment since the

Depression, from 1990 on, more newcomers than ever before were being brought in to compete with them. To make the disconnection complete, a majority of these newcomers were semi-skilled at the very same time that semi-skilled jobs were being wiped out by restructuring – or were being transferred to the far side of the Pacific and south of the Rio Grande.

To exacerbate the public's unease, the effects of a new system of refugee selection implemented in 1989 were now becoming clear. For most practical purposes, this system ended even the pretence that Canada was picking and choosing deserving cases among all those applying for asylum. A new Immigration and Refugee Board developed what amounted to a backdoor immigration system. Its approval rate of asylum claims was an incredible 70 per cent in contrast to an international approval rate of 14 per cent (in Western Europe of just 8 per cent). Even more incredible, close to 90 per cent of all original claimants remained in Canada anyway under one humanitarian provision or other. Russian Jews "fleeing" persecution in Israel were accepted as legitimate refugees, as were Jehovah's Witnesses from Portugal; a number who qualified for entry anyway as relatives of newcomers already here opted to go before the board because approval by it was so much more certain and quicker.

Some of this was the product of muddled goodwill – but thoroughly muddled since Canada took in virtually none of the world's most oppressed refugees, the Palestinians in the squalid, criminally crowded camps in Lebanon. A fair bit of it was the product of self-interested activism by immigration lawyers. Some was the product of judicial ineptitude. In a 1985 decision that almost certainly will be amended if an opportunity arises, the Supreme Court ruled that refugee claimants were entitled to the full provisions of the Charter of Rights and Freedoms. Uniquely in the world, this judgment extended national law to non-nationals. Henceforth, the rules that applied in the board's hearings were generous to a fault: "non-confrontational" questioning; approval by only one of the two board members on the panel (both had to agree on a negative decision); and limitations on secondary evidence from embassies abroad or from departmental officials who'd done earlier screening. Thereafter, failure to secure asylum required almost heroic personal incompetence, or a truly lousy lawyer. Inevitably, there was a degree of Lady Bountiful posturing by board members. Approving claims was easy because no detailed explanations were required; rejections, which might later be appealed to the courts, had to be justified by extensive, written judgements. It was also morally satisfying: One vice-chair of the board repeatedly used the term "our stakeholders" to mean only the claimants themselves, their lawyers and the refugee organizations, rather than the general public that was paying the bills.

The public's suspicion that Canada had largely lost control over its own immigration program was substantively correct. Most newcomers came here either by entitlement as relatives of earlier immigrants, or as refugees of whom, by the standards in effect in all other countries, probably one in two would have been rejected on the grounds they were really seeking to escape poverty rather than political persecution. (Escaping poverty is a wholly laudable motive; it becomes decidedly less laudable when it involves jumping legitimate immigrants in the queue.)

Only two factors kept public frustration from bursting out into raw anger: A deep-rooted conviction that as a country of immigrants we should continue to bring in as many newcomers as possible; a humanitarian urge to keep the doors open to those in need. Perhaps as significant as either of these factors was that any criticisms uttered out loud would invite a bruising accusation of "racism."

Just in time, Sergio Marchi read his polls and listened to his backbench MPS from urban ridings. Close to the end of his highly publicized review, Marchi invited critics as well as supporters of the status quo to take part in the public seminars. The impending shift in direction was signalled by a leaked interdepartmental memo warning of rising public concern about immigration levels.

Marchi's actual policy announcement of September 1994 called for a reduction in the total intake from 250,000 to about 200,000. He also announced a series of reforms such as requiring sponsors to post bonds as a guarantee they would live up to their financial commitments to relatives they had sponsored for entry. Later changes included a downsizing of the Immigration and Refugee Board to make the routine approval of claims somewhat less likely and the enactment of a $975-per-head service charge on immigrants to cover part of the ever-rising costs of integrating them into society.

These changes are essentially cosmetic. York University immigration expert James Hathaway notes that even if all the reforms are actually implemented, the proportion of "family-defined" immigrants will decline only to 67 per cent from the previous 73 per cent. "The pressure to keep the door open to relatives of Canadian permanent residents and citizens makes balanced immigration planning virtually impossible," Hathaway comments. Rather than "a symbolic reduction of family immigration," Canada's objective should be "carefully targeted independent migration (that) could contribute to the economic recovery."

Some signs suggest an internal recognition of a need for fundamental change. As soon as Marchi's review and policy announcements were safely over, the department initiated a multiyear research project titled *Metropolis*. This will be its first-ever comprehensive study of what it is that immigration actually does to and for Canada. "Migration is a powerful and inescapable agent of social change (that) affects virtually every domain of civic and family life," reads the prospectus. Policy-makers needed to make decisions "based on research rather than polemic." Detailed studies therefore would be made of the actual impact of immigration, economic, social, cultural, in Toronto, Vancouver, and Montreal. Research topics would include "the formation of ethnic, cultural or religious enclaves; the dynamics of enclaves," whether "immigrants are complementary to or substitute for domestic workers" about "the relationship between immigration and the emergence of populist parties," and, more delicately, about what the *Metropolis* researchers describe as "(their) rising expectations regarding their rights." In parallel, early in 1995, the department launched a major new advertising campaign to try to attract more independent immigrants.

It's unlikely that these kinds of tactical shifts will be enough. The protective umbrella under which immigration policy has functioned for the past three decades – essentially, the conviction that immigration is self-evidently A Good Thing and that to criticize any aspect of it is to be racist – is now full of holes. Immigration has become just another governmental policy deserving of praise or criticism no differently from all other governmental policies from trade to regional development.

For Marchi, it would be too embarrassing to undertake this kind of fundamental policy review right after having completed his own minimal one. The Liberals' dependency upon immigrant votes makes any such revisionism improbable anyway. One way or another, though, a systematic rethink is inevitable.

The nation of immigrants Canada most resembles is of course the United States. In fact, at about one million, the United States' present intake is, proportionately, only half the size of Canada's. Nevertheless, radical reforms are being contemplated there. In June 1995, a bipartisan federal commission proposed a cut in the immigration intake by more than one-third, to 550,000, and a reduction in the family class to just spouses and young children.

By eliminating existing provisions for immigrants to sponsor relatives other than immediate dependants, the commission would create an opening to admit 100,000 independent immigrants who have received specific job offers from employers.

This commission's findings represent Bill Clinton's political response to proposals for far more radical changes that now are widespread. These range from Peter Brimelow's call in *Alien Nation* for "an immediate temporary cut-off of all immigration – say for three to five years" to legislation being debated in Congress to disqualify landed immigrants (as opposed to those who've become citizens) from public services like welfare and Medicaid. Separately, Californians have voted in a referendum to cut off all illegal immigrants from any public services, from education to health care.

An equivalent to the objective analysis of the bipartisan commission's study is overdue to be duplicated here. This doesn't mean that present levels need to be lowered: A new policy of scouring the world for genuine independents with specialized skills and education, including those of language, might well result in an increase in current intake levels. It does mean that the existing policy, based largely on sentimentality and political calculation, is hopelessly out of date.

Amid today's global economy, the size of a country's population matters little because the size of its domestic market matters little. Nor does Canada any longer need to worry about attracting newcomers: Now that everyone's seen what the West looks like on TV, and now that transportation is easy, the numbers of those eager to come are virtually unlimited. The entire "reuniting families" concept has always been inspired more by political opportunism than humanitarian instincts: These families only became disunited because one member chose, voluntarily and invariably to their considerable personal advantage, to emigrate.

Apart from all of this, the nature of immigration today is light years away from that term's traditional meaning. Many newcomers no longer leave one society in order to become members of a new society. Often, the contemporary pattern is that of sojourning in a new society – the Chinese word is *huaqiao* – while retaining close connections with the "home" country, and very likely later moving on to sojourn somewhere else. American scholar Wang Gungwu writes that "new classes of people educated in a whole range of modern skills are now prepared to migrate or remigrate and respond to the pull of centres of power and wealth and the new opportunities in trade and industry. . . . These people are articulate, politically sensitive and choose their new homes carefully . . . many are masters not only in the handling of official and bureaucratic connections but also in the art of informal linkages."

The efficiency and cheapness of modern communication and transportation systems make this kind of sojourning comparatively easy; at the same time, global free trade makes it easy for newcomers to remain in intimate contact with their home country by importing specialized clothes, foods, artefacts, films, videos, and newspapers. In this sense, Canada's policy of official multiculturalism is quite out of sync with the times: While still experiencing a temporary "culture shock" after arriving, most newcomers can now easily "preserve" and "enhance" their cultures by themselves.

The change in the character of contemporary immigration doesn't in any way mean that past immigration hasn't benefited Canada immensely. Even if, as almost certainly is the case, immigration has been out of the control of the authorities for years, this has made remarkably little difference to the only aspect of the policy that matters – its real-life results. In modern times, no other country has absorbed more newcomers in greater variety with less difficulty. This inpouring has made Canada an incomparably livelier, more creative, more richly textured society. Nor had we chosen more carefully, would we necessarily have chosen any better. Most Vietnamese – the "Boat People" of the late 1970s – came here as unskilled, unilingual farmers and fishermen. A decade and a half later, their rate of employment is much higher than, and their rate of welfare much lower than, that of Canadians as a whole. Their impact upon our future will be even greater: A conspicuously disproportionate number of second-generation Vietnamese-Canadians are now on the honour lists in high schools and deans lists at universities.

Whether skilled or unskilled, unilingual or multilingual, poor or rich, what matters most about almost every immigrant is that he or she, by having had the nerve to cross an ocean, and perhaps of having outsmarted immigration officials, is self-reliant, ambitious, daring – and is all of these to a far greater degree than the native-born. Whatever their starting line, a high proportion of newcomers succeed here, and thereby create jobs and opportunities for others, simply because they came here specifically to succeed. As Richard Rodriguez remarks, it's mostly immigrants who still dream the North American Dream.

Genuine reform of immigration thus isn't a synonym for reducing the intake or for replacing generosity with mean-spiritedness along the lines now being proposed in the United States. In *Tribes*, Joel Kotkin suggests that "to cower behind the walls of a white 'fortress Europe' or 'fortress America'" would be to "repeat the tragic mistake that in the past fostered the decline of Asian societies and of their domination by Europeans." West and East need each other. Reform of immigration policy is really a synonym for Canadianizing it.

13

Civis Canadensis Sum

> *"My parents were immigrants, and my aunts and uncles as well. They were not told what it means to be a Canadian citizen. They were just told, essentially, pass the tests, pay the taxes, and that's it."*
>
> — Witness at public hearings of the Commons Committee on Citizenship and Immigration, June 1994

Anyone who becomes a Canadian by naturalization has secured the second prize in life's lottery, at the very least. More of those who become Americans will become richer faster. Everyone who comes here, though, will inherit automatically a far more closely meshed security net, including support for the culture and language of the country they've just – deliberately – left. As soon as they become citizens, they will acquire a passport with magical properties: Wherever they go, it will evoke more welcoming cries of "Good country, Canada" and considerably less hostility than the passport of any other nation.

Only those who possess Canadian citizenship by a right of birth fail to realize the magnitude of their prize. We all get misty eyed when "O Canada" is played, even if we're unsure of all the words. We like waving the flag, if not too ostentatiously. We are all well aware of the alchemy a Canadian passport confers.

Yet Canadians themselves, however unintentionally, have devalued Canadian citizenship to the point where its usefulness within Canada itself is almost non-existent. "Canadians clearly have not turned their citizenship into a source and symbol of national pride," writes University of Ottawa law professor William Kaplan in his introduction to *Belonging*. Kaplan may have been too judicious. In the same volume, Robert Sharpe, dean of law at the University of Toronto, raises the question whether "Canadian citizenship itself [has become] a highly suspect legal classification."

In law, being Canadian may now mean remarkably little – within Canada. Indeed, it's not easy even to be a Canadian in Canada: Official multiculturalism, reinforced by the kinds of questions posed in the census, pushes all Canadians into declaring themselves Italian-Canadians, Ukrainian-Canadians, Somali-Canadians, whatever, at the same time, regionalism encourages them to think of themselves first as Albertans, Newfoundlanders, whatever. The "inherent right of self-government" ceded to native people grants to them – to close to 1.25 million Canadians – a right that precedes Canada's existence as a nation-state to determine the terms of their citizenship within it. In parallel, we have ceded to Quebeckers the right of "self-determination" – a right that by international convention is limited to peoples suffering oppression and occupation like the Balts and Palestinians, but not the Scots or the Catalans. Moreover, we have accepted that Quebeckers have the right not only to decide whether they want to remain Canadians but also the wording of the question by which they will make a choice that so critically affects other Canadians; also, the timing (and the number of times) when they choose to exercise this right.

As has so often been the case with these cultural issues, all of this has happened without Canadians being told the implications of what was happening. On the evidence, few of those initiating these changes were themselves aware of the consequences. Self-government for native people, for example, was agreed to by Ottawa and the provinces during the Charlottetown constitutional negotiations without any agreement having been reached on the critical issue of whether the Charter of Rights and Freedoms would apply in full in the new self-governing territories, or about the status of non-natives living in these territories. Quebeckers have acquired the right of repetitive self-determination simply by taking it for granted that they possessed it. In lockstep, the rest of the country has been too timid to raise any objections, more useful, any conditions to the exercising of this right – provision for a parallel federal referendum for example, or for particular Quebeckers, such as native people or those in distinct regions, to exercise a reverse right to self-determine themselves "back" into Canada. The slipshod style of acquiring Canadian citizenship described by one witness to a 1994 Commons committee and quoted at the start of this chapter, has come about through progressive, almost invisible, changes in the relevant bureaucratic regulations.

The lightness of being a Canadian starts with the fact that it's the easiest citizenship in the world to obtain. That more people become naturalized Canadians, proportionately, than those in any country besides Australia, is neither here nor there. What's striking is that we ask, and expect, so little in exchange for that blue passport. The residency requirement is three years in contrast to the more general minimum of five years (twelve years in Switzerland). This residency requirement, though, doesn't necessarily require very much actual residency. Only 183 days of each of the three years need be spent within Canada's borders. Exemptions have been granted to individuals who spent only a few months here, in some instances only a few weeks. Anyway, no control system exists to confirm residency: To avoid acquiring telltale stamps in their passports, individuals need only travel south of the border, and then proceed east or west.

Canadian citizenship is a right of those claiming it rather than, as is commonly the case, a privilege extended to them by the state. All who fulfil the qualifying conditions, first of landed immigrant status, then of residency, can claim citizenship as an entitlement; the requirement for any actual knowledge of the country, including its languages, is, putting it gently, minimal.

Once obtained, whether by birth or naturalization, Canadian citizenship confers almost no benefits upon actual citizens in comparison to those possessed by all others residing here either permanently or temporarily. It's possible, although the law is unclear, that tourists who've hopped over the border enjoy the same protections as citizens. The Charter limits exclusively to citizens only the rights to vote in elections, to run for public office, to permanently enter and leave the country (a protection against deportation), and the right to minority language education in either official language.

Non-citizens, though, are entitled to vote in party nominating conventions to pick electoral candidates, which can reduce the actual election to a formality. According to a 1989 decision by the Supreme Court, citizenship isn't a necessary qualification for practising a profession. Another Supreme Court decision has extended the full benefits of the Charter and Rights and Freedoms to "every human being who is physically present in Canada," a right that certainly applies to asylum claimants and that, logically, may extend also to tourists.

In some instances, non-citizens can claim prior rights over native-born Canadians. Those who fit one of the "designated categories" are entitled (on the curious grounds of having been "historically disadvantaged" in Canada) to benefit from all employment equity programs, to the corresponding disadvantage of native-born Canadians. In her judgment on the 1989 case involving the British Columbia Law Society's claim about citizenship as a necessity for practising a profession, then Supreme Court Madam Justice Bertha Wilson argued that *all* newcomers should be classified as disadvantaged or as "an analogous category to those specifically enumerated [in the Charter]." In fact, the non-citizen whom the Supreme Court judged was being disadvantaged by being refused the right to practise law in British Columbia was a white, male, U.S. citizen educated at Oxford.

In *Belonging*, William Kaplan admits his doubts that citizenship can ever serve Canadians as "a unifying force" in the way it does in most countries. In a belated attempt to put some stuffing back into the concept, a Commons committee held hastily organized hearings in the summer of 1994. The committee's main recommendation called for the revival of a provision in earlier versions of the citizenship act for Canadian citizenship to be withdrawn from individuals who later acquire the citizenship of another country. This provoked fierce opposition from Bloc Québécois MPs who, not unnaturally, interpreted this as a pre-referendum manoeuvre to warn Quebeckers they could either have Quebec passports or Canadian ones, but not both. Subsequently, Immigration Minister Sergio Marchi drafted a revised version of the oath of citizenship, with the help of some well-known writers. The proposed new version is: "I am a citizen of Canada and I make this commitment: to uphold our laws and freedoms; to respect our people in their diversity; to work for our common well-being, and to safeguard and honour this ancient northern land." While these pieties are agreeable, they stirred up criticism from the opposite direction – the omission of any reference to the monarchy and Queen in contrast to the existing oath. Crafting out an oath of citizenship that everyone can agree on and that still means something may return the nation to the verbal contortions of Meech Lake and Charlottetown.

Before describing how we got into this pickle, it may be useful to describe the paths followed by others.

Once, the three proudest words anyone could utter were *Civis Romanus Sum*. Other than during the Republic's earliest years, to be a Roman wasn't merely to be a member of the particular tribe that had defeated the Etruscans and then the Greeks. It was to be a *somebody*.

As with so much that was Roman, the idea derived from the Greeks, specifically from Aristotle's definition of members of the *polis* as those who had accepted to be ruled and had accepted also their responsibility to help rule others democratically. The uniquely Roman idea was that of extending citizenship to encompass all kinds of people living within a multiracial empire rather than just a city-state. Centuries later, this ideal was maintained, sort of, within the Holy Roman Empire. Later still, the multiracial concept was revived, again sort of, within the British, French, and Austro-Hungarian empires. The single significant addition to the concept was Jean-Jacques Rousseau's definition of the relationship between governed and governing as being contractual and consensual, with the two parties interconnected mutually by rights and responsibilities.

The rise of nation-states tugged the definition of citizenship towards that of ethnicity. Either *jus sanguine*, or blood ties, as is still the case in Germany, or *jus soli*, location of birth, as in France, became the criterion for deciding on whom to bestow the privileges of citizenship (security, the rule of law) and upon whom to impose its obligations (taxes, conscription).

This fixity became unravelled once people started to move in large numbers. As now requires an effort to imagine, most of the "poor, huddled masses" who flooded into the United States in the 19th century had no nationality: There was then no Poland for Poles to come from, nor a Ukraine, nor an Ireland. As is equally difficult to imagine, passports came into general use only during the First World War.

It was only in this century that nation-states developed immigration programs and naturalization procedures to enable them to pick and choose among those trying to enter their societies. Clifford Sifton's decision to fill up "the last, best West" at the turn of the century with "sturdy peasants in sheepskin coats" was prompted by his calculation that newcomers from Eastern Europe would be less challenging to Canada's Canadianness – and Britishness – than the alternative of American farmers carrying the virus of republicanism northwards. Postwar Britain accepted large numbers from the Caribbean and the Indian subcontinent as a responsibility of empire, and as a source of cheap labour. The same economic imperative prompted Germany – officially a "non-immigrant country" – to develop the policy of *Gastarbeiters*, foreign guest workers, mostly Yugoslavs and Turks, who, unlike their counterparts in Britain, the United States, Canada, and Australia, themselves gained no entitlement to citizenship, nor, because of the *jus sanguine* rule, did their children. Later, France developed the same policy for North Africans. So, quite a bit later, did the oil-rich Gulf states for Palestinians and workers from Egypt and India.

For most of the postwar half-century, immigration patterns and naturalization procedures settled into more or less familiar grooves, save for the change in the sources of migrants, away from Europe and towards the rest of the world. Now, though, the very idea of national citizenship is being challenged.

The difference between past and present is that, because of communications and free trade and free-flowing finance and the rest, Marshall McLuhan's global village has become a truism. Recognition of this has prompted two responses. One is ideological: All people ought to be able to move freely within the village's marketplace. The other is humanitarian: We ought to care for the poor in other parts of the world no differently than we do for our own.

The ideological case – a libertarian one – is advanced by the Cato Institute in Washington and here by *Globe and Mail* columnist Andrew Coyne. They argue that the movement of labour should be as free within the various neighbourhoods of the extended village as is the movement of capital and of goods; only the market should decide who goes where, when, and why. That such a policy would effectively destroy nation-states does not lessen their conviction that only the marketplace matters.

Today's potential mass migration is of course driven by forces far more practical and urgent than such theoretical generalities. These are the forces of poverty, of overpopulation, and of repression. Incomparably more people are moving, or are attempting to move, or are thinking about moving, than at any time in the world's history.

The humanitarian case is that we have a duty to let them move in amongst us. Undoubtedly, members of the Immigration and Refugee Board often accept stories of persecution that are really covers for a flight from poverty both because it's terribly hard to say no to someone pleading before you to be allowed to share your advantages and because of an underlying feeling that accepting such claims is a substitute for Canada's declining contributions to foreign aid.

The problem is, how much humanitarianism can we afford before our neighbourhood comes to resemble everyone else's? In his 1995 Massey Lectures, Conor Cruise O'Brien conjured up the vivid image of a "lifeboat," inside the favoured few in the industrial countries, and grasping at its sides and certain to swamp it if allowed in, hundreds of millions of the world's desperately poor. A few years ago a brilliant BBC documentary, *The March*, depicted millions of starving North Africans setting out for Europe as their only alternative to death by malnutrition.

There's a large amount of fantasy to all this. It's today's version of turn-of-the-century alarmism about "The Yellow Peril." The practical obstacles to mass movements of population are immense, and are scarcely less so for individuals, which is why so many of the refugees who make it here are often comparatively wealthy. Forecasts that millions of East Europeans and Russians would move westwards once the Wall came down have proved groundless. As improbable are warnings that huge numbers of the twenty million refugees now being cared for by the UN will want to move to distant, foreign lands. Instead, the vast majority are waiting amid pitiable conditions to return to their own lands.

Even developed countries' traditional incentive for encouraging immigration – the benefit of cheap labour – has been lessened significantly now that the global economy enables transnationals to pick and choose which low-wage country in which to locate their factories.

Nevertheless, incomparably more people than ever before in human history are now aware of the possibilities of migrating, and of the immense advantages of doing so, and of the ways to do it. In one defensive response, the member-states of the European Union have signed the Schengen agreement, which balances reductions in the barriers in-between them with much higher barriers to all outsiders. As part of his response to rising criticisms of U.S. immigration policy, Bill Clinton has found the funds to increase the number of border guards by fifteen hundred. Congress is debating legislative proposals to disqualify not just illegal immigrants but landed immigrants from welfare and Medicaid. (In Canada, the scale of illegal immigration is unknown, and in the absence of any effective deportation system, tends to get dealt with by periodic general asylums.)

Besides its potential scale, contemporary immigration and, consequently, the character of national citizenship are being affected by two more subtle factors. One involves migrating as an end in itself rather than as means to secure a new citizenship. The presence in the United States of some five million illegal immigrants, principally Mexicans, regularly gives rise to alarmist comments. Less often remarked on is that the great majority eventually return home after earning the money they need to look after their families. On a smaller scale, the same phenomenon occurs in Europe, especially with North Africans and Turks. In Germany, bureaucratic obfuscation aside, the reason few Turks exercise the right to claim German citizenship that some in fact possess is because they would then lose Turkish citizenship by that country's own rules, and therefore would lose the right to own property there.

The other factor, described in the previous chapter, is that of "sojourning." Even when acquired, the second citizenship may serve principally as a commercial convenience that, ironically, is often most useful for providing protection in the former "home" country and a guarantee of easy departure from it. In itself, dual citizenship isn't new. Indeed, for the better part of a century after Confederation, Canadians were categorized as British subjects and thereby could claim to have been the world's first mass dual citizens along with all others in self-governing territories in the British Empire. Today, cheap and efficient transportation and communications systems, reinforced in Canada's case by official multiculturalism, have made the concept of dual citizenship into a potentially general one.

Dual citizenship can mean dual loyalties, and thus erode the substance of citizenship. These other loyalties may be political, so that what happens in the Middle East, in former Yugoslavia, in the Indian subcontinent, can matter more than whatever may happen politically in Canada. Commonly, the second loyalty is to commercial imperatives. According to one recent survey, one in four Chinese-Canadian families in Toronto include at least one member who performs as an "astronaut," flying regularly back across the Pacific, to Hong Kong, Taiwan, or China. Often, the deeper loyalty is cultural. In *The Caribbean Diaspora in Toronto*, Frances Henry writes of a phrase frequently used among those who've moved here: "Canada is where you live. 'Home' is where you come from." Dual loyalties don't have to mean loyalties in conflict: the Greek-Canadian youths who cheered Greece's basketball team over Canada's when they met in an international competition in Toronto were just giving themselves an excuse to cheer. But they can mean attenuated loyalty to Canada. And they can reduce citizenship to a convenience.

In pursuit of its objective of "preserving" and "enhancing" the cultures of all those who have come to Canada – voluntarily after all – official multiculturalism enhances and preserves dual loyalties. Important parts of our immigration program have the same effect. We've turned Canadian citizenship into an export industry, selling it to so-called "investors" (pretty cheaply, at $250,000 over five years as against the $1-million requirement in the United States). Uniquely in the world, our citizenship act specifically encourages newcomers to retain their previous passports. (While a U.S. Supreme Court decision has recognized dual citizenship – to the great advantage of American-born university professors and other Americans here – American immigration officers deliberately raise as many bureaucratic obstacles as they can to the continued possession of two passports.)

Celebrating our citizenship has never come easily to Canadians. It took us eighty years to create a distinctive nationality for ourselves by the Citizenship Act of 1947 (even while retaining, as a kind of safety net, the pre-existing category of "British subject" for another three decades). Nor, as historian J. L. Granatstein writes, has Canada been prepared to impose what he calls "hard obligations" upon its citizens. Taxes aside, the principal hard obligation of citizenship has always been that of fighting on behalf of one's country; in turn, the rock-hard form of this obligation has been conscription. It was only close to the end of both world wars that we imposed upon ourselves this great, if brutal, experience in collective participation. The opposition of French-Canadians to "British" wars was the primary obstacle in the way of its imposition, but a subsidiary consideration was that by picking and choosing among the volunteers we avoided having to take into our armed forces all "others" who would have applied – Germans and Austro-Hungarians in the first war, and also Italians, Japanese, Sikhs, in the second. We redefined our citizenship, this is to say, to suit our own ethnicity.

Ethnicity has now become the principle challenge to our citizenship. In a powerful essay in *Belonging*, titled "The Fragmentation of Canadian Citizenship," University of British Columbia political scientist Alan Cairns raises the question whether it is possible to have "a citizen body lacking the bond of a standardized citizenship nevertheless participating in common civic endeavours." Writing at a time – 1991 – when Quebec nationalism was in the ascendancy, and similarly that of native people, Cairns sees a "three-nation," fragmented Canada developing within which major segments of the population would redefine citizenship to suit their particular purposes. As an additional threat to "standardized citizenship," Cairns identifies "the political articulation of various social, ethnic and gender diversities of modern society."

The referendum will decide whether Quebeckers really want to redefine their citizenship to the extreme of creating a new one for themselves. By contrast, the divisiveness of official multicultural-ism is entirely our own creation.

The absurdity here is that almost no one from Italy, say, or Somalia, comes to Canada to be an Italian or a Somali. They come here to be Canadians. As soon as landed, though, their new state in effect tells them that rather than becoming Canadians they must remain Italian-Canadians, Somali-Canadians, and so on. Natural-ly, ethnic politicians want to keep their constituents apart from the mainstream; if everyone integrates, these politicians would lose their power as gatekeepers and fixers. Our state, though, encourages these gatekeepers to maintain what amounts, at worst, to an apartheid form of citizenship, at best a "differentiated citizenship."

The real absurdity is that little evidence exists that this is what most newcomers really want. We've listened too much to self-appointed ethnic spokespeople, too little to the newcomers them-selves. Perhaps the most eloquent expression of what newcomers think was contained in an article by Devo-Jaiikoah Dyette for one of the "Diversities" columns published in the *Toronto Star* during the winter of 1994-95. "I am a black Canadian living in a society to which I believe I belong by right," writes Dyette. "I refuse to be called an African based solely on the colour of my skin. I am a

Canadian first, who happens by the luck of the draw to be black
... I am very proud of my colour and I am very proud of my
country."

On behalf of those Canadians most likely to be marginalized
by negative stereotyping, Dyette says, "Treat me like one of you,"
not as a black Canadian or as an Afro Canadian but as a Canadian
who happens to be black.

For one group of Canadians, though, this ideal of an undiffer-
entiated and equal Canadian citizenship can never encompass all
of reality. Putting it bluntly, native people are Canada's blacks. We
haven't treated them in the same atrocious way Americans once
treated blacks, nor have we ever called out the cavalry. But, to our
own enduring national shame, we have treated them more de-
meaningly than Americans have treated their own native people.

In Canada, recognition of a right of native people to self-
government dates back only little more than a decade; by contrast, in the United States, it has existed for more than a century
following a 1830 Supreme Court ruling that aboriginals constituted "dependent, domestic nations." Here, the rate of unemployment among Indians on reserves is triple that of the national rate;
in the United States, it is "only" twice the level of a national rate
that itself is far lower than Canada's.

In a modernized version of Rousseau's "noble savage," native
people are now perceived through the distorting lenses of political correctness. Disney's soft-focus 1995 movie *Pocahontas* is the
consummate example of this sentimentalism.

Self-abnegation by the descendants of those who "won"
confers no benefits upon contemporary native people. The truth
is that any contact between a nomadic hunter-gatherer culture
and a technologically advanced, rational, and confident culture was
bound to be bruising, if not fatal. The epic achievement of native
people has been that, even though "defeated" and dispossessed,
they yet preserved their memories and myths so that, like seeds of

grain preserved in the dry air of ancient Egyptian tombs, these eventually could be brought back to life.

How real this rebirth can actually be is an open question. Indians are Canadians now. They watch TV, ride snowmobiles, depend upon rifles to kill their winter's meat. Yet Indians, and Inuit, are a fundamentally different kind of Canadian. They *were* here first. They *are* at one with the land and with nature in a way that only the most environmentally minded European-Canadians can achieve. Their consensual style of decision-making is utterly different from ours. Native people can do naturally what European-Canadians are incapable of doing – remain silent when they have nothing to say.

Whatever can be said about the reality of those elements of the original hunter-gather culture that still persist at the turn of the millennium, the central fact is that we dispossessed them. Indeed, until the 1970s, our national policy was to abolish them. Our motive was kindness. Convinced that native culture could not survive amid European-Canadian culture, successive politicians and officials, and also most ordinary Canadians, accepted that native people should be treated, in their own best interests, as dependent children rather than as "dependent domestic nations." Governments would protect them by keeping them away from other Canadians, on reserves. Governments would nurture them by providing the funds they could not, for lack of natural commercial capabilities, generate themselves. Above all, through residential schools and the Christian religions, we would train them to grow up to be Canadians just like everyone else.

In the pursuit of these policies there were more good intentions and exceptional, at times heroic, endeavours by individuals than it's now fashionable to recognize. The only reality that matters is that these policies failed: In every material respect, most critically in self-esteem, native people have been disadvantaged Canadians from our first contact with them.

By the early 1970s, native people themselves had begun to repudiate these policies. A new generation of young leaders, such as Harold Cardinal and George Erasmus, many university educated, all with an understanding of white man's ways, emerged and began to speak out. First, they rejected the "assimilationist" white paper of 1969 that proposed to abolish the Department of Indian and Northern Affairs. Then, in mid-1970, after a first-ever face-to-face encounter with Pierre Trudeau and his cabinet, they demanded negotiations on their own terms, over land claims and self-government. By this time, Indian ways had come to represent to the ever-increasing number of environmentalists the way all Canadians should follow. Even as native people began to see themselves differently, we began to perceive them differently, and also our collective selves.

Native people have since travelled an immense distance. Key consciousness-raising events along their way have been Ovide Mercredi's successful securing of a place at the table where the Charlottetown Accord was hammered out, Elijah Harper's role in actually blocking the Meech Lake Accord, the uprising by the Mohawk at Oka, the achievement of the Cree of northern Quebec in November 1994 in forcing the Quebec government to abandon, at the very least temporarily, its plans for a James Bay II hydro project.

At the same time, though, native people have been caught up by the same "rights frenzy" as everyone else. Following the enactment of the Charter of Rights and Freedoms, they, like so many other interest groups, have devoted a disproportionate amount of time and energy to concocting legal solutions to their problems – their success in securing acceptance of an "inherent right to self-government" in the 1992 Charlottetown Accord negotiations representing the summit of this legalistic achievement.

That 63 per cent of Indians on reserves then voted against the accord that Mercredi had so triumphantly secured for them is neither here nor there. Native politics are as bruising and as personal as those in university faculties. Within most native groups, political legitimacy resides not in the band or council or among chiefs, elected or appointed, but only within extended families, thereby making consensual decisions excruciatingly difficult to achieve. Natives are divided further between their own nations, these being as distinct as francophones and anglophones, and between their own kind: Many status Indians opposed the Charlottetown Accord because it extended the right of self-government to non-status Indians and Métis.

A specific problem here is that self-government is a misnomer. What is at issue is really *self-administration*. The portentous phrase "self-government" conjures up illusionary images of quasi-independence and of a right to self-determination. The Mohawk of Kanesatake thus have taken the phrase "inherent right of self-government" to its literal and logical conclusion by proclaiming themselves an independent state, possessed of its own passports and with the power, by "blood quantum," to determine who is or is not a Mohawk and so entitled to live on the reserve.

Self-administration is less glamorous and more difficult. The risk is that other Canadians will exploit this term as an opportunity to dump their moral obligations to native people, saying in effect, "Here's your last cheque; good luck with it." The hard truth is that only a minority of native groups yet possess the necessary administrative expertise, know-how, and experience in imposing "hard obligations" upon their own members, such as paying taxes to native governments. Self-government, so-called, thus may be imposed upon native people before they are ready for it. The December 1994 "framework agreement" granting self-government to all status Indians in Manitoba and abolishing the Department of Northern Affairs there was signed by the federal government even before agreement had been reached on such crucial issues as the status of non-natives living in these areas or about the overriding authority, or otherwise, of the Charter and federal and provincial laws.

Some painful arguments are going to break out over whether self-governing native people must observe general environmental and conservation laws, as well as the gun registration regulations. Other more difficult issues have yet to be faced. The past practice of solving the native "problem" by throwing money at it cannot be sustained for long. The current federal budget for native affairs of some $5 billion is at risk at a time of general cutbacks, all the more given the rapid rise in the native population (one in two are under twenty).

The second issue, yet more painful, is that native people's ability to twinge the conscience of other Canadians is nearing its limit. As native self-government approaches reality, others will become more acutely aware of what they may lose, a phenomenon especially sharp in British Columbia where land claims encompass, in theory, 95 per cent of the province. Amid downsizing and recession, all Canadians have less and less time and inclination to worry about the problems of others. Few among the ever-increasing numbers of new Canadians are likely to bond emotionally to such Old Canada issues as native versus non-natives, or for that matter English versus French or East versus West.

The transition native people are making now from rhetoric about past wrongs and from the rights frenzy to practical self-administration will not be an easy one. Serious administrative mistakes are bound to be made – although by no means necessarily worse than the financial mess all other Canadians have managed to get themselves into. Ultimately, only one thing needs to be said: Whatever problems native people may create for themselves can never exceed the harm we have done to them.

In a presentation to the Senate Committee on Social Affairs, Alan Cairns warned native people not to put too much emphasis on their right to decide themselves the terms of their Canadian citizenship: "If they remove themselves from that 'we' community, I do not say they become like people who do not live in Canada, but they do not then have the same capacity to tug at our civic heart strings in terms of supporting the kinds of funds they will require if they are to develop in the way they would like."

Cairns's warning applies equally to Quebeckers, to all the racial, ethnic, and gender-identity groups, and indeed to all provinces and regions. Those who "remove" themselves from the community by claiming special rights to be more equal than others in self-defined circumstances lose their moral claim to be treated as equal citizens in all other respects.

In an introduction to the collection of essays *Theorizing Citizenship*, University of Toronto political scientist Ronald Beiner makes the same point in a different way. After reviewing all the demands for special treatment on the grounds of having been excluded historically, Beiner asks, "Included in what? If a community of citizens doesn't involve a kind of universality, how can there be a community of citizens to which the hitherto excluded and marginalized can gain entry?"

The "what" that all these groups want to be included in, even while demanding the right to partially "remove" themselves from it on their own terms, is of course the Canadian community. In turn, that community is the product of all the habits, assumptions, and values accumulated and shaped over the decades by people who happened, principally, to be white males of European origin. This isn't to say that all they once did was admirable. It's to say that these habits and assumptions are the community's centre. Without ever stating it, perhaps without being aware of it, more and more Canadians want to take from that centre all the while taking for granted that that centre will always be there for them. Beyond some indefinable point, though, there will no longer be a "there, there" to Canada.

Who will be left then to say with pride *Civis Canadensis Sum*?

PART IV

The Heart of the Matter

14

Postmodern Dominion

*"Two black brothers from the land of the snows. What will the
foreign pundits make of that."*

— Stephen Williams, filmmaker, on hearing that his
film, *Soul Survivor*, had been chosen for the 1995
Cannes Film Festival Critics Week

Wilfrid Laurier got it wrong when he said that the 20th century
might belong to Canada. Instead, Canada belongs to the 21st
century. We are the world's first postmodern state.

Postmodern has become a hot-button word. Journalists and
editors toss it into stories to make themselves seem up-to-date.
Perhaps the first popular use of the word appeared in a *Newsweek*
article in the fall of 1992 describing Bill Clinton and Al Gore's
travels through the heartland in a bus as America's "first postmodern campaign." Even that early, the writer took for granted
that readers, even if they didn't know the literal meaning of the
term, would understand that it implied something daring and
unusual. Since then, all kinds of quirky events have been hyped-
up as examples of the postmodern.

This scattershot labelling is justified. Postmodern can be
applied to just about anything. A coherent theory of postmodernist architecture exists, for example; in practice it's mostly a sales
gimmick to justify to clients buildings that don't look like cereal
boxes and that therefore might appeal to Prince Charles.

My own use of the term is just as imprecise. I use postmodern to mean a radical break, a discontinuity, in our national evolution. Nothing more than that, but also nothing less.

The Canadian society of the mid-1990s is quite different in texture and temper from that of a decade ago, perhaps even from only a half-decade ago, no matter that the underlying changes have been building up for a long time. The national economy no longer exists; in its place we work, or try to find work, in a local production site of, and market for, the global economy. Demographically, we are no longer the old anglophone and francophone *deux nations* plus aboriginals; instead, we are well on the way to becoming a global nation, or a microcosm of all the world's peoples. Always the world's most decentralized nation-state, we have become decentralized further – more accurately "de-centred" as is a key term in postmodernist theory – no longer just into our historic regions and provinces but more and more now into all our new "identity" communities.

The old Canada – if not the old Canadian economy – still exists and in many respects is flourishing. The founding anglophone and francophone communities are still large, are culturally influential, and retain the greater part of the political, economic, and financial power. Hence the title of this chapter: "Postmodern Dominion." We have one foot in the future and one in the past. The phrase isn't mine. I lifted it from a paper delivered by journalist and critic Robert Fulford to a conference on citizenship sponsored by the University of Ottawa in January 1992, and reprinted later in *Belonging*. Not counting works of literary scholarship such as Linda Hutcheon's 1988 book, *The Canadian Postmodern*, Fulford was the first, I believe, to use the term to describe Canada's national condition. His bracketing of the hot-button word with the archaic "Dominion" especially caught my fancy.

A serious and comprehensive theory of postmodernism exists. It flourishes in North American universities; all students of the humanities will encounter it during their studies.

The doctrine dates back to the 1960s. Its origins are French; its first gurus were Jacques Derrida and Michel Foucault. It crossed the Atlantic in the early 1970s. One of its most formidable contemporary advocates is Habib Bhahaba of the University of Chicago.

The doctrine's source and the timing of its importation here aren't coincidental. The 1960s amounted to a false break or discontinuity. For a time, it seemed that rebellious youth could change everything; then nothing changed. Postmodernism amounts to an attempt at a second revolution – but only an intellectual and verbal one. Its advocates launch their thunderbolts, especially against patriarchal Eurocentric wisdom, from behind the protective ramparts of university campuses. Postmodernists analyse, criticize, deconstruct, reducing the inherent meaning of Shakespeare's folio, for example, to not much than that of a telephone directory. All this revolutionary talk becomes a substitute for real, and thereby risky, revolutionary action. Postmodernists are deeply concerned with "the structures of oppression," especially as these bear down on the identity minorities of women, gays and lesbians, and ethnic and racial groups. They are not concerned with socio-economic class nor, most certainly among the many who are tenured academics, are they greatly troubled by income disadvantages.

Indeed, postmodernism amounts to Marxism reduced from economics to culture. The sideways shift occurred after the New Left revolutionaries of the 1960s gave up on their dream of forging an alliance between the peace and youth movements and the stolid, conservative, pro-Vietnam War workers whom, as Herbert Marcuse had correctly diagnosed, had succumbed to the "repressive tolerance" of secure jobs and ever-higher wages. Today, so at least goes the theory, potential revolutionary consciousness resides in race and gender-identity groups. The famous slogan of the New Left of the 1960s, "Never Trust Anyone Over 30," has been updated to "Never Trust Anyone European and Patriarchal."

As for the doctrine itself, actually comprehending it requires a familiarity with critical theories like structuralism and deconstructionism and an ability to fake an understanding of words like "incommensurability" and "signifier." Much is pretentious posturing. Yet the postmodernists are onto something. The modern era, of standardization, homogenization, centralization, of lifelong jobs with comfortable pensions at their end, of familiar gender roles, has clearly come to an end. Nation-states may be becoming obsolete. The family, that primal building block of humanity, is no longer what it was and may now be anything.

Postmodernists have no better idea than anyone else what may emerge as a new social order. Bhahaba talks about a new "Third Space"; this is a slogan without content, much like the old "Consciousness Three" of the 1960s. Yet when all is in flux, or is "de-centred," uncertainty may be the only certainty. Postmodern analysis is about the end of structure, coherence, authority, hierarchy, narrative, and history, of general truths of all kinds. All is relative; nothing is absolute. It is about a denial of the validity of separating subject from object, of a distancing between observer and observed. It's about the rejection of rational analysis and its replacement by anything from sheer playfulness to the ego of the individual. Irony is integral to postmodernist expression. That's of course a quintessentially Canadian quality. Scholar Linda Hutcheon writes astutely about this Canadian character tic: "Irony Self-Deprecating is Irony Self-Protective."

Our aptitude for irony aside, it may seem a stretch to connect all of this to contemporary Canada. In fact, the connections are well-grounded. We've always been decentralized, or de-centred." The multiple identities that are so central to postmodernist analysis existed here long before official multiculturalism: Historically, aside from the ingrained ambivalence of the *Canadiens,* most English-Canadians thought of themselves as simultaneously Canadians and British up to at least the Second World War. Canada's single genuinely original thinker, Marshall McLuhan, compressed much of the essence of postmodernism into two of his most famous lines: "The global village" and "The medium is the message." Even earlier, Harold Innis, also a trail-breaker, was puzzling through the de-centring implications of the new communications technology. Novelist Robert Kroetsch has argued that Canadian literature skipped the modernist period of all other literature, going straight from the Victorian to the postmodern.(Kroetsch was co-editor of the first North American magazine to use the term in its title, *A Journal of Postmodern Literature,* first published in 1972.)

When I titled the November 1994 lecture at Brock University "Canada as the First Postmodern Nation," I thought I was being daring, even better, original. Later research led me back to Fulford, then sideways towards quite a few others who'd been following the same trail. In his 1992 book, *A Tremendous Canada of Light,* critic and essayist Bruce Powe writes of Canada as "the first country in the post-industrial economy to be more a state in process than a nation-state." Powe concludes, as is about as postmodern as you can get that, "Canada's very impossibility is its hope and its possibility." The same year, Stephen Schecter, a Quebec political scientist, in his book *Zen and the Art of Post-Modern Canada,* described this country as "a society with no over-arching ethic . . . the first state that will do something about its post-modernity." In *Lost in North America,* playwright John Gray writes that "We may have found ourselves at the leading edge of a very large human experiment, charting new territory as model citizens of the Global Village." Lastly, in his 1993 book, *Post-National Arguments,* critic and poet Frank Davey analyses sixteen major works of Canadian fiction published since 1967, and concludes, "What this array of post-Centennial Canadian fiction appears most strongly to announce is the arrival of the post-national state – a state invisible to its own citizens, indistinguishable from its fellows, maintained by invisible political forces and significant mainly through its position within the grid of world-class cities . . . collectively, they suggest a world and nation in which social structures no longer link communities or regions, political process is doubted, and individual alienation has become normal."

The common denominators these commentators detect between postmodernism and contemporary Canada are those of impermanence, mutability, plasticity, and fragility. Canada is no longer a nation-state but a postmodern something. Canadians are "charting new territory" without knowing what or where it is. The United States is of course proceeding similarly, but less confusedly than Canada, and thereby still behaving more in a modern rather than postmodern manner, because Americans are marked indelibly by their Americanness while to be a Canadian can now mean just about anything.

Postmodern isn't the only way to describe our circumstances. Political scientist and author Stephen Clarkson applies the term "post-sovereign state" to Canada and to other comparable countries. Japanese economic analyst Kenichi Ohmae uses the term "post-national regional state" to describe the condition of countries midway between being old-style nation-states and futuristic global ones. The late critic George Woodcock called Canada an "anti-nation." British historian David Cannadine calls us "a nation-less state." Most piquantly, Mexican-American writer Richard Rodriguez calls Canada, "The world's largest country that doesn't exist."

Because our de-centring is now as much cultural as geographic and political, postmodern fits our condition better than any other term. We may finally arrive at the long-sought Holy Grail of our national identity by discovering that, uniquely in the world, we have an identity that is impermanent, mutable, plastic, fragile, and both opaque and transparent. That's to say, anything and everything.

There's another reason why we should apply the label post-modern to ourselves. While Canadians are known to be uncommonly good at civility and tolerance, what we really shine at is talking. We are a society that communicates with itself, endlessly, repetitively, discursively, doggedly, and with inexhaustible good-will. It's said that on arriving at the Pearly Gates, all Canadians automatically follow the sign pointing to "Seminar on Heaven and Hell." Canadian public discourse is a never-ending Couchiching Conference, and like that annual event, our debates never end in any conclusions (which would be confrontational).

All inventions and innovations in communications happen first in the United States. But they cross the border almost instantly. We're the most heavily cabled country in the world, and the most compulsive makers of long distance telephone calls. The first pilot projects in what's now called "transactional TV" or "on-demand video" were done here in the 1970s, in the more prosaic form of pay TV. New Brunswick's fibre optic network is one of the most advanced in the world. The world's first wired community has been built at Blackburg, Virginia. An equivalent, with all the homes on-line to the Internet, will open soon in Orangeville, Ontario. It's no coincidence that McLuhan was Canadian nor that his student, Derrick de Kerckhove, has just published a new analysis of the electronic age, *The Skin of Culture*.

One theory now popular – with House Speaker Newt Gingrich among others – is that we're on the cusp of a new era in human history, or are already into it. The creed's authors, Alvin and Heidi Toffler, call it the Third Wave of the Information Age. The first wave happened when humans discovered the techniques of culti-vation, liberating themselves from the hardships of life as hunter-gatherers. The second arrived when humans discovered how to

trap the power of steam, liberating themselves from the unvary-
ing cycle of agricultural life and projecting themselves into an
extraordinary era of endless, industrial progress. Now, because of
telecommunications and computers, we're about to be sub-
merged by a third wave, "a quantum leap forward" in which the
centralized, standardized society of the industrial age will be de-
massified, de-centred, de-synchronized. According to the Tofflers,
the political consequences will be the replacement of majority
rule by "minority-based democracy," of representative government by "semi-direct democracy" (by way of electronic
plebiscites), and of the application of the new rule of "decision
division" or of decision-making being devolved from the centre to
the states, communities, and individuals. Gingrich buys almost all
of this. He isn't just out to cut back government, he explains, he's
out to create a new "future-conscious politics."

It's hard to separate the practical exigencies shaping many contemporary events, like the debt and deficit, from the Tofflers' and
Gingrich's blue-sky generalities. The Internet's potential is truly
revolutionary: It can bring people face-to-face, right across continents, liberating them from the reach of all authorities, in the way
that automobiles and paved roads first did. Despite the potential
and the hype, the Internet isn't yet used as much more than a
sophisticated and cheap form of telegraphy – "CB radio with
typing" as it's been called – for pornography (alt.sex.spanking)
and for cranky messages like those from militia members urging,
"Bury your guns and use the codes" after the Oklahoma City
bombing. The Internet is even encountering the practical con-
straint that as its usage (now about thirty million subscribers)
increases, its response time is slowing, at least temporarily. Simultaneously, the more individuals and businesses use it to publicize
their wares, the longer it takes to find anything worthwhile.

Clearly, though, our communications condition is qualitatively
different from that of any earlier society. Sales of computers now

top those of TV sets. By the year 2000, laptop computers will cost less than a bicycle. Enthusiasts, like *Wired* magazine's Nicholas Negroponte, proclaim that "computing is not about computers any more. It's about life."

Soon, the five-hundred-channel TV universe will engulf us. We'll all be able to "cocoon" as we watch videos on our TV screens or receive E-mail messages on our computer screens (the two screens, eventually, becoming one). As replacements for our neighbourhoods and communities, some of us are already becoming part-time citizens of "virtual communities," forming bonds with other virtual citizens in San Francisco, London, Sydney, Tokyo, Hong Kong. Many of us will be able to work from our homes, "commuting" to the office by fax and modem. Many more will be able to shop from our homes; in the United States, in-home shopping is estimated to be a $5-billion industry by the year 2000.

Some of this may in fact never happen. All those VCRs blinking endlessly "00.00" confirm that much that can work perfectly well is unworkable. A survey by Anderson Consulting found little interest among Canadians in home shopping and on-demand videos: Only electronic education achieved a high rating. A major appeal of Internet E-mail (cost aside) is that it is anonymous: users can change their sex, status, ethnicity, and colour. That's also its great defect. Communicating by typing in real time is a sterile substitute for actually talking to someone else. Telecommunications is about transmitting information. Real communications is about connecting directly with other human beings, by trial and error, amid hurt and delight. As for the endlessly touted information superhighway, global media magnate Rupert Murdoch, who ought to know, says that even in North America and Europe it's still the better part of two decades away.

Nevertheless, much of all of this *will* happen – and already is happening. One of the reasons why companies have been able to de-layer their middle management is because they've at last figured out how to restructure themselves around the computer rather than using it as a kind of super-typewriter. Hence the unnerving phrase "virtual corporations." The Information Era destabilizes all the old structures because the only asset that matters now is knowledge rather than, as in the Industrial Era, factories, machinery, loyal workforces. Negroponte was getting carried away in proclaiming that computing is "about life." But he was being astute in observing that "an entire segment of the population will feel disenfranchised," not only the semi-skilled as they watch the technologically educated soaring off into cyberspace but also the middle-aged computer illiterates watching ten-year-olds communicate across continents. Israeli scholar Elihu Katz has warned of "the vanishing of public space" as more people turn away from neighbourhood, community, and nation to their TV and computer screens; with so many churches now empty, what collective social experiences remain other than sporting events?

While it's easy to assume that the Tofflers, Gingrich, Negroponte, de Kerckhove, and all the other techno-groupies are widely exaggerating the capacity of black boxes to actually change individual and societal behaviour, let alone to solve all our economic, social, and cultural problems, these futurists do possess one shining quality. They are all optimists. At a time when scepticism, cynicism, and pessimism about the present and future are more prevalent than they've been in decades, these techno-groupies are the last believers in the Victorians defining presumption of the possibility of human progress.

All of this is going to affect many peoples other than Canadians. But much will happen more directly to us than to anyone else, even Americans. In a five-hundred-channel TV universe, Canadian signals will fade to the margin, like Canadian magazines on today's newsstands. Our telephone companies have had to reorganize themselves on American lines because intercontinental calls can so easily be first routed southwards and then east or west to take advantage of the cheapest rates. The Internet, although nominally global, is an American system in design and style; certainly, the Canadians who surf it aren't doing so only to communicate with other Canadians. Canadians sense this: In the Anderson survey, a remarkable 62 per cent expressed a fear of the impact of the Information Superhighway upon the Canadian identity.

In an essay titled "As Canadian as Possible . . . Under the Circumstances" after the famous winning entry in a "This Country in the Morning" competition, Linda Hutcheon describes postmodernism as "questioning any notion of coherent, stable, autonomous identity (be it individual or national)." That's about as good a description of contemporary Canada as it's possible to get – under the circumstances.

Hutcheon quotes poet Al Purdy as having written that "Certainty of nationality and personality is an illusion since there is no permanence in anything, anything at all." Purdy continues, though, "Yet we cling to this shifting and uncertain self, this rag of aging bone, this handful of dust, to which we've given a loved name."

Truly, we have arrived at some kind of historical discontinuity, some radical break from our earlier evolution. What will individual physical identity mean when after today's cosmetic surgery comes the genetic engineering of tomorrow? What will human intelligence mean when computers become intelligent? To return to the theme of this book, what will happen in a virtual, interconnected world to a nation-state to which we've given "a loved name," and that, anyway, is the only one we've got? Either we reinvent it, or we watch it unravel.

15

A Reinvention Agenda, Part One

"Our hope lay in our belief that in the northern half of this continent we could build a country which had a stronger sense of the common good and of public order than was possible under the individualism of the capitalist dream."

— George Grant, *Lament for a Nation*, 1965

A state-nation rather than a nation-state. A nationless-state. A post-sovereignty state. A postmodern one. Benedict Anderson's evocative term "imagined community" fits us better than any of these. But he applies it to most nation-states and nation-peoples. The quality that makes us truly one of a kind is that we are an *invented* community.

Rather than being a political entity constructed out of the conventional building materials of ethnicity and history, these themselves being as much imagined as real, we are our own creation. We exist because we willed ourselves into existence behind the fragile walls of lines drawn arbitrarily across the continental map and, back then, because of a certain monarchical sentiment, and, even more, a fear of mob rule. We continue to exist because we continue to will our existence. Most nation-states *are*. We are always *becoming*. We are doomed forever to have to reinvent our community.

Our community is at risk now of being disinvented – of being deconstructed, to use that fancy postmodernist term. External forces are pulling us apart. So are internal ones. We can't halt the former at our borders; we can at least try to understand their nature, and, within the limits of the possible, temper them. As for the internal forces fissuring our community, the choice is entirely our own whether we allow them to continue to pull us apart. To be a Canadian is to be unbearably light, in terms of identity and nationality. So we have to be lightfooted, and supple and quick.

Of the new forces, the most important by far is the conjoined effect of the global economy and financial system and of technology, all interacting with the prevailing dominance of neo-conservative, free-market ideology. As winds running contrary to the old wisdom of the paternalist provider-state, some of these forces have been liberating and constructive. The neo-conservatives have energized contemporary political debate. They have challenged encrusted assumptions and they have exposed quite a few hypocrisies. They have dared to talk about social and moral responsibilities as liberal democrats long ago lost the nerve to do. But when neo-conservatives read out the lesson that Canada should transform itself into a sort of northern Hong Kong, they are being absurd – except to the extent they serve their own self-interest.

Thatcher's comment that "There is no such thing as society" may have been terribly prophetic. If the 1970s were about the self-indulgent "me" and the 1980s were about greed, the 1990s may be about the existential I, alone in the jungle.

Canada's nature is not that of an "I" nation, though. As individuals each of us is of course egocentric, as is the human condition, most particularly the North American condition. But the raw materials out of which we have invented our community have been those of a rough and ready egalitarianism combined with an animating liberalism (in its reformist sense). These are our sustaining myths. They are our substitutes for the conventional commonalities of ethnicity and history. We are a political community, not a sociological one.

This is the source of the central, otherwise inexplicable, difference between Canadians and Americans. We read the same books and magazines, watch the same films and TV, correspond as much on the Internet, work at the same kind of jobs: we both go south during the winters to Florida or Hawaii.

Yet Canadians and Americans are quite different people. Neither is better; each is what they are. Moreover, it isn't just anglophones and francophones who, out of their historical experiences, have worked out by trial and error a value system that makes them North Americans in a distinctively un-American way. "New" Canadians claim they can spot other "hyphenated-Canadians" at international ethnic conferences, perhaps by a greater diffidence, a greater readiness to listen to others, even by a proclivity for apologizing when someone steps on their foot.

We have invented a different kind of North American community. In some part, the source of this distinctiveness is just northernness. A good part resides in the now deeply rooted Canadian sensibility. Unlike Americans, foreordained to be individualistic and competitive, the Canadian community is inherently collectivist, egalitarian, and liberal, or Red Tory, or social democrat. Our core ethic is that everyone should be included fully in the community by the community itself rather being required (also being challenged, it must be added) to hack out their own space in the jungle.

The universality in Canada's social programs and the program of equalization are expressions of this ethic. So also is our commitment to national bilingualism, to self-government for native people, and to official multiculturalism. Our Constitution encompasses a Charter of Rights that is the most liberal and pluralist in the world, if also the most politically correct. In parallel, the magnitude of our immigration program and the generosity of our refugee program, along with the leading role we once played in helping to end apartheid in South Africa, and our contributions to peacekeeping, extend our ethic outwards.

Our community is no longer simply our creation. We have become it, and we are perceived by others to embody it. If we ceased to be a community, others would notice and would regret the passing of a distinctive idea about how different people can live together.

Some qualifications to our uniqueness must be stated. It's been easy for us to be nice to others because we have no external enemies and few international responsibilities except those we choose voluntarily to exercise. A fair part of the agreeableness of the habits and attitudes towards each other developed by the Canadian community have been the by-product of effortlessly acquired surplus resource wealth. That's over now. Barring a prolonged global boom, we will remain, at best, roughly where we now are for quite some time, even as we have to run a lot harder to hold our present position.

There's also the fact that it's been only comparatively recently – the near half-decade since the enactment of free trade – that we've had to adjust ourselves to the harsher realities of the global marketplace. Still, we're showing more political and personal resilience than we tend to give ourselves credit for. Politically, many of today's populist proposals for new forms of direct democracy, like referendums and recall of MPs, were part of the Reform platform long before the Republicans drafted their Contract with America. Paul Martin's comprehensive attack on the deficit in his February 1995 budget preceded the proposals still being debated in the Senate and House of Representatives.

At the level of the personal, the national mood today can perhaps be described best as unsentimental. Topics once off-limits in public debate – immigration, multiculturalism, welfare, and a rejection of any special deals to satisfy Quebec – are discussed candidly, and no longer only in living rooms and taverns. Canadians are no longer in awe of those in authority over them.

Survivalist may be an even better descriptive term. As noted earlier, since 1990 a great many Canadians have had to contend with the ultimate personal challenges of unemployment, personal bankruptcy, sharp contractions in their incomes. They've come through, most of them, after learning to cope in ways they haven't used, nor have needed to use, in decades. Indeed, to the ever-increasing number who are self-employed in one way or another, the old provider state looks like an antique. To many young Canadians, well aware they are going to have to both provide for themselves and pay off the bills piled up by earlier generations, the old provider state has turned into a succubus state.

The challenge that now confronts us is to match this survivalist and unsentimental temper with the traditions that shaped this country. Unless we can match temper and tradition it becomes an open question, not just whether the community can be preserved but whether it is worth preserving at all. Without our ethic of egalitarianism and our sense of collectivism, we will become simply a poorer version of the United States. Once akin to them, we would have no reason not to become them. Indeed, if Canada did join the United States – were allowed to join – most Canadians would benefit considerably economically. In terms of purchasing power, the cross-border gap is about 20 per cent. All Canadians thus could make themselves one-fifth richer by exchanging their blue passport for a green one. If Canadian neo-conservatives were logical rather than ideological, they would be calling for Canada to become America rather than merely for it to become Americanized.

Although it quite often comes up into private conversations, this existential issue has so far intruded into the Canadian public debate only at its outer margins. Occasionally, public figures attempt to raise the topic indirectly: Saskatchewan Premier Roy Romanow's call for a national debate about "core values" as an example, and Reform Leader Preston Manning's call for a national debate about how to sustain medicare by picking and choosing treatments to be included and excluded. Paul Martin's minting of the phrase "nationalism without walls" reveals an awareness of the urgency of the issue.

Instead, the greater part of our mental energy has been directed at national unity and deficit reduction. These are over-arching concerns all right. The first, though, will be settled almost entirely by Quebeckers themselves. The second has been miscast. It's an issue about means, not about ends. Deficits do have to be reduced, drastically. What matters, though, is the nature of the society after the deficit has been eliminated.

What follows are some thoughts on this topic. Whether or not they are valid, they at least derive from a particular perspective.

Their starting point is the conviction that no community can continue to be a true community if it allows itself to polarize into two economic nations. The binding glue of mutual interdependence, of a sense of "reciprocal obligations," in Christopher Lasch's phrase, will evaporate. Without that glue there is, indeed, "no such thing as society." We could become the national equivalent of a condominium apartment building in which owners and tenants greet each other politely and warmly, and periodically deal sensibly with common practical concerns like maintenance and landscaping, but have no sense of belonging to an enterprise with values and purposes larger than their individual self-interests.

At its end point, the perspective assumes that multiplying the polarizing effects upon us of contemporary economic forces by constructing new cultural walls will make it certain that no communal sense of reciprocal obligations can remain, nor, sooner or later, any community.

The balance of this chapter will address the economic issues. The succeeding one will try to confront our cultural challenges.

In recent years, we've discussed at great length, and often passionately, economic issues like the deficit, free trade, deregulation and privatization, government downsizing, the market economy. We've said scarcely a word about the kind of society that is likely to emerge once all these programs and policies have been implemented – other than to assume, or to cling to the belief, that, magically, a whole lot more money will appear. Not since the 1990 *Good Jobs, Bad Jobs* study by the Economic Council of Canada has there been a serious analysis of the probability that we are dividing ourselves into two Disraelian nations.

Instead of examining what may be happening to us, we are, to a considerable degree, in a state of denial about it. Studies about the extent of income polarization look at the immediate past rather than at the future. It took an American economist, Edward Wolff, to point out that we've accepted passively ever-growing disparities in wealth, principally by taxing wealth far less than is done in the United States, even less than Switzerland.

One reason for our complacency is that we know we've come through the shocks of deep recession and of restructuring with our incomes still decidedly more equal than those in the United States. Endlessly comparing ourselves to the United States to our own self-advantage may be like proclaiming that all is still well as we fall past the fourteenth floor. Indeed, if the socio-politics of the 21st century are going to be about income inequalities, the United States may be in better shape to cope with this kind of future than ourselves. Americans believe in the marketplace, and accept that personal failure in it is their own fault. We've always assumed we would be looked after; once out in the cold we may more easily get frostbite and certainly will be quicker to blame others for it.

While we've survived the first shocks, many more are yet to come. Our social safety nets are shrinking. The effect of this upon our income distribution has been masked because so many thousands of workers have retired early on modest or better pensions. As well, many tens of thousands of young people are still "hiding" in schools and colleges and universities. The very government deficits now being eliminated are sustaining our economic activity to a greater degree than is realized – one that won't be appreciated until all the deficits are gone.

The really important statistics are those about *employment* inequalities rather than those about *income* inequalities. External forces are transforming us inexorably into two categories of people, one made up of high-paid, internationalist knowledge workers, the other of economic gypsies who make their way through life by way of part-time and short-term jobs and contracts, sometimes self-employment, sometimes moonlighting. The net incomes of most of these gypsies will be reduced further by their having to pay for their own sickness benefits, vacations, life insurance, dental plans, pensions.

It isn't necessary to get quite as paranoid as Michael Lind, who argues in *The Next American Nation* that the United States "is being renovated as a New Honduras or a new Belize," and that "Homogeneous and nomadic, the overclass is the first truly national upper class in American history." He does make the very shrewd point that "The American ruling class spares no pains in promoting the belief that it does not exist" and that the claim that exceptional financial rewards are justified is largely specious since it's not "multi-lingual physicists" who are becoming spectacularly wealthy but members of the traditional élite of "bond traders, corporate vice-presidents and partners in law firms" who've learned the new global tricks.

It's not paranoid at all to observe that the free market and the global market and unconstrained capitalism all lead inevitably to income polarization. That income gaps in China and in Russia are wider today than they were before the communists took power in those countries can be put down to the necessary raggedness of early, Wild West capitalism. Nevertheless, in countries like China, Vietnam, North Korea, no doubt soon Cuba, communism's last historical function has become to provide capitalists with a docile proletariat to exploit.

What cannot be dismissed is that in the world's most advanced market-oriented nations, the United States and Britain, income gaps are now wider than at any time in the last half-century. The same widening of income gaps is happening globally despite all the chatter about how the global economy will diffuse wealth. In 1960, the richest 20 per cent in the world received incomes thirty times those of the poorest one-fifth; today they receive sixty times. Only those ignorant of history, or spectacularly self-interested, would argue that unconstrained global capitalism, unless headed off, is headed anywhere other than back to the future of ten-year-olds in mines and of robber-baron-style wealth.

We have entered the era of postmodern capitalism. It has taken the place of the postwar era of state capitalism, in which all Western societies were structured around a triad of government, business, and unions. Now that the nation-states that once contained them and nurtured them have become porous, unions are on their way to vanishing. Governments are fast-losing their ability, also their nerve, to mitigate the polarizing effects of the marketplace. This leaves corporations, above all transnational ones, free to reshape the world to suit their convenience. About these institutions, there are two cardinal characteristics. They are unaccountable, unlike governments. Their single operating principle or value is, in Eric Kierans's phrase "accumulation."

If in the cultural sense we are nearer to being postmodern than any other country, we are still a comparative laggard when it comes to postmodern capitalism. Unions here, while far weaker than in the past, are still stronger comparatively than those in the United States, representing 18 per cent of the non-public labour force (in fact, the lowest percentage since the 1930s) as against 11 per cent there. Our capitalists aren't as vocal as those south of the border, not least because so many can speak only as echoes of their American owners. Canadian neo-conservatives are braggartly noisy these days, yet remain inhibited by a curious sense of political illegitimacy that reveals itself in their endless whining about the "liberal media." Most importantly, our governments are still supported by our tradition of being a state-nation rather than a nation-state; indeed, with entertainment and sports now so

Americanized, politics – and the arts – remain our only real source of national heroes, and of villains.

Increasingly, though, we are different from others, most particularly the United States, in degree rather than in kind. As nation-states lose their ability to protect their own citizens and as corporations become more non-national and hence more unaccountable, capitalism is everywhere returning to the conditions of its early years. Despite Nobel economics laureate Wassily Leontief's foreboding, human beings aren't really likely to become as irrelevant to the production process as are horses to modern agriculture. There's no question, though, that an ever-growing number of citizens in developed countries are now at risk of becoming as marginalized economically as the greater part of the work forces in Third World countries have always been.

From out of all this angst, fear, and unease, the neo-conservatives have emerged with a clear, comprehensible, formula for economic success: "Government bad; market infallible." To return to a point made previously, the great appeal of this formula is that it *is* clear, simple, and self-confident. Its core concept, once the attractive wrappings about individualism and self-reliance have been removed, is that of trickle-down economics: Income redistribution by way of the marketplace rather than by government.

It's hard to believe that those who proclaim this theory actually believe in it. Even the *Wall Street Journal* has commented uneasily about the number of wealthy Americans who've opted to become citizens (non-tax paying ones) of places like the Turks and Caicos and Belize. Similarly, an ever-increasing number of Canadians are transferring their assets abroad. Those still at home are ridding themselves of the old egalitarian tic. Pay packages at the top are the largest ever: The new all-time Canadian record of $32 million set in 1992 by Peter Munk of Barrick Resources has been topped since by the $41 million of Magna's Frank Stronach in 1994.

It's only comparatively recently, however, that neo-conservatism has set the agenda in the United States and Canada. As David Frum describes – censoriously – in *Dead Right*, Ronald Reagan talked a good neo-conservative game but was really a softie ex-New Dealer. In Britain, though, neo-conservatism as a serious political creed dates all the way back to Thatcher's victory in 1979. What is telling is that having entered the future first, many British neo-cons have now started blinking.

In a report, *Civic Conservatism*, published in the summer of 1994, David Willets, once a key intellectual adviser to Margaret Thatcher and now an MP, expresses his "deepest fear about the direction our country is taking." This was that "somehow, we are becoming worse people – more self-centred, more aggressive, less civil, less willing to give time and effort to any cause greater than ourselves."

Here, Willets is touching on a cardinal characteristic of the effect of free-market economics upon contemporary societies. In legitimizing individualism it legitimizes selfishness. It also delegitimizes any sense of social responsibility. Hence the change in the face of the politics of paranoia. Once, this manifested itself on the left, among members of the peace movements, the environmental movement and the feminist and anti-racists movements, all of whom were convinced the élite was excluding them. Paranoia has now become a manifestation of the right, expressing itself in the anti-tax, right-wing populist, white-male backlash against the liberal provider state, in the extreme by the formation of militias. The critical new element is that of violence. While the old movements of the left sought to change society, those of the right seek to demolish society.

Another example of British neo-conservative revisionism is contained in John Gray's 1994 book, *Beyond the New Right*. Gray expresses his worry that all of the "civilizing connecting chords" within community and of extended family obligations are fraying away. Most tellingly, Gray quotes the philosopher Ludwig

Wittgenstein: "Trying to repair a broken tradition is like trying to mend a broken spider's web."

Besides denying human nature – essentially, finder's keepers – the neo-conservative trickle-down formula denies history. Capitalism without government is like a one-wheeled bicycle. On its own, it's certain to crash. As Marx pointed out, capitalism's inherent contradiction is that accumulation by the few pauperizes the very consumers whom corporations depend on to purchase their goods. Indeed, it's a safe bet that just about the time deficits get eliminated, corporate leaders will pick up a new song sheet and begin demanding that governments exercise their social responsibilities by pumping money into the pockets of consumers so they can again buy the available products.

Nevertheless, until some unknown economist puzzles his or her way towards a new Keynesian paradigm, the neo-conservative market ideology is going to dominate our politics, not least because liberal democrats have as yet lacked the imagination to do more than cling to the past.

Chapter Six advanced some suggestions for how we might at least slow our fracturing into two economic nations. Work-sharing has to be worth a serious study: Unless the marketplace, in a departure from all historical experience, creates enough jobs spontaneously, the only alternative to work-sharing is a guaranteed annual income system, or lifelong welfare. New forms of partnership between governments and public institutions and the voluntary or "social sector" are a necessity. As necessary is a systematic review of our educational programs: These are the second most expensive in the world; they most certainly are not the second best.

Only one suggestion really matters. We must do what we have to do: Reduce the deficit in order to remove ourselves from the computer screens of the "stateless legislators" and also reinvent government in order to make it lean and keen. But we should not do too much. The traditions we break may be irreparable. Subsequent legislation can always summon dismantled institutions back into existence, but their institutional memory and spirit will have vanished. If by ideology and specific government action we legitimize inequality and delegitimize our public institutions, we risk destroying the Canadian spirit beyond recall.

One other proposal in that chapter is as important, but much harder, for Canada to act on. "The fates of all democratic capitalist states are dependent upon how well we collectively civilize stateless money with a new international concept of world monetary rules, norms and policy actions," declares Steven Solomon in his 1995 book about international finance, *The Confidence Game*. Chrétien tried to raise the topic at the G-7 meeting in Halifax in June 1995, but his own voice was too small. In the end, if nation-states can no longer regulate international finance, they themselves no longer have a purpose. Indeed, some observers are calling for a single international currency and monetary system.

In the ether beyond national boundaries, though, democracy vanishes. So does accountability. Nation-state governments are the only institutions that can curb the inherent excesses of global capitalism and thereby prevent the old oppression of state bureaucracies being replaced by a new tyranny of corporate apparatchiks. It is only nation-state governments that can save capitalism from self-destruction as it proceeds mindlessly towards accumulation as a self-justifying end.

Here, one last useful comment can be made about the nature of our present condition. Once the realization takes hold that income gaps are going to widen inexorably from now on and that evermore workers are going to be marginalized permanently, an explosion of populist outrage is bound to happen. The stepchild of today's in-your-face economics is bound to be in-your-face politics.

This anger is going to be directed at corporate leaders and against global capitalism itself rather than against today's "soft" targets of bureaucrats and mainstream politicians. The realization that the promised land of the neo-conservatives is, largely, a wasteland, will provoke a political outburst that will be far angrier, and more violent, than today's often grumpy rejection of the provider state. If, at that time, nation-states are unable to summon up the energy and political will to re-enter the political centre as the only institutions that can save global capitalism from itself, and their own societies from political turmoil, they will condemn themselves to history's graveyard.

One thing is certain: If Canada divides into two economic nations, we ourselves will not long survive as a nation-state. The breaking of our social contract would release Canadians from their loyalties to their community. Unless its citizens believe they belong to a more or less egalitarian community, their loyalty to it will ebb inexorably away. Unlike Ireland, Portugal, or Denmark, say, we are not a "natural" nation. If these countries – even Britain and France – eventually become no more than provinces within a federal Europe, their memory and spirit will still endure, just as it has in Catalonia within Spain, or Scotland within Great Britain. The United States, as an idea nation, possesses the stuff of permanence.

As an invented nation, either we reinvent our traditions of egalitarianism and liberalism to accommodate the realities of today's global economy or, some year, some decade, we will simply fade away – either to become a northern echo-image of the United States or to become a region within it, like a kind of more northerly New England.

This is our primary challenge. Compared to it, all others are secondary. Complicating it significantly, though, is that even as our external walls have vanished, new walls have sprung up within our own community.

16

A Reinvention Agenda,
Part Two

"Have we survived?
"If so, what happens after survival?"

— Margaret Atwood, *Survival*, 1972

Geography, of which we have "too much" as William Lyon
Mackenzie King once observed in one of his rare soundbites, has
always ensured that Canadian identity would be as much, or
more, local than national. The Rockies, the Canadian Shield, the
upthrust of Maine, the straits of Cabot and Northumberland,
keep most of us at a distance from one another. The central
Canadian conspiracy Westerners forever rail against is mostly the
product of geography: Ontarians and Quebeckers, clustered
together with no physical barrier between them, can easily con-
spire to do so in the Prairies and British Columbia. The feature-
less character of the continent itself, delineated on an East–West
axis only by a relatively short stretch along the Great Lakes and St.
Lawrence, turns our gaze away from ourselves, and southwards,
where it's warmer. Nevertheless, we fashioned a national community and a national market from out of our unpromising portion
of the North American landscape.

The nature of geography's grip upon us is different now. It's
pulling us right out of ourselves. The Canadian national market

has become a subdivision – more exactly, five of them – within the continental economy. Canadian industries, wherever located, function as production centres for the global economy rather than for whatever remains of the domestic market.

At the same time as Canadians are having less to do with each other economically, our government, the foundation of our distinctive political construct as a state-nation, is less able to provide for Canadians economically, socially, culturally. Our national government will always be around. Together with the provinces, it accounts for 45 per cent of the GNP. Once deficits are shrunk down to a bearable size, governments may again dare to be innovative. At a guess, they will first turn their attention to trying to help young people, the group hardest hit of all by the current socio-economic changes. As for government itself, reinventing bureaucracy needn't only be a euphemism for downsizing it: A skilfully reinvented bureaucracy really can do more with less.

Government, though, will no longer be there for Canadians in the way it has been through the lifetime of almost every Canadian adult. Outside of areas like foreign policy, defence, and trade, the responsibilities of the federal government may become increasingly symbolic rather than substantive: today's operating slogan of "think global, act local" doesn't leave much for a national centre to do. In the limit, the entire Ottawa apparatus may function increasingly like a kind of enlarged Governor Generalcy.

Canadians seem to have figured out instinctively that the purposes of their national government will become increasingly symbolic. Ekos Research found that, outside of Quebec, Canada itself rather than the provinces, or any ethnic or other subcommunities, is, excepting only the family, "the strongest source of belonging for the general public." Far more than is generally realized, most Canadians are Canadians first.

As for just what it is Canadians want to belong to, Ekos judged that "Humanistic and idealistic values top the list of the preferred government values among the Canadian public, while the more economic-material issues are placed much lower in their hierarchy." Because of the very absence of walls around us, Canadians want their government to establish moral and cultural bulwarks that will define us as a distinct society. This sense of the symbolic value of our nationality is distinctively Canadian, quite probably is uniquely Canadian.

Sustaining this kind of idea-state is of course exceedingly difficult to do without external walls. We lack the raw power of that other idea-state, the United States, to command the global tides to every now and then stop. Simultaneously, our commitment to "humanistic and idealistic values" is going to be tested to the limit by the polarizing impact upon incomes and jobs caused by today's global and technological forces. People who are themselves struggling as self-reliant survivalists can reach out only so far to others in difficulty.

Our values are also being tested from within. The more our various subcommunities remove themselves from the general community by insisting on dictating the terms of their citizenship, the less other Canadians will be inclined to share with them or to care about them. By granting a kind of licence to groups to do this – so seldom challenging their demands for rights without asking for an offsetting commitment to the community as a whole – we have added a whole new set of internal cultural walls.

The attempt by Quebec nationalists to build a wall between themselves and other Canadians isn't new of course. What is new is that few Canadians now care much about this threat. To oversimplify, but not by much, few outside Quebec feel any need or urge to do anything except wait for the phone call: "We've voted and we're In/Out."

Barring a dramatic turnaround towards sovereignty in the polls – quite possibly not even then – this attitude isn't likely to change in advance of the referendum. In many ways, though, other Canadians have been getting off too lightly. Circumstances seem to justify our making scarcely any contribution to the preservation of our community other than to shut up.

As suggested in Chapter Seven, we could contribute by being generous. One possibility would be to offer to recognize Quebec as a distinct society in the preamble to the Constitution. This would represent a symbolic recognition of Quebec's self-evident distinctiveness, but one with no political and legal implications. Jacques Parizeau would of course refuse any such offer contemptuously. Ordinary Quebeckers, though, would know that it had been made. Symbols do matter.

The hard truth is that symbols are about all that's available to Quebec now. Nationalist and sovereigntist leaders have misled Quebeckers into believing that their wholly legitimate anxieties as a minority can be exorcised by obtaining *something* – distinct society, special status, sovereignty-association – from the rest of Canada. This has always been an illusion. As soon as Quebec became special or distinct legally, Quebeckers would become less than equal politically at Ottawa. In any imaginable sovereignty-association they would be minor partners, and largely powerless ones. Nor can outright independence alter demographic reality: As soon as alone, Quebeckers would be totally alone in an Anglo-Saxon continental sea.

Only Quebeckers themselves can assuage, even if never entirely escape, their anxieties. In their quite different ways, Pierre Trudeau and René Lévesque understood this. Trudeau went to Ottawa and showed that a francophone could best, easily, the best that the rest of the country could put up against him. Lévesque stayed home, and by nationalizing the power companies and creating Hydro-Quebec, showed that Quebeckers could run and manage huge enterprises as well as any anglophones or Americans. This kind of assertive self-confidence rather than a retreat into the convolutions of sovereignty-association is, surely, what Quebec needs now.

A symbolic "distinct society" offer by the rest of the country would be only a gesture. But it would be a gesture of welcome, and of respect. It might also – who knows? – lower the wall between anglophones and francophones.

The wall going up between native people and other Canadians is similarly new only in the sense that it is now native people who are building it themselves, and with far greater self-confidence, and much higher, than before. We ourselves built the previous wall – around their reserves.

In any consideration of native affairs, the moral bottom-line is clear. No matter how many mistakes they may make in their self-governing territories, it is impossible for Indians and Inuit to do more harm to themselves than we have done to them.

As remarked in Chapter Thirteen, though, it would be a mistake of a different kind for self-government to be built on the illusion that this is self-government in any sense comparable to the kind achieved by a people after exercising their right to self-determination. What's called "self-government" is really self-administration, and should have been so described during all the guilt-ridden constitutional negotiations.

We have deceived native people about the possible, and the real. History cannot be rewritten. Centuries of inexorable, osmotic assimilation cannot be undone. Natives do have a special sense of themselves, a distinctive ancestry, a special relationship to the land and to all the animate creatures and creations on it. But they are Canadians now. While it is right to recall the assimilationist wrongs done to them in the old residential schools, it would be foolish not to recognize the integrative effects of the ever-increasing numbers of native people – more than twenty-two thousand today – now enrolled in universities and colleges.

As Canadians, even if self-administering ones because of their unique culture and history, native people must abide by the same rules as bind all other Canadians – all relevant federal and provincial laws and the Charter of Rights and Freedoms. As important, for self-administration itself to be real, native governments must tax their own people. To continue to rely principally on funds from outside, as many native communities wish to do, is unrealistic; it's also a decision to remain dependent on outsiders.

In any case, the supply of outside funds is nearing its limit. It's bound to fall behind the curve of the rapid population growth of native people. As a warning sign, during the mid-1995 election in Saskatchewan, the Conservatives proposed for the first time an end to the tax-free status of Indians on reserves.

As relevant to the future that awaits native people is that the moral debt to them is owed by anglophones and francophones. As the numbers of these "old" Canadians dwindle proportionately, so will the political will to continue cancelling that debt financially. To many among the ever-growing number of newcomers, the native issue, like those of national unity and of East versus West, is yesterday's issue.

The walls being built between Canadians by all the "identity" groups as they claim separate entitlements to dictate the terms of their Canadian citizenship are entirely new.

The specific policies involved are those of multiculturalism and employment equity. Each is intended to make Canadian society more inclusive. Each institutionalizes new forms of exclusiveness.

The central fact about multiculturalism is that Canada *is* multicultural now, and multicoloured, and postmodern. Compared to this cardinal sociological fact, official multiculturalism is as much beside the point as would be a Multi-Religion Act and a Department of Multi-Religionism. One of our nation-building achievements was to separate church and state; we've now smudged it by conjoining state and race. Indeed, if the Baptist religion, say, can flourish here without its adherents demanding to be known as Baptist-Canadians, so can the Italian culture, say, continue to enrich the mosaic without it having to be hived off as Italian-Canadian.

The real reason for multiculturalism's obsolescence is that it assumes that our future is to be multicultural, multiracial, multicoloured. Instead, our future is likely to be – should be – crosscultural, cross-racial, cross-coloured: Eventually, we'll all be coffee-coloured. By treating differences of race, ethnicity, colour, as integral to identity rather than as manifestations of heritage, official multiculturalism encourages apartheid, or, to be a bit less harsh, ghettoism.

Which leads to a critical point. Quebec's policy of "cultural convergence" (the same one that applies in all European countries) is a far more imaginative and creative creed than the one in effect in the rest of the country. It means that newcomers should absorb the values, myths, and traditions of the society they've come to – voluntarily – even while contributing their cultural particularities to the larger society. Out of this can come multicultural synergy in contrast to the multiple monoculturalism produced by official multiculturalism.

A case in point is the kind of creative proposal advanced in the 1994 policy paper, *Euroislam or Ghettoislam*, by the Swedish diplomat Ingmar Karlsson. Karlsson calls for "The Islamic community in Europe [to] become a bridge between Europe and the immigrants' countries of origin . . . [by] transferring democratic approaches and liberal ideas to their native countries." Building Karlsson-style "bridges" – since adopted as official policy by the Swedish government – between multicultural groups and their "kin" back home (also between multicultural groups here that traditionally have been political and cultural rivals) would be a far more creative way of making Canada distinctive than our antique policy of official multiculturalism.

The same kinds of bridges need to be built between the old Canada and the rapidly emerging new Canada. Official multiculturalism makes it harder for the two Canadas to get together. It

makes the one defensive. It encourages the other to claim seemingly limitless entitlements. The consequence isn't multiculturalism: it's multiple monoculturalism.

A good way to begin moving across that bridge would be to
listen to some of the voices on the other side. One, quoted earlier,
was Devo-Jaiikoah Dyette's comment: "I am a Canadian first, who
happens by the luck of the draw to be black." Indeed, a fascinating feature of the *Star*'s "Diversities" column was the large
number of multicultural voices who used it to say they didn't like
multiculturalism. "Multiculturalism is the sharing of cultures. It
isn't about bottling up a culture and preserving a culture through
the colonization of city districts," writes Vinay Menon. "The vital
question is, 'In your heart, where's home?' Are you concerned
with Canadian issues? Do you exist in a cultural vacuum where
news from your country of origin always receives first priority?"

Of all the multicultural groups, black Canadians are of course
the most vulnerable to negative stereotyping and outright racism.
They are also the most divided psychically, pulled back towards
their ancestral homelands in Africa and towards the United States
where all the epochal experiences of the black diaspora have
occurred and, lastly, towards the curious country of Canada that
has welcomed them in, yet often keeps them at a distance. These
contradictions were addressed by André Alexis, a writer born in
Trinidad who came to Canada at the age of three, in an eloquent
essay in the May 1995 issue of *This Magazine*: "Canada is a place
that has been for the most part sung, danced and constantly re-
imagined by white Canadians." Alexis recalls the effect upon him
of reading Margaret Laurence's *The Stone Angel* in high school: "I
can yet recognize essential things: the earth, the sky, certain
people, the way they talk. . . . The feeling of recognition is all the
more vivid because I *don't* live in her version of our homeland."
He concluded, "I miss black Canadian writing that is conscious of
Canada, writing that speaks not just about situation or about the

earth but rather *from* the earth. After all, it is our country and it is our responsibility to add our voices to the white voices that are articulating Canada."

Alexis's essay merits being quoted at length because he employs phrases so seldom used in commentaries about multiculturalism: "our country," "our homeland," and, most rare, "our responsibility."

Ending official multiculturalism is, surely, the way to create a community within which everyone can refer uninhibitedly to "our country" and "our homeland," above all, can talk about "our responsibilit(ies)" to each other – even while all who are multicultured can retain as much of their cultural distinctiveness as they choose, no differently from Baptists or believers in any other religion or creed. It's the difference between being of a community and merely being in it.

Employment equity programs are entirely new. Even at their peak, they've never been that important. It's sheer guess how many – or how few – of the "designated groups" have actually gained jobs and promotions they would not have achieved on their own. Universities, although hyper-politically correct, have no enrolment equity programs. Yet more women (55 per cent) are students than "should be," and similarly racial minorities (23 per cent in contrast to their 14 per cent share of the population).

Alan Borovoy's argument that the purpose of these programs should be to "end future discrimination" rather than mete out punishment for the sins of the past, is surely the only point worth making. Well-conceived programs of information and education, stiffened by the stick of spot-checks of selected corporations and institutions with the results being well publicized, could achieve most of what needs to be achieved. "Merit" of course should be made an explicit criterion, as should poverty or unemployment, whether by members of the "privileged" class or by anybody else, be made a criterion for exemption. Programs founded on the ideological swamp of "historical disadvantage" were bound to sink from sight, as, in one way or another, they are doing now.

Immigration of course isn't a new program. Nor, in itself, is it in any way divisive.

Our present immigration policy is divisive though. By a combination of political opportunism and bureaucratic ineptness, it has evolved into a program structured to benefit principally immigrants themselves (more exactly, their relatives) rather than the community as a whole. Simultaneously, our current refugee program exploits Canadians' humanitarian instincts to operate what amounts to a parallel and largely unaccountable immigration program: Our rate of asylum claims in comparison to that of even ultraliberal countries like Denmark and Holland is inexplicable in any objective terms.

The issue here has nothing to do with numbers, demographics, or cost. It has to do with self-respect. A community too timorous to make choices about who is eligible to enter can no more protest undesirable consequences than a householder who randomly invites in passersby.

Even when multiculturalism, employment equity, and immigration are all combined, they are only of secondary socio-political importance. The relative proportion of immigrants within the population – about one in six – is no higher than during earlier postwar years (if a good deal higher when compared to the population's current birth rate). Official multiculturalism has been part of our landscape for a quarter-century, and its financial size is shrinking steadily.

New, though, is the increasing sense of entitlement by "identity groups," matched now by an increasing sense of disentitlement, even of disenfranchisement, by native-born Canadians or

English-speaking Canadians (a term used here to encompass the large numbers of those of other ethnic origins who have engaged in the "cultural convergence" of identifying themselves with English-Canadian values and myths).

Entitlements by definition, above all when sanctified repeatedly by the highest court in the land, carry with them no sense of "reciprocal obligation." Even if each demand is fully justified, responding to all of them takes us down a path we've already taken – to our considerable cost.

For roughly the last two decades, almost every demand by this or that group, industry, or region for financial compensation or advantage was responded to in some way or other. The bottom-line of all of that is today's national debt of $550 billion.

What we've done to ourselves fiscally, we may be doing to ourselves culturally. The promiscuous handing out of rights without ever checking on their cumulative effect upon the community's sense of cohesion and solidarity is disturbingly similar to our past practice of redistributing wealth without checking on the effect of this upon our capacity to create wealth.

Moreover, demands for cultural rights are quite different in their character from demands for financial assistance or subsidy. Financial demands are merely about advantage or catchup. Rights are about moral absolutes. Without realizing it, we've abandoned the Canadian tradition of compromise, of log-rolling, of give and take. Increasingly, we rely on the law to solve societal conflicts of interest. The law, though, is about black and white, win or lose: It is inherently adversarial. Politics of course is often adversarial too. But it is accountable – elections; the official opposition; the media – in a way that the law is not. The law, constitutional law above all, is about absolutes; politics is about accommodation.

One of the shrewdest analyses of the predicament we've got ourselves into was provided by York University political scientist Reg Whitaker in a 1992 analysis of the Charlottetown Accord negotiations and subsequent referendum. "The symbolic politics

of difference recognition raise serious questions about the fragmentation of the democratic community," he writes. Whitaker
notes that while native leader Ovide Mercredi won for himself
both a seat at the bargaining table and agreement on an "inherent
right of self-government," he was ultimately rejected by his own
constituency who, partly because they'd seen him at the high
table, took for granted that he'd been co-opted. By contrast,
National Action Committee leader Judy Rebick lost both her bid
for a bargaining spot and her demand for a gender-equal Senate,
yet came away a hero. Often, to be on the inside trying to make
the community function is to be suspect; staying on the outside is
a safe way to remain pure.

A variant on this theme of what's been called "the death of
conversation" is the new popularity of "shouting heads" discussion panels, one on the left the other on the right, neither listen-
ing to the other in a quest for solutions but each propounding
whatever ideology or identity cause they happen to espouse. The
old, distinctively Canadian, Couchiching-style of debate has been
replaced by absolutism and posturing. These are entertaining;
they also are deeply divisive.

Of its very nature, identity politics fractures a community.
That's a very high price to pay for the additional "inclusion" that
has been achieved over the past decade, not least because, given
Canada's naturally inclusive character, it's hard not to believe that
virtually all of it of it wouldn't have happened anyway.

If the community continues to be hollowed out in this way, its
centre will no longer be able to hold. The moment could be closer
at hand than is generally assumed. English-speaking Canadians,
or Anglo-Celt Canadians, or culturally converged Canadians, or
whatever may now be the proper term, may decide that the community isn't their community any longer.

This topic is an exceedingly delicate one. But it's one of the most
troubling aspects of contemporary Canada. Far more "cultural

anxiety" exists about all the changes now going on than the governing class is either aware of or has been able to bring itself to recognize by discussing publicly. In recent years, the political antenna of the élite have been at best weak, or have been completely switched off. It has been surprised time and again – by everything from the defeat of the Charlottetown referendum to Reform's electoral success to the extent of opposition to high immigration levels that forced the Chrétien government to retreat from its plans to increase the intake to Harris's sweeping election victory in which resentment at employment equity played a part. Most recently, the governing class has been taken by surprise by the strength of rural opposition to gun registration. Often, it seems that only Chrétien's near-miraculous personal popularity is protecting the political class from the same kind of massive rejection that swept Mulroney from office.

Having raised a difficult topic, it's necessary to cut to its core. A key characteristic of English-Canadians (or whomever) is that they are the only people in the country who have only one country. All immigrants are linked to their ancestral homeland. All Quebeckers have *deux pays*, Canada and that part where they feel themselves *maîtres chez nous*. All native people retain, at least in their memory, an image of another country. Only English-Canadians are here alone, emotionally and psychically.

This vulnerability of English-Canadians is seldom appreciated or recognized. Instead, their contributions to building a country that the UN keeps saying is the most agreeable in the world to live in have been subjected, for example, to the facile revisionism of CBC-TV's *The Valour and the Horror*. This is in glaring contrast to the way Australians have used their military disasters and accomplishments to *imagine* their community. The prevailing doctrine of "historical disadvantage," sanctified by the Supreme Court during its sojourn into trendiness, presumes that historical Canada was a seething cauldron of racism and sexism (as it no doubt was, in the prevailing fashions of those times). In a typical example of this kind of "presentism" or hindsight, the Meech Lake Accord was attacked constantly as the product of a bunch of white men in suits in a back room. This was quite true. True also was that the Charter of Rights and Freedoms, that bible of every identity group in the country, was also written by guys in suits.

This isn't an argument for a return to the past, which in any event has vanished. Nor is it to argue that "representation" is not now an essential instrument for achieving political legitimacy, even though it's never been clear whether the dogma of "cultural appropriation" would limit each member of the most scrupulously representative board or commission to speaking only on behalf of their own special-interest group.

Yet the problem is real. From the junking of the word "Dominion" to the fact that English-Canadian is now the only hyphen banned from official usage, the sense of disenfranchisement felt by many English-Canadians is acute. Many young people are of course delighted to be inheriting a newer world. Black Canadians, even though the most disadvantaged economically of all racial minorities, possess "the psychological affluence" of exerting over young white Canadians the appeal of their music, their "cool" clothes style (such as baggy, sagging trousers), and just their projection of authentic street cred. Many older Canadians, though, mourn the passing of their familiar world. This is what the one in two who told pollsters they felt they were becoming "strangers in their own land" were trying to say, not least because, unlike Quebeckers, native people, and immigrants, they are provided with no outlets to express their sense of loss – except in angry calls to hotline radio shows.

Sooner or later, they will find a way to say it out loud. A backlash isn't the Canadian way. A passive-aggressive withdrawal is. At some point, English-Canadians may decide that they are simply one more multicultural group within the apartment complex rather than the legatees and guardians of the myths and values of the building as a whole. The vote, by 20 per cent of Canadians, for the Reform Party in the 1993 election was a warning signal. So was the election, in the country's most "diverse" province of Harris's Conservatives. Another warning signal is the quiet, and so very Canadian, shift of "old stock" individuals away from some central parts of Toronto and Vancouver, along with the new popularity of walled estates. There have to be connections between this cultural anxiety and the prevailing cynicism about politics in general. Similarly, there's a message implicit in the anti-tax protests: The link here is that taxes paid by one person always benefit other persons who are strangers; the more these really are strangers, or "differentiated citizens," the greater the unwillingness to part with one's money.

The Canadian community simply will not hold together unless it is animated and sustained by the English-speaking Canadian sensibility – outside Quebec. If we cannot forge some kind of partnership between the old and new Canadas, framed by those "tramlines" laid down long ago by English-Canadians, our future may become that of a kind of northern Los Angeles.

"Newcomers to Canada find themselves in a curiously pastless country," writes journalist and critic Robert Fulford in an exceptionally eloquent essay for *Belonging*. Often detached in his analyses, Fulford this time was passionate. Canadians were "slowly obliterating the country's symbolic landscape"; we had "for the most part written off our history as unimportant," reducing it to "little more than a series of picturesque and unconnected anecdotes."

A people who have no collective past can have no collective future. Milan Kundera understood this. In *The Book of Laughter and Forgetting*, he writes, "Destroy its books, its culture, its history.... Before long the nation will begin to forget what it was, and what it is." Mexican-American writer Richard Rodriguez understands this. "Don't teach me about my ancestors," he writes.

"Teach me about the 16th century Puritans, so I can understand today's America."

Canadians, many of them, don't understand this. It's possible to graduate from high school without taking a course in Canadian history. The standard text for university students, the two-volume *The History of Canada's People*, deals with the First World War, in which Canadian consciousness was born and during which sixty thousand Canadians died, in just seven pages. In no other country, especially in contrast to Europe and the U.S., are so few references made in public debates to events and figures from the past.

Indeed, we positively scorn the greater part of our history, not merely as dull – un-European and un-American that's to say – but also nowadays as an unending chronicle of racism, sexism, homophobia, militarism, environmental-degradation. Identity politicians often sound as if they imagine themselves to be the first moral Canadians.

Canadian historians share a considerable part of the blame for this. Instead of "probing the ways in which the past can equip us for Canada's future," in the phrase of historian Michael Bliss, they have retreated into the politically correct and the local; "The history of housemaid's knee in Belleville in the 1890s," as historian J. L. Granatstein writes scornfully. Indeed, Bliss, Granatstein, and Desmond Morton are among the few with nerve enough to still attempt the ennobling purpose of historians – to help their community become what it should be by describing and interpreting what it was.

The absurdity of this historical indifference is that it leaves Canadians with the impression that their country has become probably the most agreeable in the world (or so the UN says), by some fluke rather than as the distinctive achievement of Canadians.

It's time, surely, to revise the endless revisionism, whether about Canada's wartime military errors or about its long-ago mistreatment of immigrants or about its usually well-intentioned failures in trying to accommodate the interests of the descendants of a nomadic hunter-gatherer culture with the realities of a rationalist, technological civilization. The alternative to booing isn't cheerleading: it's the intelligent search for connections between past, present, and future.

There are connections, for example, between today's official multiculturalism and mass immigration and the turn-of-the-century decision to bring in hundreds of thousands of "men in sheepskin coats," and before that to fill up our empty spaces with all those Irish and Scots fleeing poverty just like so many of those now knocking on our doors. Similarly, there are connections between the turn of the century Social Gospel movement that produced J. S. Woodsworth and Tommy Douglas, later of the son-of-the-manse tradition of public service personified by Lester Pearson, and the kind of liberal, pluralist society that we've become. The 1982 Charter of Rights and Freedoms is the successor of John Diefenbaker's 1961 Bill of Rights and of his call for "un-hyphenated Canadianism" that in turn came out of anti-élitist prairie populism. Employment equity, however ineptly implemented, was preceded by *de facto* affirmative action for francophones in Ottawa, and before them for the veterans of both world wars. If many Canadians now feel rootless, it's because we've so rarely explored our roots.

History can only be a foundation. We'll still need to build substitutes for walls around us.

Neo-conservatives have made one signal contribution to contemporary public debate. They have dared to reinject back into it that long-unfashionable word "responsibility." By this, neo-conservatives mean that individuals should take responsibility for the consequences of their actions (such as illegitimate children) and of the consequences of their non-actions (failure to seek employment). By contrast, contemporary liberalism has largely lapsed into a boneless non-judgementalism.

Neo-conservatives, though, are concerned only with the individual, the self, the ego. Without ever caring to admit it publicly, they agree with Margaret Thatcher that "There is no such thing as society" and that it is only individuals, and their families, that matter.

Humans are social beings, though; if not, they are just atoms. It's the value placed on the community that divides today's conservatives who proudly wear the prefix "neo" from those conservatives, Joe Clark and Dalton Camp as examples, who still adhere to the older creed of Red Toryism that itself comes right out of Canadian history (George Grant as the archetype) and, in its very contradictions, comes the closest Canada has ever come to defining a distinctive political philosophy.

If liberals and social democrats and Red Tories are going to have anything worthwhile to say to Canadians – other than a continued clinging to a past that itself was more dependent upon endless economic growth than anyone then recognized – this, surely, is going to happen only when they can articulate the kinds of responsibilities that it takes to sustain a diverse community as an integrated whole. Also in need of articulation is a new concept for the governance of public institutions. Creating these was the great achievement of liberal democrats. Their crashing failure was never to figure out how to renew public institutions, so that many have long since degenerated into expensive, unresponsive bureaucracies. If a new concept can be defined it is going to have to hinge on the notion of a partnership between public institutions and the public at large and the non-profit agencies of the voluntary or "social sector."

Personal responsibility is an important value, and an appealing one. *Civitas*, a sense of obligation to the community, not just in the now jaded sense of "caring and sharing" but also in that of a

civic duty to give back to the community a part of what one has
earned by living in it, is a higher value; today, it is a far more necessary one.

Above all, this kind of moral dimension to contemporary politics would give voice at the millennium to what it is that
Canadians want to hear said, because it articulates the Canadian
essence, its sustaining myth. A discernible hunger exists in the
country for this sense of *civitas*. The extent of public rage at Brian
Mulroney is one measure of it. Objectively, he doesn't deserve the
contempt with which he is regarded. His record wasn't that bad.
Yet in some undefinable way, Canadians came to judge Mulroney
as un-Canadian. This is why Stevie Cameron's best-selling book,
On the Take, touched a national nerve. Ekos Research's pulse-
taking is also revealing. It found that Canadians are "thirsting for
a celebration of shared symbols, ideals, and sources of pride."

Trying to define what is Canadian about Canada is of course a
fool's game. This isn't because people don't know what being
Canadian is; it's that they are embarrassed to say it out loud. As
everyone in fact knows full well, it means trying to live by the
ideals of tolerance, civility, and decency. It's a lot harder, for lack
of the anchor of ethnicity, being a Canadian than being Irish,
Danish, Polish, whatever. Only those things difficult to do are
worth doing. This is why our lightness of national being can be at
times almost unbearable.

Turning generalities about *civitas* into daily-life practicalities is
of course excruciatingly difficult. Suggestions have been made
that the Charter of Rights should be matched with a Charter of
Responsibilities. How, though, to know whether someone's uncut
front lawn is a disgrace to the neighbourhood or an environmentally pure wildlife meadow? (The Swiss have snuck a few social
responsibilities into their Civil Code, such as that everyone must
contribute to the maintenance of indigent relatives). No doubt
a national debate about civic responsibilities would make the

Meech/Charlottetown debates look like a choir practice. While it was happening, though, Canadians would be talking to one another about each other.

We must also talk to others about ourselves. As the world's first postmodern nation, no matter that we arrived here by accident, we have a distinctive story to tell.

In a 1994 presentation to the Senate–Commons Committee on Foreign Affairs, writer John Ralston Saul made the important point that Canada is known abroad neither for its politicians nor its businesspeople nor for its exports but "for its culture. That is our image. This is what Canada becomes in people's imagination around the world." Our cultural expressions *are* us. They transmute values, attitudes, and myths into words and images. We've found ways to do this that if not distinctive to us in the sense of being uniquely Canadian are very much our own style: Our film and TV documentaries, satires from "This Hour Has 22 Minutes" to the "Royal Canadian Air Farce," comedy from SCTV to *Wayne's World* to "Kids in the Hall," the cartooning at which we're unusually deft, are all suffused with a decidedly un-North American irony. It's our writers of fiction, that ever-lengthening international list from Margaret Atwood and Robertson Davies to Michael Ondaatje, Rohinton Mistry, Alice Munro, Mordecai Richler, Carol Shields, and M. G. Vassanji, who express mostly clearly the Canadian voice. The 1994 competition for the first Giller Prize, of $25,000, for Canadian fiction marked a kind of epiphany in modern Canadian writing. In the phrase of Munro, who was one of the judges, the task was to select "the truest voices." Those voices turned out to tell of a postmodern nation: Of the five finalists, three were born outside the country, two were writers of colour, two were women, one was gay.

Of course we no longer have the money we once had for the arts, or for anything. To govern, though, is to choose. We could, for example, take a cue from Australia, a nation undergoing a similar change in its consciousness, in its case from being a former British nation to being an Asian one. In November 1994, the Australian government announced a three-year, $250-million Creative Nation program to expand its arts council, to fund additional TV programs, and to establish a new Academy of Music in Melbourne, a gallery of aboriginal art in Canberra, and an Institute for Indigenous Performing Arts Training in Brisbane. Tellingly, a major share of these funds is being used to create three new institutions; just as Australians are ahead of us in understanding that their past speaks to their present, they are ahead of us in understanding the role of institutions in nurturing a sense of *civitas*.

We can also tell others about ourselves through our diplomacy – specifically by what we do to help keep the peace for others and by what we do to promote and protect the human rights of others. From Haiti to Bosnia, we are doing more of the first than we have ever done. As for the second, the government's new policy, in the words of Foreign Affairs Minister André Ouellet, is that it's "Boy Scout[ish]" to intrude any softness about human rights into the hard practicalities of winning exports.

Certainly, we have to be practical. But if we lose our ideals, we lose everything. As always, it's outsiders who've recognized what few Canadians can bring themselves to say. In forecasting Canada's demise, even though he hoped it wouldn't happen, Lansing Lamont writes in *Breakup* that if Canada vanished, "The world would lose a moral voice." In *The Independent*, British writer Jan Morris (more accurately, a Welsh one) writes, "The end of Canada would mean the end of Canadianness.... The general Canadian sense of public kindness and concern would be overwhelmed by the general American sense of dog-eat-dog." It's our collective responsibility to others as well as to ourselves to go on being, if not Boy Scouts then, in Lester Pearson's phrase, "honest brokers."

At different places in this book I have tried to suggest specific responses that may help to both reimagine our community and to reinvent it. Why bother? Inertia, the same force that keeps all institutions going long after their original purpose has been fulfilled, will sustain us for quite a while. When that runs out, we could bid to join the United States – however reluctantly, they'd eventually accept us – thereby raising our incomes if not necessarily improving our lifestyles.

The reason, I believe, is because the Canadian values of tolerance, civility, and decency are precious and are becoming more and more rare the world over. To allow these to vanish for lack of energy and nerve would be, in Pierre Trudeau's famous comment about the possible end of Canada, "a crime against humanity."

Sources

Three sources have been referred to in a number of chapters and should be mentioned at the outset. Other books, reports, and articles are listed under the chapter headings where they are first quoted.

Granatstein, J. L., and McNaught, Kenneth, eds. *"English Canada" Speaks Out*. Toronto: Doubleday Canada, 1991.

Kaplan, William, ed. *Belonging: The Meaning and Future of Canadian Citizenship*. Montreal: McGill-Queen's University Press, 1993.

Rethinking Government. Ottawa: Ekos Research Associates, Inc., April 1995.

Introduction

Lamont, Lansing. *Breakup: The Coming End of Canada and the Stakes for America*. New York: W. W. Norton, 1994.

1. L'État C'est Nous

Anderson, Benedict. *Imagined Communities: Reflections on the Origin and Spread of Nationalism*. 2d ed, rev. London: Verso, 1991.

Ball, George W. *The Discipline of Power*. Boston: Little, Brown, 1968.

Coyne, Andrew. "Support for the Arts: burden or boon? The audience as partners." *Globe and Mail*, December 31, 1994, C1.

Ignatieff, Michael. *Blood and Belonging: Journeys Into the New Nationalism*. Toronto: Penguin, 1994.

Keynes, John Maynard. *Yale Review*, 1933.

Naylor, Thomas H. "Downsizing the United States of America." *Challenge Magazine*, November-December 1994.

Ohmae, Kenichi. "The Borderless World." *Harvard Business*, 1990.

2. Associating with the Yanks

Grant, George. *Lament for a Nation*. Toronto: McClelland & Stewart, 1965.

Gwyn, Richard. *The 49th Paradox: Canada in North America*. Toronto: McClelland & Stewart, 1985.

McCallum, John, and Helliwell, John F. "The Extraordinary Trade-Generating Powers of the Canadian Economic Union." Royal Bank of Canada, May 1995.

Rotstein, Abraham. *The Precarious Homestead: Essays on Economics, Technology and Nationalism*. Toronto: New Press, 1973.

3. À *la Carte* Americans

Blank, Stephen, and Krajewski, Stephen. "U.S. Firms in North America: Redefining Structure and Strategy." The National Planning Association, 1995.

Canadian International Development Agency (CIDA). "Canada in the World." Ottawa: CIDA Information Services, 1995.

Gray, John. *Lost in North America: The Imaginary Canadian in the American Dream*. Vancouver: Talon Books, 1994.

Hart, Michael; Dymond, Bill; and Robertson, Colin. *Decision at Midnight: Inside the Canada-U.S. Free Trade Negotiations*. Vancouver: UBC Press, 1994.

Morris, Jan. "Jan Morris Blows Canada's Trumpet." *The Independent Magazine*, March 24, 1990.

Pfaff, William. *Wrath of Nations: Civilization and the Fury of Nationalism*. New York: Simon & Schuster, 1993.

Valpy, Michael. "Trading Tradition for a Few Measly Bucks." *Globe and Mail*, November 18, 1993, A2.

4. Into the Wide World

Courchene, Thomas. "Social Canada in the Millenium." C. D. Howe Institute, 1994.

Drucker, Peter F. "The Age of Social Transformation." *Atlantic Monthly*, November 1994.

Goldsmith, Sir James. *The Trap*. London: Macmillan, 1994.

Helleiner, Eric. *States and the Re-Emergence of Global Finance: From Bretton Woods to the 1990s*. New York: Cornell University Press, 1994.

Kerckhove, Derrick de. *The Skin of Culture: Investigating the New Electronic Reality*. Toronto: Somerville House, 1995.

Reich, Robert. *The Work of Nations: Preparing Ourselves for 21st Century Capitalism*. New York: Random House, 1992.

5. The New Two Nations

Beach, Charles, and Slotsve, George. "Are We Becoming Two Societies? Income Polarization and the Middle Class in Canada." C. D. Howe Institute, 1995.

Bridges, William. *Jobshift: How to Prosper in a Workplace Without Jobs*. London: Nicholas Brealy, 1995.

Disraeli, Benjamin. *Sybil: or The Two Nations*. 1848.

Economic Council of Canada. *Good Jobs, Bad Jobs*. Ottawa: 1990.

Lasch, Christopher. *The Revolt of the Elites and the Betrayal of Democracy*. New York: W. W. Norton, 1995.

Rifkin, Jeremy. *The End of Work: The Decline of the Global Labor Force and the Dawn of the Post-Market Era*. New York: Putnam Publishing Group, 1994.

Wolff, Edward. *Top Heavy*. New York: Twentieth Century Foundation, 1995.

6. Feuding with Feudalism

Kierans, Eric. "Corporations and the Cain Culture." *Policy Options*, September 1989, 17-20.

"Workers in an Integrating World." *World Bank*, 1995.

7. The Nation That Dares Not Speak Its Name

Akenson, Donald Harmon. "The Historiography of English-Speaking Canada and the Concept of Diaspora: A Skeptical Appreciation." *Canadian Historical Review*, September 1995.

Bercuson, David J., and Cooper, Barry. *Deconfederation: Canada without Quebec*. Toronto: Key Porter, 1991.

Cairns, Alan C. "The Fragmentation of Canadian Citizenship." In *Belonging: The Meaning and Future of Canadian Citizenship*, edited by William Kaplan, op. cit.

Desbiens, Jean-Paul. *Les Insolences de Frère Untel*. 1965.

Freeman, Alan, and Grady, Patrick. *Dividing Up the House: Planning for a Canada without Quebec*. Toronto: HarperCollins, 1995.

Gibson, Gordon. "Plan B: The Future of the Rest of Canada." The Fraser Institute, Vancouver, 1994.

Gwyn, Richard. *The Northern Magus: Pierre Trudeau and Canadians*. Toronto: McClelland & Stewart, 1980.

Resnick, Philip. *Thinking English Canada*. Toronto: Stoddart, 1994.

Royal Commission on Bilingualism and Biculturalism. "Interim Report." Ottawa, 1965.

Salutin, Rick. "Adieu Quebec." *Saturday Night*, March 1991.

Whitaker, Reg. "With or Without Quebec?" In *"English Canada" Speaks Out*, op. cit.

8. Our Cold War

Atwood, Margaret. *Survival*. Toronto: Anansi, 1972.

Laforest, Guy. *Trudeau and the End of the Canadian Dream*. Montreal: McGill-Queen's Press, 1995.

9. More Equal Than Thou

Buckley, Melina. "Touchstones for Change." The Canadian Bar Association, Toronto, 1994.

Fekete, John. *Moral Panic: Biopolitics Rising*. Montreal: Robert Davies Publishing, 1994.

Gibson, Dale. *The Law of the Charter: Equality Rights*. Scarborough: Carswell, 1989.

Joseph, Clifton. "On Your Mark! Get Set! Go Multi-Culti!" *This Magazine*, December 1994-January 1995.

Taylor, Charles. *Multiculturalism and "The Politics of Recognition."* Princeton, N.J.: Princeton University Press, 1992.

Tocqueville, Alexis de. *Democracy in America*. 1835.

10. A Frenzy of Rights

Abella, Rosalie. "The New 'Isms.'" In *"English Canada" Speaks Out*, op. cit.

Borovoy, Alan. "Brief to Ontario Standing Committee on the Administration of Justice." September 1993.

Martin, Robert. "Challenging Orthodoxy: A Critical Analysis of Racially-Based Job Quotas." *The Canadian Labour Law Journal*, Vol. 1, Spring 1993.

Simeon, Richard. "In Search of a Social Contract: Can We Make Hard Decisions as if Democracy Matters?" Benefactors' Lecture, C. D. Howe Institute, September 13, 1994.

11. Dividing the Culture

Bissoondath, Neil. *Selling Illusions: The Cult of Multiculturalism in Canada*. Toronto: Penguin, 1994.

Gwyn, Sandra. "Multiculturalism: A Threat and a Promise." *Saturday Night*, February 1974.

Mukherjee, Bharati. *The Middleman and Other Stories*. Toronto: Penguin, 1989.

12. A Nation of Immigrants, or For Them?

Brimelow, Peter. *Alien Nation: Common Sense about Immigration*. New York: Random House, 1995.

Gungwa, Wang. "Sojourning: The Chinese Experience in Southeast Asia." Jennifer Cusman Lecture, 1992.

Hathaway, James C. "The Immigration Reform That Wasn't." *Canada Watch* (York University) November-December, 1994.

Kotkin, Joel. *Tribes: How Race, Religion, and Family Determine Success in the New Global Economy*. New York: Random House, 1992.

Rodriguez, Richard. *Days of Obligation: An Argument with My Mexican Father*. New York: Viking Penguin, 1992.

Stoffman, Daniel. "Towards a More Realistic Immigration Policy for Canada." C. D. Howe Institute, 1993.

13. *Civis Canadensis Sum*

Beiner, Reginald. *Introduction to Theorizing Citizenship*. Albany, N.Y.: State University of New York Press, 1995.

Cairns, Alan. "Citizenship and the New Constitutional Order." Brief to the Senate Standing Committee on Social Affairs, April 28, 1992. *Canadian Parliamentary Review*, Autumn 1992, 2-6.

"Canadian Citizenship: A Sense of Belonging." Report of the Standing Committee on Citizenship and Immigration. Ottawa, June 1994.

Dyette, Devo-Jaiikoah. "Black Canadian, Not African." *Toronto Star*, March 7, 1995, A21.

Granatstein, J. L. "The 'Hard' Obligations of Citizenship." In *Belonging: The Meaning and Future of Canadian Citizenship*, op. cit.

Henry, Frances. *The Caribbean Diaspora in Toronto: Learning to Live with Racism*. Toronto: University of Toronto Press, 1994.

Kaplan, William. Introduction. In *Belonging: The Meaning and Future of Canadian Citizenship*, op. cit.

Sharpe, Robert J. "Citizenship, the Constitution Act, 1867, and the Charter." In *Belonging: The Meaning and Future of Canadian Citizenship*, op. cit.

14. Postmodern Dominion

Davey, Frank. *Post-National Arguments: The Politics of the Anglophone-Canadian Novel Since 1967*. Toronto: University of Toronto Press, 1993.

Fulford, Robert. "A Post Modern Dominion: The Changing Nature of Canadian Citizenship." In *Belonging: The Meaning and Future of Canadian Citizenship*, op. cit.

Hutcheon, Linda. "As Canadian as Possible . . . Under the Circumstances." Lynch, Gerald, and Rampton, David, eds. *The Canadian Essay*. Toronto: Copp Clark Pitman, 1991.

Negroponte, Nicholas. *Being Digital*. New York: Knopf, 1995.

Powe, Bruce. *A Tremendous Canada of Light*. Toronto: Coach House Press, 1993.

Schecter, Stephen. *Zen and the Art of Post-Modern Canada: Does the Trans-Canada Highway Always Lead to Charlottetown*. Montreal: Robert Davies Publishing, 1993.

Toffler, Alvin, and Toffler, Heidi. *Creating a New Civilization*. New York: Turner Publishing, 1995.

15. A Reinvention Agenda, Part One

Frum, David. *Dead Right: The End of the Conservatism of Hope and the Rise of the Conservatism of Fear*. New York: HarperCollins, 1994.

Gray, John. *Beyond the New Right: Markets, Government, and the Common Environment*. New York: Routledge, 1993.

Lind, Michael. *The Next American Nation: The Origins and Future of Our New National Identity*. New York: Collier, 1994.

Solomon, Steven. *Confidence Game*. New York: Simon & Schuster, 1995.

16. A Reinvention Agenda, Part Two

Alexis, André. "How a Canadian Black Identity Became a U.S. Cultural Franchise." *This Magazine*, May 1995.

Bliss, Michael. "Privatizing the Mind: The Sundering of Canadian History." *Journal of Canadian Studies*, Winter 1991-92.

Finkel, Alvin; Conrad, Margaret; and Strong-Boag, Veronica. *History of the Canadian Peoples, Vol. II, 1867 to present*. Toronto: Copp Clark Longman, 1993.

Fulford, Robert. "A Post Modern Dominion." In *Belonging: The Meaning and Future of Canadian Citizenship*, op. cit.

Karlsson, Ingmar. "Euroislam or Ghettoislam." Paper delivered at the Bertelsmann Symposium, June 16-17, 1994.

Menon, Vinay. "Canadian Identity Should Transcend Ethnic Preferences." *Toronto Star*, April 11, 1995.

Saul, John Ralston. Brief to the Senate-Commons Committee on Foreign Affairs, 1994.

Whitaker, Reg. "What is the Problem with Democracy? The Failure of Constitutional Politics." Paper delivered at the Democratic Politics Conference, Carleton University, November 1992.

Index